Writing the Siege of Leningrad

Writing the Siege of

PITT SERIES IN RUSSIAN AND EAST EUROPEAN STUDIES

JONATHAN HARRIS, EDITOR

WOMEN'S
DIARIES,
MEMOIRS,
AND
DOCUMENTARY
PROSE

CYNTHIA SIMMONS AND NINA PERLINA
WITH A FOREWORD BY RICHARD BIDLACK

UNIVERSITY OF PITTSBURGH PRESS

Title photo: Courtesy of The Central State Archive of Film, Photographic,
and Audio Documentation, St. Petersburg

All primary source documents have been reprinted with the permission of their authors.

Published by the University of Pittsburgh Press, Pittsburgh, Pa., 15260

Library of Congress Cataloging-in-Publication Data

Simmons, Cynthia, 1949–
    Writing the siege of Leningrad : women's diaries, memoirs, and
documentary prose / Cynthia Simmons and Nina Perlina ; with a foreword
by Richard Bidlack.
        p. cm. — (Pitt series in Russian and East European studies)
Includes index.
    ISBN 0-8229-4183-X (cloth : alk. paper)
    1. Saint Petersburg (Russia)—History—Siege, 1941–1944—Women.
2. Saint Petersburg (Russia)—History—Siege, 1941–1944—Sources. 3. Women
in war—Russia (Federation)—Saint Petersburg. I. Perlina, Nina, 1939–
II. Title. III. Series in Russian and East European studies.
    D764.3.L4 S56 2002
    940.54'21721—dc21

                                                        2001006540

Ђлокадницам

For the *blokadnitsy*

CONTENTS

FOREWORD: HISTORICAL BACKGROUND TO THE SIEGE OF LENINGRAD

RICHARD BIDLACK

THE SIEGE OF LENINGRAD BY GERMAN AND FINNISH ARMIES DURING World War II was one of the most horrific events in world history. According to the most recent and reliable estimate, fighting in the Leningrad area from the summer of 1941 to the summer of 1944 and during the 872 days of blockade and bombardment of the city itself took the lives of somewhere between 1.6 and 2 million Soviet citizens (not to mention enemy casualties). The entire range of this estimate exceeds the total number of Americans, including military personnel and civilians, who have perished in all wars from 1776 to the present.[1] While no one knows how many Leningraders perished during the siege, it is reasonably estimated that within the city and its immediate suburbs, no fewer than one million civilians died, mainly during the terribly cold winter of 1941–1942.[2] The exact death toll, however, may have been considerably higher.

The prolonged siege possessed elements of epoch, epic, and monumental tragedy that transcend the temporal and spatial boundaries of World War II. For the USSR at war, the defense of Leningrad held strategic significance. It was one of the nation's largest centers for manufacturing munitions. More important, however, is the fact that if Leningrad had fallen in the late summer or early autumn of 1941, Germany could have redirected hundreds of thousands of additional troops and war machines toward Moscow. If Moscow had in turn been taken in short order, the war might have ended. Holding on to Leningrad and defending the eastern adjacent region of Karelia also protected the lend-lease corridor southward from Murmansk. Although American-manufactured lend-lease materials played little role in Soviet

ix

I wish to thank the International Research and Exchanges Board (IREX) and the Dean's Office of Washington and Lee University for supporting the research on which this foreword is based.

defense through 1942, they did greatly facilitate the eventual Soviet triumph on the eastern front.

Victory in the "Great Patriotic War" (to use Soviet parlance that has carried over to the present in Russia) became an integral part of the USSR's self-justification and propaganda. On average, about one book per day on the war was published in the USSR between 1945 and 1991. These works, though often rich in detail, followed prescribed themes and were subjected to heavy censorship. Soviet-era books on wartime Leningrad number about four hundred. Few of them were published before the death of Stalin, who always regarded the "second capital" with suspicion.[3] Attention to the siege in post-Soviet Russia has dropped dramatically due to the material impoverishment of the historical profession, but the quality of research has risen sharply, particularly in the publication of previously classified documents.[4] Outside of Russia, the best general histories of the siege are Leon Goure's *The Siege of Leningrad* and Harrison Salisbury's outstanding best-seller, *The 900 Days: The Siege of Leningrad.*

A conspicuous void, however, has remained in the historical literature: description and analysis that focus specifically on the activities and attitudes of women, who made up a large majority of Leningrad's civilian population during the siege. The diaries, letters, memoirs, oral accounts, and accompanying commentary assembled here in *Writing the Siege of Leningrad* help fill that void. Several memoirs and diaries have been published in English by female siege survivors, but what has been missing before *Writing the Siege of Leningrad* is a scholarly work in any language that attempts to define female perspectives on the siege and to trace those perspectives through a number of first-hand accounts. *Writing the Siege of Leningrad* is also a very timely book, because it contains many accounts based on recent interviews. The number of blockade survivors is dwindling rapidly, and their personal histories need to be written down while there is still time.

To understand the type of city that Leningrad was at the start of the Soviet-German War and how women came to play a major role in sustaining the city during the siege, one has to go back to at least 1929. That year marked the start of Stalin's programs for rapid construction of the nation's heavy industrial base in the First Five-Year Plan and collectivization of agriculture. Hundreds of thousands of peasants fled the mass starvation that followed state seizure of their land. Many were drawn to the new and expanded factories in heavily industrialized Leningrad, where they could receive both a salary and a food ration card. Rapidly rising prices, caused by the famine and a severe shortage of consumer goods, meant that families generally needed a second salary to make ends meet. This prompted many women who had not previously worked outside the home to enter the city's work force. The expanded educational opportunities of the early Soviet decades also enabled women to seek employment in many new fields.

In the late 1930s political terror swept through Leningrad. Whether or not Stalin actually ordered the murder of Sergei Kirov, Leningrad's Communist Party leader, on 1 December 1934, he used the murder as a reason or pretext to purge thoroughly the city's party organization and industrial elite. By 1937 and 1938, the purges had become widespread in Leningrad. Most of those arrested were men, which created more jobs for their wives, widows, sisters, and daughters. Work opportunities for women increased further between 1938 and the first half of 1941, because many new defense plants were opened in Leningrad during the Third Five-Year Plan. By 1940, Leningrad was producing approximately 10 percent of the nation's total industrial output in more than six hundred factories, and women made up some 47 percent of the city's industrial work force, which comprised about 750,000 people altogether.[5]

Soviet histories of the war exaggerated the changes that took place following the start of the German invasion by implying that the USSR had previously been a society at peace. In fact, Leningrad's economy was highly mobilized and militarized in 1939 and 1940. The Soviet Union attacked several nations during the two years of the alliance with Nazi Germany. Leningrad served as the arsenal for the offensive war against Finland during the winter of 1939–1940 (which claimed the lives of at least 127,000 Soviet military personnel); fighting in the Winter War took place just north of the city. Once again, more women went to work in Leningrad's factories to replace men who had been drafted into the armed forces. Contending with shortages that accompanied the war economy in 1939–1941 provided specific lessons for Leningraders that would prove useful during the siege years.[6] At the same time, however, the fact that production of goods and services for the civilian population had been sacrificed to expand military production before 1941 made it that much more difficult for Leningraders to bear further militarization of their economy during the war with Germany.

Leningrad was experienced in preparing for war and waging it before 1941, and a series of new, massive mobilization drives commenced as soon as Germany began its invasion on 22 June 1941. Probably no city in the world ever steeled itself for war to a greater extent than did Leningrad. In the process, hundreds of thousands of men had to leave the city. Military reservists, all men, were called up for active duty. By 1 October 1941, 298,700 had responded, and most went to the front.[7] In addition, during just the first week of the war another 212,000 Leningraders who had not been drafted volunteered for what eventually became known as the "people's militia" (*narodnoe opolchenie*). In some cases, people were under pressure to volunteer, as Ol'ga Freidenberg describes in the part of her memoir that is included in *Writing the Siege of Leningrad*. Militia units were formed in Leningrad throughout the summer of 1941. Most volunteers were men, though women were officially encouraged to volunteer in August. All told, about 130,000 volunteers were hastily formed into ten divisions and other units that fought alongside regular army formations.[8] The volunteers received little or no training and were often armed only with hunting rifles, hand grenades, or bottles filled with gasoline. Their mission was to stop the advance of the armored divisions of German Army Group North. It is no wonder that the volunteers suffered extraordinarily high casualty rates. Another 14,000 Leningraders, mainly men, were trained as partisans and sent behind enemy lines.

With so many men taken from the city at the start of the war, women were relied on to carry out subsequent important tasks. Untold thousands replaced their husbands and brothers in factory jobs at the same time that many industries were retooling to produce war munitions. They worked at least eleven hours each day and then toward the end of summer received training in "worker battalions" in off hours to prepare to defend their city factory by factory if necessary. Factory workshops were armed and windows bricked up. Moreover, in one of the largest mobilization efforts, roughly one-half million civilians, of whom probably the large majority were women, were drafted during the summer of 1941 to build defense fortifications along the Pskov-Ostrov and Luga River defense lines (180 and 60 miles southwest of Leningrad, respectively) and in areas much closer to Leningrad. Before 1941, Stalin had refused to construct defenses in rear areas. Official propaganda had stated that any invader of Soviet territory would be immediately repulsed. Hence, the southwest approaches to Leningrad had been left largely undefended. During the first summer of the war, women, teenage girls and boys, and old men were ordered to dig huge tank-trap ravines and to build other defenses. They received very little food and often had to sleep under the stars. They had little shelter against enemy fighter aircraft, which strafed their anthill-like construction sites. The efforts of the labor conscripts, however, were not in vain. The fortified zones between Pskov and Leningrad slowed what had been up to that time a very rapid German advance along the Baltic and thus were an important part of the reason why Leningrad became the first city on the continent that Hitler failed to conquer.

Despite all of this activity, ordinary Leningraders had no reason to suspect that their city was in great danger until 21 August, when their main newspaper, *Leningradskaia pravda*, finally informed them that German armies might try to take Leningrad. An evacuation of industrial machinery, skilled workers, and nonworking dependents, which had started in July, had not made much progress before the last rail line out of Leningrad was severed on 29 August. Altogether, only about 636,000 people (including about 147,000 refugees, who had fled into the city from the southwest) of a prewar population of around 3.3 million were evacuated before the start of the blockade. Around one million mothers and children, who should have been evacuated, were left trapped in the city.[9] At the same time that so many remained inside the blockade ring, others were forcibly exiled. Several tens of thousands of former criminals, army deserters, and the so-called "social-foreign element"—former nobles, White Army officers, kulaks, and passport violators—were rounded up and sent to various locations east of the Urals. In addition, mainly during the first week in September 1941 and again in March 1942, there were mass deportations of ethnic Finns and Germans, some of whose ancestors had resided in and around Leningrad for the past couple of centuries. By the end of the summer of 1942, the People's Commissariat for Internal Affairs (NKVD), or secret police, had exiled eastward a recorded 58,210 Germans and Finns (mainly the latter).[10]

The siege of Leningrad began on 8 September, when German troops reached the southern shore of Lake Ladoga and thereby severed any land route out of Leningrad to the south. With front lines established just two and one-half miles south of Leningrad, Hitler opted to besiege the city rather than attempt to seize it. Finnish troops, meanwhile, reoccupied the boundary north of Leningrad that Finland had held before the Winter War of 1939–1940. The Finnish government refused Hitler's entreaties to continue the southerly advance beyond the 1939 boundary along the eastern shore of Lake Ladoga to link up with the German armies.[11] Thus Europe's largest lake remained Leningrad's only surface route of supply and escape during the siege.

On 8 September German aircraft fire-bombed Leningrad for the first time, destroying, among other things, the Badaev Warehouse, where much of the city's food reserves was stored. Leningrad's situation grew desperate during the autumn months. Air and artillery bombardment continued to pulverize and burn the city, which received very little food, fuel, or raw materials from the "mainland" (as Leningraders referred to the rest of the USSR, from which they were cut off). German artillery spotters could peer right into Leningrad from hills south of the city. Livestock and bread had actually been directed away from the Leningrad region at the start of the war. However, by mid-July, food rationing was introduced (see Table of Rations). Workers (*rabochie*) in "hot" workshops, such as steel smelting, received the largest rations. The other three categories, in descending order of the size of their rations, were: workers, engineers, and technicians; other employees; and nonworking dependents. During the autumn, rations were cut four times. Supplying the city with food became most precarious between 8 November and 9 December, when Germany temporarily held the rail junction city of Tikhvin, thereby forcing Soviet food convoys to lengthen their circuitous supply route to Leningrad over Lake Ladoga by about eighty miles. Starting on 20 November, the top category of rations was cut to 375 grams per day of bread, which was the only food that was regularly available. Inedible elements such as sawdust were added to the bread to make the rations seem larger. At the same time, the ration for nonworking employees and dependents was slashed to only 125 grams, or slightly more than a quarter pound, of the adulterated bread. Infants and the elderly began to die from starvation in November. By year's end, roughly 100,000 had perished. Men succumbed to the effects of hunger before women did, because men have less body fat and their cardiovascular systems are not as strong.

At the same time that starvation set in, Leningraders had to continue to work several hours of overtime each day. Stalin wanted Leningrad's war plants to produce as much war matériel as possible and send a large portion of it to Moscow to bolster the capital city's defenses. Some of the arms and raw materials were airlifted out of the city in American-made DC-3s. In the fall, Moscow's defense held top priority, and Stalin ordered resources from the entire nation sent there regardless of the effects elsewhere. As replacement workers were being killed by enemy shells and bombs and starving to death, Leningrad's factories continued to retool for war production and to manufacture as many artillery guns and mortars and as much ammunition as possible until the city's one remaining power plant practically ran out of coal in December. Some enterprises closest to German lines relocated their workshops to regions farther away from German artillery. The emphasis put on war production destined mainly for Moscow left Leningrad almost entirely unprepared for the coming winter under siege.

Not until December did Leningrad's political leaders turn their main attention to the city's emergency needs. During that month and in January 1942, the first small self-standing metal stoves (*burzhuiki*) and power generators were manufactured, and public baths, laundries, heating stations, and convalescent centers (*statsionary*) opened. For many, these measures were too little and taken too late, though starvation rates would have been high in any case without an increase in food shipments to the city. Close to half of Leningrad's civilian population that was not evacuated would perish from hunger and cold in the first winter and spring of the siege. Evacuation provided the best hope of survival. By late January, with the temperature reaching as low as -40° F, ice on Lake Ladoga froze thick enough to permit heavy truck traffic. All told, approximately 590,000 Leningraders, most of whom were nonworking adults and children, were evacuated over the "Road of Life" during the first winter of the siege. No large-scale air evacuation of civilians seems ever to have been considered.[12]

In general, the food rations by themselves were insufficient to sustain life, particularly during such a cold winter. Many blockade survivors have noted in their diaries and memoirs that the generosity of others—a relative, friend, or even a stranger—enabled them to survive. Adamovich and Granin stated in their memoir collection that "each had a savior," such as parents who saved food rations from work to give to their starving children. It is hardly surprising that Leningraders also developed a range of techniques to enhance their own chances of survival.[13] It would seem that nearly everyone relied to some extent on black-market barter trade, though it remained technically illegal. At the city's central markets during the worst of the winter, people would exchange a gold watch for a handful of turnips or a Persian rug for a couple of chocolate bars.[14] There was much trade between civilians and the several hundred thousand soldiers stationed inside the blockade area. Soldiers exchanged their larger food rations, which were roughly double those of most civilians, for clothing and other items.

Leningraders sought out opportunities to visit troops near the front in any sort of official capacity as part of a factory's "goodwill delegation" or to provide cultural entertainment. Although there were instances of starvation among the troops of the Leningrad Front (or army group), in general the soldiers generously shared their food with the civilians who came to visit them. *Writing the Siege of Leningrad* contains a menu of the meals served to a group of entertainers during a visit to the front on 12 December 1941. Tamara Nekliudova recorded the menu, which includes many foods that at that time were generally unavailable to civilians, such as pork fat, sunflower seeds, and cocoa. In another of the book's entries, Kseniia Matus described in an interview from 1996 her day trip in early November 1941 to the front lines with a group of musicians from her conservatory. At dinner she feasted on meat cutlets, small pies, bread, and vodka.

Leningraders also took advantage of special privilege or influence (*blat*) to find a way to leave the city or to obtain more food if they remained in it. For instance, factories often had "closed" cafeterias and a "director's" cafeteria, which provided a little extra food. Cafeteria No. 12 at party headquarters at Smolnyi distributed bread, sugar, cutlets, and small pies throughout the winter. Employees were strictly forbidden to take food from the cafeteria for fear that its bountiful supply would become widely known. Communist Party members as a whole may be considered an elite group that benefited from various forms of privilege. During the first half of 1942, 15 percent of all members of the Leningrad Party Organization starved to death, which was less than half of the city's civilian mortality rate.[15]

The most desirable jobs were in bakeries, candy factories, other food-processing plants, cafeterias, buffets, and hospitals. There was fierce competition to get on their payrolls, and the starving begged for food on their premises. These places became excellent havens for their employees, and their starvation rates were very low; at several food plants no one died. Some quality control experts were even overweight. Of the 713 people employed at the start of the winter at the Krupskaia candy factory, none starved to death. On the eve of the German invasion, 276 people, mainly women, were employed at the Baltika bakery. By the beginning of the winter, the work force had grown to 334. Twenty-seven Baltika employees (8 percent) starved to death; all were men. At the city's only margarine factory, there were large quantities of linseed, sunflower seeds, and even coconuts during the winter. (On the eve of the war this plant had obtained two thousand tons of coconuts from the Philippines.) Employees lived off the oil-bearing crops, and not one starved to death.[16] In her diary that is replicated in *Writing the Siege of Leningrad*, Anna Ostroumova-Lebedeva recounts how a friend of hers during a visit to the public baths in the spring of 1942 ran into "well-fed Rubenesque young women," all of whom worked at food shops, soup kitchens, and children's homes.

Throughout the siege, workers, engineers, and technicians received considerably more bread per day—twice as much for part of the period—than did other employees and nonworking dependents. Some factories also provided soup and other hot food in addition to the higher ration. Most of the siege survivors profiled in *Writing the Siege of Leningrad* were teachers, musicians, dancers, and intellectuals in other cultural fields, which meant that they were in the lowest ration category. Those in that category often tried to secure the higher worker ration or even to persuade city authorities to grant them "worker" status for rationing purposes.[17] At the beginning of January 1942, of 2.2 million civilians in Leningrad, 800,000 (or 36 percent) received worker ration cards. When factories ceased production, as most did in December, workers nevertheless generally continued to receive the higher rations through the spring of 1942. In her oral account included in *Writing the Siege of Leningrad*, Valentina Bushueva describes how she remained in bed for the months of March and April 1942 with her body swollen from starvation, but she continued to receive her worker bread ration.

Factory employment provided other benefits. The largest defense plants received access to special stockpiles of food and also were allowed to send their own food trucks across frozen Ladoga. Many factory workshops became large mutual-support centers, where workers pooled their strength to carry out essential chores. Some took up living round-the-clock at their workplace. Workers formed brigades to clean living space in workshops, mend torn clothing, repair shoes, and to set up laundries, baths, showers, and warming stations. It was primarily girls and women who composed these brigades, which also took food to those too weak to come to work, cleaned their apartments, attempted to place orphaned children in homes, set up child care centers in their factories, and arranged for burial of corpses.[18]

Soviet histories of the siege and works written in Russia since the collapse of the Soviet Union have emphasized the heroism of ordinary Leningraders who had to endure unimaginable suffering. True heroes by anyone's standard of measure were in abundance. Russian president Vladimir Putin recently told several journalists that his father's legs were shattered by shrapnel during the winter of 1941–1942 on the far side (left bank) of the Neva River. A fellow soldier who happened to be an old neighbor saved his life by hauling him on his own back through a battle zone and across the frozen river all the way to a hospital in Leningrad. Putin's mother nearly starved to death around the same time and at one point was presumed dead and actually laid out with corpses. Her brother fed her his own rations, and Putin's father while recovering in the hospital also secretly passed his rations on to his wife.[19] The extraordinary deprivations and ever-present threat of enemy bombardment, however, prompted others to engage in many sorts of illegal, immoral, and depraved activity. Theft of food was widespread. Starving teenagers snatched rations in and around dark and crowded bread shops. Armed bands occasionally looted shops. Workers and administrators in bakeries and food stores systematically stole large quantities of food. At one food shop, the director, assistant director, and warehouse manager were arrested for stealing seven hundred kilograms (1,540 pounds) of food. Thieves were punished severely and swiftly. Some were shot for stealing just a half-loaf of bread, but the threat of execution did not deter desperate people. Murder and cannibalism became a significant problem. According to recently declassified Russian documents, about two thousand were arrested for cannibalism (which was classified as "banditism" in the criminal code) during the siege. Most often the accused were young, unemployed women, with no prior conviction, who were born outside of Leningrad and therefore probably did not possess ration cards. They were simply starving people pursuing any means possible to feed themselves and their children.[20]

How did Leningraders react to their government's failures in feeding and protecting them during the first year of the war? The partial opening of Russian archives over the past decade has enabled historians to combine surveys from party and NKVD organs with independent eyewitness accounts (like those in this book) to assess the popular mood. The city's security apparatus employed an army of informants throughout each district of the city to monitor and control public expression.[21] The most critical period of Leningrad's defense was mid-September 1941, when NKVD sappers mined several defense plants and other key installations in the city's southern districts in anticipation of a German ground assault. Overheard comments reveal that it was rather widely presumed that party personnel and the city's large Jewish population[22] would be eliminated if Germany took Leningrad,

but opinions were divided over what would happen to the rest of the popu-
lace. Some Leningraders were not alarmed at the prospect of German occupation; others more boldly expressed their hope that the city would fall.
Swastikas occasionally appeared on courtyard walls. Anti-Jewish epithets
were heard most frequently during the first days of the war and in late summer, when Leningrad's defense was most in doubt, but it would appear that
such sentiment never became widespread or systematically articulated.

During the first six months of the war, the Leningrad Party Organization lost far more members to the front than it was able to take in as new
candidates. The party actively sought replacements and even resorted to
readmitting some who had been expelled. The number of new entrants
was especially low during the precarious month of September, a time when
members often tried subtly to dissociate themselves from the party without
drawing the party's attention. There was much fence sitting in terms of political loyalty when the city's fate hung in the balance. By the end of 1941,
party membership was cut in half and Komsomol membership was down
90 percent. By early 1942, the composite profile of party members and candidates had changed: they were older and slightly less educated, and women
composed a greater percentage than on the eve of the war. Party functions
were curtailed, and numerous party cells (primary party organizations) had
disappeared. At the same time, official propaganda de-emphasized communist ideology in preference for themes that extolled patriotism and the
heroics of the Red Army. Party organs and communist ideology revived in
Leningrad only in the latter half of 1943.[23]

During the autumn of 1941 when food rations were repeatedly cut, informants noted a sharp rise in vocal criticism of the authorities. Professional
agitators were taunted and heckled when they had to explain why rations
were being reduced. On several occasions, small groups of employees refused
to work overtime without additional food. Party leaders also received a
number of anonymous letters demanding the surrender of the city.[24] Verbal
expressions of pro-German sentiment and open appeals to authorities to
surrender continued to be made through the winter, but appear to have diminished in frequency. At the same time, however, the letters that were censored by the NKVD for "defeatist" comments reached a peak of around 20
percent during the winter. Much of the censored correspondence was between men at the front and their families in Leningrad.[25] At no time did
opposition sentiment coalesce into a formidable threat to the authorities.

Leningrad did not collapse into chaos, as the German leadership had hoped. Order was preserved for a number of reasons. Most Leningraders despised the enemy's genocidal siege tactics, feared the possible effects of German occupation of their beloved city, desired to support friends and relatives at the front, and continued to hope that the city would soon be liberated, especially after the Red Army's counteroffensive outside Moscow began on 5 December. The fact that Leningrad's leaders during the winter actively tried to protect the general population probably also played a part in maintaining residents' loyalty. Moreover, the rigors of trying to survive the winter tended to numb and mute feelings of political dissent.[26]

A prominent theme in studies on the Soviet home front is that spontaneous initiative and personal freedom increased during the war and did so largely because state and party organs were preoccupied with matters directly linked to waging war and lacked resources to deal with other peripheral matters.[27] This theme applies well to Leningrad, particularly from the time of the hungry winter through late 1943. The brigades described above that organized emergency services at factories are an example of increased local initiative. Another area in which there was greater freedom of expression was religion, specifically, the practice of Orthodox Christianity. There were ten functioning Orthodox churches in the blockaded territory, and throughout the siege they were very active in a number of ways (as Valentina Petrova notes in her interview from 1995, which is included in *Writing the Siege of Leningrad*). Services were held daily, and they were well attended. During the summer and fall of 1941, the Cathedral of St. Nicholas donated 355,000 rubles to the Red Cross to be used for aiding wounded soldiers. It was around that same cathedral that Metropolitan Aleksi courageously walked in procession with an icon each day of the siege, even during air raids. Volunteers protected churches against incendiary bombs during air raids. Church activity increased as the city's population declined, and only one church was closed, temporarily, during the hungry winter. Churches tried as best they could to assist their parishioners during the starvation winter. In 1943, the year that Stalin allowed the Church to reinstate a patriarch, Leningrad's churches even raised funds for a tank column.[28]

Leningrad's cultural and intellectual communities, which are so well illuminated in *Writing the Siege of Leningrad*, displayed extraordinary dedication to their work during the bleakest periods. This reflected their overall seriousness of purpose, but their devotion was also a way to discipline their minds to persevere and avoid falling into a state of listless depression and resignation. During the first blockade winter, many of Leningrad's institutes and libraries remained open. Every day the main reading room of the city's public library attracted readers. Doctoral dissertations continued to be written and defended during the winter in air-raid shelters and basements. One of the best known examples of cultural creativity and determination during the siege was the composition and performance of Dmitrii Shostakovich's Seventh Symphony. Shostakovich finished the third movement of his famous work, dedicated to Leningrad, in the late summer and early autumn of 1941; at that time he also worked as a fireman during the air blitz. In early October, after having repeatedly refused to leave the city, he finally obeyed a command to evacuate. His symphony received its premier in the city of Kuibyshev in March 1942 and was first performed in Leningrad on 9 August 1942 by an assortment of emaciated musicians, who were joined by others summoned from the front.[29]

If authorities allowed greater freedom of expression in some areas, that policy did not apply to political dissent. As already noted, pro-German and anti-Soviet sentiment directed toward authorities was most frequently expressed between September and November 1941. The NKVD tried as best it could to eliminate that sentiment. Arrests for counterrevolutionary activity were most numerous in the fall of 1941. Altogether, between 1 July 1941 and 1 July 1943, a total of 3,799 Leningrad civilians were convicted of counterrevolutionary crimes, and 759 (20 percent) of them were executed. The rest were imprisoned, which, during the fall or winter of 1941–1942, practically amounted to a death sentence. Between the start of the war and 1 October 1942, a total of 5,360 civilians were executed in the city for various offenses.[30]

Throughout the starvation winter, city authorities worried about the possibility of an outbreak of typhus and other diseases due to the accumulation of refuse, excrement, and unburied corpses. There were several failed attempts to clean up the city starting in late January. In late March, when the temperature finally rose above freezing, the authorities became more concerned. For twelve days starting on 27 March, hundreds of thousands of Leningraders, mainly women who were practically walking skeletons, cleaned up the city, and the only form of mass transportation, the trams, started running again. The feared epidemics never materialized.

At the same time, a city-wide gardening campaign was launched. Seedlings were distributed, and practically every courtyard and vacant plot of ground in the city was planted with cabbages, lettuce, beets, tomatoes, cucumbers, and other vegetables. Cleared excrement was used as fertilizer. All previous taxes and rent payments for gardens were discontinued. Former collective farms outside of Leningrad but within the siege area were planted by workers from city factories, though most preferred to work on their own gardens. The gardening campaign proved so successful that by November Leningrad had amassed a four-month supply of food.

Leningrad's mortality rate peaked in late January or early February. By the end of the spring, starvation was ending, although half of all workers were still remaining at home on sick lists. From the spring of 1942 through the rest of the year, Leningrad continued to adapt to its blockaded existence. Important tasks left over from the preceding summer were completed, and additional measures were undertaken to protect the remaining population. The evacuation by ship of nonworking people across Ladoga resumed in late May, a month after the ice road began to break up. By the end of the year, the city's population was pared down to 637,000, of whom a recorded 82 percent were employed.[31] People were dispatched to cut firewood and dig peat in anticipation of a second siege winter. Electrical cables and pipelines were laid under Ladoga to supply Leningrad with electrical power and fuel from the "mainland." Leningrad was much better prepared for the second blockade winter.

Leningrad could not ignore the possibility of a renewed German effort to take the city in 1942. In fact, in late July Hitler ordered his armies to occupy Leningrad by the end of September, but eventually abandoned the plan when the pivotal battle for Stalingrad began to take shape. The Red Army's attempts to relieve the city, however, were also thwarted. In June, 45,000 Leningraders, mostly women, were ordered to complete construction of defense works started in 1941.[32] During the summer, dozens of defense plants in Leningrad resumed manufacturing millions of artillery shells, bombs, and mines and thousands of small arms. It was primarily women who produced these munitions. By 15 December, in different sectors of the defense industry, they accounted for between 60 percent and 80 percent of all workers; in light industry and textiles, about 95 percent. At this time, women made up 76.4 percent of all of the city's industrial employees and 79.9 percent of all factory workers. Most of these women were new to their jobs since the start of the war. Men, however, continued to predominate in more skilled jobs. They composed about two-thirds of engineers and technicians at this time.[33]

In October 1942, the Leningrad Front, located inside the siege zone, began receiving reinforcements, including tanks and artillery, to increase its size from three to four armies. On 12 January those armies began to fight their way eastward along the southern coast of Ladoga toward the Volkov Front armies, which in turn simultaneously drove westward into the German "bottleneck" toward Leningrad. The two fronts linked up on 18 January and opened a corridor into Leningrad along Ladoga's shore that was just six miles wide. At 10:09 A.M. on 7 February, the 517th day of the siege (and five days after the victory at Stalingrad), the first train pulled in to Leningrad's Finland station having passed through the narrow corridor and crossed the Neva River on tracks laid over the ice. Its arrival marked the beginning of the last stage of the siege, in which the blockade ring was pierced but remained largely intact for almost another year. Through the rest of 1943, 3,105 trains would run the gauntlet of the "corridor of death" (also called the "road of victory"), which German artillery continually shelled from short range. Repair crews fixed the tracks some 1,200 times in 1943.[34]

Despite the continuation of enemy artillery fire in 1943, Leningrad came remarkably close to becoming a "normal" city in 1943. The rail connection allowed more food, raw materials, and fuel to enter the city and manufactured products and more people to be sent out. Cattle were brought in to build up livestock herds. Leningraders continued to devote as much time as they could to their private gardens. It was calculated that the city's total vegetable harvest in 1943 was more than twice as large as in 1942, even though the city's population was smaller. By the end of 1943, per capita food consumption in Leningrad was on par with that of the rest of the nation (where millions were going hungry in some areas). The city's death rate continued to drop; the only widespread deadly disease was hypertension, which was a long-term consequence of severe malnutrition. As many Leningraders had died in individual days in early 1942 as died in all of 1943. Toward the end of 1943, for the first time since the start of the siege, the birth rate surpassed the death rate (an accomplishment that Russia today cannot come close to claiming).[35]

During the second half of the year, industrial production accelerated, and work norms were raised, as the city resumed the role it had played up to December 1941 as industrial supplier to other areas of the nation. In late 1943, Leningrad began to manufacture large turbines, generators, and other machines needed to rebuild industrial regions, such as the Donbass, that the Red Army had recently retaken. At the same time, artillery shells and other ammunition were produced and stockpiled in Leningrad for the anticipated offensive that would finally smash through the blockade. Party cells were reactivated throughout the city, and party propaganda devoted more attention to communist ideology. Several months before the end of the siege, therefore, Leningrad was experiencing its own return to normalcy: the restoration of communication and command links with Moscow. This transformation occurred as the enemy stepped up its bombardment. German bombers returned to Leningrad in 1943 and flew more than two hundred sorties, and enemy artillery fire reached its greatest intensity of the war in September.[36] Leningraders tended to view the bombardment as an expression of futile vindictiveness; most seemed to realize that liberation from the siege was not far off. By this time, the Red Army had already retaken most of pre-1939 Soviet territory, and Soviet troops had crossed the old border with Poland.

When the Leningrad Front launched the long-awaited offensive on 14 January 1944, many Leningraders, who by this time numbered only 575,900,[37] scrambled onto rooftops to watch the awesome and terrifying spectacle of thousands of Soviet artillery shells screaming over their heads. The last German shell hit Leningrad on 22 January. Five days later German forces had been driven back out of firing range. The siege was over.[38]

The Red Army refrained from launching a simultaneous offensive north of Leningrad against Finland. Instead, the Soviet government in February secretly offered Finland peace terms and bombed Helsinki to intimidate the Finnish government into accepting its offer. Through intermittent negotiations during the latter part of the winter of 1944 and into the spring, the Soviet government spelled out its harsh terms. They included Finnish recognition of Soviet territorial annexations during the Winter War, a huge indemnity, and the reduction by half of Finland's armed forces, among other things. Finland, which was under severe pressure from Germany not to sign a separate peace, refused to comply. On 9 June, three days after its western allies invaded Normandy, the Soviet Union employed over 1,000 aircraft and a pulverizing artillery barrage in launching a surprise attack against Finnish positions on the Karelian isthmus. By 19 September, Finnish field marshal and president Gustav Von Mannerheim had accepted the Soviet price for peace. This deal allowed Finland to avoid Soviet occupation and retain its independent, democratic government, although the USSR would essentially control Finnish foreign policy for the following half century.

A massive celebration took place in Leningrad when the siege ended. However, during the seven and one-half years between the end of World War II and Stalin's death, the main Soviet archival collections dealing with the siege remained closed, preventing Soviet scholars from conducting detailed research. (The most prominent revelation in this period occurred at the Nuremberg Trials in 1946, where the Soviet government cited a figure —generally acknowledged to be far too low today—of 649,000 civilian deaths in Leningrad during the war.)[39] Stalin seems to have feared allowing discussion on the politically sensitive issues of why Leningrad was not better defended in 1941 and why the siege lasted so long and so many died, as well as the prospect of cultivating a heroic reputation for the city and its inhabitants.

Stalin's deep-seated mistrust of the former imperial capital extended back at least to the mid-1920s, when his rival Grigorii Zinoviev was the head of the city's party organization; it developed further during the Kirov affair and the subsequent purges in Leningrad in the late 1930s. One effect of the siege was that while Leningrad's party leaders and prominent intellectuals were cut off from the "mainland," they enjoyed a fair amount of autonomy from Moscow. Once the war ended, however, Moscow sought to gain greater control over, and in many cases eliminate, Leningrad's political and cultural figures in what has become known as the Leningrad Affair. The intellectuals were attacked first. Stalin put Leningrad's former party leader Andrei Zhdanov, who had been transferred from Leningrad to Moscow in 1944 (and would die, apparently of natural causes, in 1948), in charge of a broad cultural offensive against works that were deemed to have departed from the socialist realist norms of the 1930s. In 1946 Stalin personally issued a decree against the Leningrad journals *Zvezda* and *Leningrad*. The satirical writer Mikhail Zoshchenko and the city's most famous poet, Anna Akhmatova, both of whom had resided in Leningrad for at least part of the siege, were severely and crudely criticized during the *Zhdanovshchina* for their writings and were expelled from the Writers Union.

The bloody political purge commenced three years later. In the immediate postwar period, Leningrad's second party secretary, Aleksei Kuznetsov, who had emerged during the siege as a more effective leader than his boss, Zhdanov, was a rising star in the Soviet political firmament. A young and outspoken leader, he did not refrain from raising controversies from the past. For instance, he charged that the investigation into Kirov's murder had not revealed the real instigators. Another prominent Leningrader, Nikolai Voznesensky, who had been one of the main organizers of the Soviet wartime economy as the head of Gosplan and after the war been elevated into the Politburo, was also known for his uninhibited and direct manner. Their budding careers naturally drew the attention of the ever-suspicious Stalin and those closest to him, Lavrentii Beria and Georgii Malenkov. The Kremlin leaders may have actually convinced themselves that these prominent Leningraders and others were conspiring to take power, though no proof of any such conspiracy has ever surfaced. Approximately two hundred Leningrad leaders were arrested and put on trial in 1949 and 1950. Many of them, including Kuznetsov and Voznesensky—as well as Voznesensky's brother Alexander, the rector of Leningrad State University, and his sister Maria, a party worker—were executed.[40] During the same period, the Museum of the Defense of Leningrad, a huge exhibit that filled thirty-seven rooms, began to close for extended periods and then was shut down altogether in 1953. Some items in the collection were sent to other museums; others were destroyed.

Thus, in the postwar years, the Kremlin sought to squelch both the history of the siege and Leningrad's best known cultural and political leaders. To some extent, the Kremlin succeeded in silencing that which the cold, hunger, and enemy bombardment of the blockade could not. At least the writers could regain their reputations, and some of their works were published in the Soviet Union after Stalin's death. The Museum of the Defense of Leningrad finally reopened in 1989, though with only part of its former possessions, as Ol'ga Markhaeva, a senior researcher at the museum, notes in *Writing the Siege of Leningrad*. The history of the siege is still being written. This book broadens significantly our understanding of that most horrible ordeal by drawing us intimately into the lives of many women who suffered it.

THE ACTUAL GATHERING OF THE PERSONAL NARRATIVES WITHIN THIS book took place during two successive summers. In 1995, Nina Perlina and Cynthia Simmons began conducting interviews in St. Petersburg and copying documents in the Russian National Library (formerly the Saltykov-Shchedrin Public Library) and the Museum of the Defense of Leningrad. Arlene Forman and Nina Perlina continued this work in the summer of 1996. The entire process of gathering, analyzing, and compiling these documents spanned approximately five years. It is apparent in retrospect, however, that the project was developing in incubation over a much longer period of time.

Born and raised in Leningrad, Nina Perlina knew the official and a good deal of the unofficial history of the Siege. American contributors to this volume (Arlene Forman and Cynthia Simmons), both children of the cold war, were less informed with respect to the particulars and scope of the catastrophe—Soviet losses in World War II were less emphasized in American schoolbooks. Yet a confluence of factors and events came to convince everyone involved of the urgency and significance of this endeavor.

Certainly the fiftieth anniversary of World War II precipitated the reconsideration of this crucial period. In many cases it has led to revisionist attacks on official history. This process coincided with what might be considered the final phase of the humanistic movement—our postmodern and millennial privileging of the individual voice. This volume will take its place among a growing number of private accounts of the war years, including those from a woman's perspective (for example, *Frauen, Women in the Holocaust*, and *War's Unwomanly Face*).

The anniversary stocktaking of World War II coincided, tragically, with war and siege again in Europe. As if the historical retrospective were not enough, television images of war in Yugoslavia fueled without fail the memory of anyone who had endured the "last world war." Watching lines of refugees, bundled up against the cold and treading carefully over snow and ice, Nina Perlina immediately recalled her childhood in Leningrad.

Earlier yet, the phenomena of glasnost (from the late 1980s) and the fall of the Soviet Union (1991) incited researchers and private citizens alike to question the writing of history under communism. They demanded access to the official documents on which that history was (or intentionally was not) based and to other public archives that might shed light on the past. Unfortunately, the institution that was created in 1942 to serve this function, the Museum of the Defense of Leningrad (*Muzei Oborony Leningrada*), fell into official disfavor in 1949 as a result of the Leningrad Affair, and was closed in 1953 (until glasnost). The holdings of the Russian National Library, which were never officially closed, remained an obvious resource for such an inquiry. Siege documents took on greater significance as the growing interest in private accounts of history coincided with the impetus to reexamine the official history of the Siege. Of equal importance, the atmosphere of openness in Russia after 1991 also made it possible for people to convey personal reminiscences and private archives of the Siege to anyone interested to read or listen. Primary documents became more accessible at the same time that researchers were coming to value their contribution to new perspectives on the war.

The History of the History

During the Siege and soon afterward, within the official Soviet parameters of valor and preordained heroic perfection, some *blokadnitsy* (women who suffered the Siege of Leningrad) contributed their perspectives. Anna Akhmatova was among the first of the poets to give voice to the city's grief. Her cycle of poems *The Wind of War* (*Veter voiny*), written in 1941, captured the terror and suffering of the first months of the Siege. In *Leningrad Speaks* (*Govorit Leningrad*, 1945), Ol'ga Berggolts published poems that she wrote during the Siege. Her inspirational words were broadcast over the radio throughout the Siege and served as a lifeline among the city's inhabitants.

As soon as early spring, 1942, the well-known artist Anna Petrovna Ostroumova-Lebedeva was commissioned to compile a pictorial account of the Siege for the women of Scotland. As was often the case in the Stalinist period, her work in *The Scottish Album* (*Shotlandskii al'bom*) was appropriated for use as propaganda.[1] Ostroumova-Lebedeva's officially sanctioned accounts of the Siege—in her artistic depictions and in her memoirs *Autobiographical Notes*[2]—differ significantly from her unexpurgated diary, available in the Russian National Library, which is excerpted in this collection.[3] Candid personal accounts did not pass uncensored into the annals of Soviet history, because the official position on the Siege was that it was a trial not only of women and children, not only of Leningraders, but of all Russians.

Vera Inber's diary *Almost Three Years: Leningrad Diary* (*Pochti tri goda: Leningradskii dnevnik*) was published in 1946.[4] Her radio broadcasts of civic poetry and her recitations at poetry readings during the Siege had had a resuscitative effect on the city's inhabitants, and certainly her verses, bearing such titles as "A Woman's Nurturing Hand" (*Zabotlivaia zhenskaia ruka*), "To Woman!" (*Zhenshchine!*), and "Our Native Girl" (*Devushka rodnaia*), hailed the almost superhuman effort of the besieged women of Leningrad. Although Inber concedes in her diary that criminal acts occurred occasionally, the predominant tone of the memoir is "officially" patriotic. She describes Stalin's speech of 11 October 1941 as "one great shining consolation"[5] and later speaks of the irresistible quality in his voice that convinces one of his knowledge and sincerity.[6] As the diaries of Ol'ga Freidenberg and Liubov' Shaporina attest, such an attitude toward Stalin was not necessarily shared by those whose memoirs were never published during the Stalinist period.

In the West, accounts not strictly "Soviet" began to appear: Alexander Werth, *Leningrad* (1944) and *Russia at War* (1964); Konstantin Kripton (pseudonym), *Osada Leningrada* (The Siege of Leningrad, 1952); Leon Goure, *The Siege of Leningrad* (1962); Harrison Salisbury, *The 900 Days: The Siege of Leningrad* (1969).[7] Goure described Leningrad as a city that endured "thanks to the work and suffering of women";[8] Salisbury's riveting history included accounts by survivors that were more revealing than anything previously published of the nonheroic aspects of Siege life (such as cruelty, crime, and cannibalism).[9] Yet none of the authors confronted gender as a defining issue of the Siege experience.

In the waning years of the Soviet Union, the publication in 1982 by Ales Adamovich and Daniil Granin of *A Book of the Blockade* (*Blokadnaia kniga*) marked a turning point in the official Soviet account of the events of 1941–1944.[10] The impetus to publish the book, as Adamovich and Granin explain it, had to be troubling enough. The postwar generations were beginning to question why Leningrad had not surrendered and where the proof was that these events had really occurred.[11] The authors refer to those who doubted or who had tired of hearing about the Siege as "moral dystrophics" ("dystrophy" is a medical term for starvation, although some considered it a wartime euphemism for a crime against Leningraders).[12] *A Book of the Blockade* is based on several hundred interviews (many conducted in the Saltykov-Shchedrin Public Library—see the interview with Nataliia Rogova). Those interviewed are often quoted directly. It is broader in scope and the accounts are more varied than in any previously published testimony.

At first the editors perform their requisite nod to the myth of valor:

> Some stories came our way—vague, second-hand ones—about bread being stolen (by adolescents or men, who suffered most from hunger pains and proved to have the least power of endurance). But when we began to question people, to ascertain how many times they had themselves seen it happen, it turned out, nevertheless, that there were not many instances. In such a big city, of course, all kinds of things happened.[13]

Yet survivors proceed to recount surprisingly numerous incidents of theft (Nataliia Petrushina's bread ration was stolen from her hands several times, by both men and women),[14] forgery ("all manner of thieves and Fascist agents" tried to disrupt the work and forge the ration cards of the Volodarskii Printing house),[15] and military incompetence (Mariia Motovskaia recalls faithfully supervising the evacuation of young children to the Novgorod region—into the path of the attacking German army).[16] Despite the editors' disclaimer, these interviews undoubtedly came closer to the "whole story" than any that had yet made it to the Soviet printed page. Most disturbing, from our post-Soviet perspective, is the editors' admitted censorship —the hundreds of pages of testimony that they chose not to include. These oral histories most likely would have added another dimension to the history. Despite its breadth and its disclosures, *A Book of the Blockade* falls within the valorous "canon" of Siege history, a work of the "thaw" variety, restricted, nonetheless, by the political considerations of its day and by the undefined editorial decisions of Adamovich and Granin.[17]

At the same time, memoirs by émigrées were being published in the West. These augmented and substantiated what was reported in Salisbury's

The 900 Days and were much more revelatory: Elena Skriabina's *Years of Wandering: From the Diary of a Leningrad Woman* (this memoir figures in Salisbury), Elena Kochina's *Blockade Diary*, and Galina Vishnevskaia's *Galina*.[18] By 1984, when Vishnevskaia published her memoir, the inequities and atrocities of the Siege were already so familiar to western readers that she recounted briskly, in just two pages and with no sense of revelation, that her father, who later abandoned her when he left the city, ate well from provisions that he stole from the military warehouse, that her classmate, who ate human flesh, stole her ration book, and that "one often saw corpses with the buttocks carved out."[19] Only with the advent of glasnost did such "unvarnished" accounts appear in print in the USSR. In some quarters, they have evoked long-repressed sentiments concerning Leningrad's tragic fate. Today, in the St. Petersburg area, the history of the Siege of Leningrad, and particularly of the perceived neglect or even ill will demonstrated by the Soviet government in Moscow (Stalin) toward the city, inspires citizens and young people to take pride in their region (*krai*)—at the expense, it would seem, of a commitment to the country as a whole.[20]

Most important of all in the evolving history of the Leningrad Siege, glasnost also gave voice to a number of women—perceptive observers and gifted chroniclers whose diaries and memoirs had remained unpublished, or unpublishable. These included accounts of some better-known women, such as the literary scholar Lidiia Ginzburg, the classicist Ol'ga Freidenberg, the artist Liubov' Shaporina, and the ballerina Vera Kostrovitskaia, as well as those of little-known women, whose words lie in private collections and in the manuscript divisions of libraries and museums. Lidiia Ginzburg's "Notes of a Besieged Person" (*Zapiski blokadnogo cheloveka*) is not included in this collection as it is now available in translation. It deserves special mention, however, because it is emblematic of what we have found characterizes women's accounts of the Siege. She speaks of how people incited to the common cause (*obshchee delo*) contribute to it even involuntarily, just by accomplishing their *personal* tasks.[21] She is critical of all, including herself and her class (the intelligentsia), who acted less than honorably and betrayed the almost mythic Russian conception of spiritual and societal connectedness (*sobornost'*). Finally, she recognizes the outer limits of the battlefield in the changes occurring in her own body and her loss of womanhood.[22]

Personal Narratives and History

The shift in focus from global, political relations to the individual's relation to history is neither new nor surprising, for in intellectual history one can find many proponents of this purportedly "nonhistorical" approach, be they chroniclers of past events or scholars whose reinterpretations of the past have refined our understanding of the role of the individual experience within the broader cultural context. The latter have furnished the interpretive strategies most appropriate to this study of the Siege. Our theoretical approach is built on the affinities shared by a diverse group of literary critics, historians, and philosophers of culture, in works as varied as Ivan Grevs's *Essays on the History of Roman Landownership*, Nikolai Antsiferov's *The Soul of Petersburg*, Mikhail Bakhtin's *The Dialogic Imagination*, Marc Bloch's *The Historian's Craft*, Isaiah Berlin's *Russian Thinkers*, Nicola Chiaromonte's *The Paradox of History*, and Viktor Vinogradov's *On the Language of Literary Prose*.[23]

All these scholars consider the ordinary individual and the vicissitudes of his or her private experience in life as an infinitesimally small, integral unit—the common denominator of world history.[24] The minutest detail of the actual "where" and "how" or the smallest peripeteia of an individual decision must then be reintegrated into the whole of historical knowledge. This is what Hegel termed the *Weltgeist*. "Every corner of space," writes Chiaromonte, "hides a multitude of individuals, each of which represents the historical process in a way that is incomparable to others. For a single one of these individuals each moment in time is infinitely rich in physical and psychological incidents, each of which plays a role in the way he experiences history and conceives it."[25]

Furthermore, these scholars assert that all forms of art, economics, material culture, religion, and philosophy enter history as autonomous creative cognitive activities, through the assimilation and internalization of the very core of each other's contents. Conceptualizing cultural history as a nonhierarchical system built by a multitude of symmetrical, autonomous, yet interconnected cognitive experiences, these thinkers were compelled to look beyond the limits of their respective disciplines to find new methods and materials outside their given fields.

This study of the Siege of Leningrad was inspired by the interdisciplinary nature of all these works and by their implicit suggestion that a closer relation be established between history and literary studies. The gaps in our present understanding of the history of the Siege demand precisely this kind of augmentation: the inter- and intratextual examination and interpolation of a variety of personal accounts, oral histories, and local lore, as well as documentary fiction, metafiction (the writer's meditation on her text), and autobiography.

Newly obtained materials demonstrate that temporal distancing from the dramatic events of the Siege, as well as the protective mechanisms of memory that bring them closer, have left their imprint on people's recollections. Siege diaries from the forties provide chronologically verifiable information, while in the majority of retrospective diaries and oral histories, factual data and discrete chronological events become restructured and homogenized into a sort of documentary fiction.

It is our overriding concern for the variety of contexts of experience and the mutability of any context over time that underlies the arrangement of the accounts that follow. We might distinguish and classify these texts as "immediately lived experience" (diaries and letters), "experience as remembered and revivified" (memoirs and oral histories), and the "aesthetic exploration of experience" (documentary fiction).[26] These materials may be examined along various parameters (gender, ethnicity, profession, socioeconomic status), and these will certainly be considered when relevant. However, the loci of genre and time have been chosen over other considerations in the schema of organization in order to foreground some fundamentals of cultural history: the nuances of context, the shift of context in time, and the conscious individual attempt to explore and interpret history through fictionalization.

The *Blokadnitsy*

Our contributors represent a variety of socioeconomic classes, ethnicities, and professions. Although some who were young women during the war describe their experiences as manual laborers (Valentina Bushueva's work in the peat bogs, for instance), most sought white-collar positions. This was a simple matter of survival—hospital workers and caregivers in orphanages got more bread than unskilled laborers. After the war many of these women became doctors and teachers and naturally contributed to the feminization of those fields. Receiving advanced training in education and medicine, they continued the dedicated work they performed during the Siege of caring for the young and the ailing. The memoirs and diaries we have translated were often written by women already recognized as the cultural elite of Leningrad. It stands to reason that these women in particular would feel compelled to ponder the tragedy and to express their thoughts in writing.

We made contact with our informants in a number of ways. In some instances we followed references to individuals mentioned in the documents we found in the Russian National Library and the Museum of the Defense of Leningrad. Other Siege survivors were recommended to us by the staff members of these institutions. Other *blokadnitsy*, hearing of our work through veterans' groups and meetings, or in some other way, sought us out themselves. More than once in a bookstore, when we simply asked a salesperson to show us new books on the Siege, we were immediately approached by customers standing nearby, Siege survivors who offered right then to tell us their personal stories.

∞

As outlined above, much has been written about the Siege of Leningrad. Recently historians have been taking advantage of increased access to Soviet government documents and other archival materials to contextualize and corroborate our information to date. This volume adds to these new sources various *unofficial* documents and testimonies from the segment of the population that was most successful in keeping the city itself alive—the women. While starving, these women worked for and protected their city and their families. And in response to their biological imperative—to preserve body fat or energy and nurture—they survived. For their courage and fortitude they have received, as most Leningraders who suffered through the Siege have, the medal "For the Defense of Leningrad." Yet there is a courage that they continue to exhibit and that has often gone unrecognized. They remember. As Lidiia Ginzburg wrote, they have heeded Alexander Herzen's dictum: "The one who can survive must have the strength to remember." This book is intended not only as a resource for those learning and revising the history of the Siege of Leningrad. It is also a tribute to these women and their valorous remembering.

WE WOULD LIKE TO THANK THE INSTITUTIONS THAT FUNDED TRAVEL to Russia and other research expenses related to this project: Boston College, for a Research Incentive Grant and numerous Research Expenses Grants (CS); and the International Research and Exchanges Board for GIST Short-Term Travel Grants (1993-CS; 1994-NP).

Very special thanks to our families, friends, colleagues, and students, who contributed to this collection and who aided and supported us in our work at home and in St. Petersburg (Leningrad). Arlene Forman played a key role in the early years of this project, conducted interviews and gathered materials at the Museum of the Defense of Leningrad in the summer of 1996, and translated several of the documents ("O. M. Freidenberg," "E. O. Martilla," "T. P. Nekliudova," and "L. I. Veshenkova"). She also brought her editing skills (and wit) to bear as the preface was evolving during one summer's reunion of three old friends. Alla Zeide translated excerpts from V. V. Miliutina's diary and her "Ode to Grass" as well as "V. I. Bushueva," "K. M. Matus," and "L. V. Shaporina." A number of undergraduate and graduate students at Boston College contributed over the years to the volume. Robert Matthews and Natalia Glazman worked with primary sources, and Natalia cotranslated "N. V. Stroganova." Graduate students Yulia Skoroupskaia and Megan Malinowski worked at indexing and Danuta Bujak Czubarow at editing. Katherine Hardin Currie, a student in the Department of History at Indiana University, took an interest in our collection, which proved useful in the writing of her honors thesis. In the course of that work, she translated "L. S. Razumovskaia."

Valentina Petrova, Natal'ia Rogova, and Valerii Sazhin of the Russian National Library, Natal'ia Ashimbaeva, Director of the Dostoevsky Museum, and the museum staff helped us to obtain various essential documents and photographs and the rights to publish them. Without their assistance, this often intricate and delicate procedure would, in some cases, have been impossible and would have delayed the publication of our work considerably. We are grateful to all the staff members of the Russian National Library and the Museum of the Defense of Leningrad for their assistance in locating and obtaining documents as well as the context they provided for the history of the Siege as they described to us the work of their institutions in this regard.

We are grateful as well to the State Hermitage Museum, the Russian National Museum, the Central State Archive of Film, Photographic, and Audio Documentation, and the Museum of Bread for permission to reproduce photographs and other works of art.

Margaret Higgonet read an early version of our manuscript and offered suggestions from the perspective of her pioneering work on women and war. Darra Goldstein read the penultimate variant, made many helpful suggestions, and enlightened us on some of the more obscure concoctions that had to pass as food during the Siege. We wish to thank the other known and anonymous reviewers of our manuscript. We hope that in dialogue with them we have refined and enriched the context we have provided for these documents.

Colleagues at Boston College lent considerable support to our project. Michael Connolly, Roberta Manning, and Maxim Shrayer offered encouragement over the years and valuable advice as we prepared our work for publication. Thomas Epstein was so kind as to ferry vital resources between Boston and St. Petersburg. Stephen Vedder, assistant director of the Boston College Photography Production Service, generously lent his expertise to the reproduction of archival photographs. His efforts then received the careful attention of Ann Walston at the University of Pittsburgh Press. Our sincere thanks to everyone involved in the editing and production of this volume at the Press, especially to Niels Aaboe, editorial director, and Deborah Meade, production editor. Special thanks to Deborah M. Styles for her careful editing of the manuscript and her ability to lend clarity to the occasionally convoluted.

We are grateful to Richard Bidlack for agreeing to write the historical background to the Siege, for sharing his knowledge, and for supporting efforts to tell more of the Siege's stories.

Above all, we want to express our profound gratitude to the survivors who agreed to meet with us, to recall such a tragic period in their lives, and to give voice to the unspeakable. We extend our deep sympathy to the families of Ol'ga Grechina (1922–2000), Antonina Maslovskaia (1925–2000), and Avgusta Saraeva-Bondar' (1925–2000), with our regret that these women did not live to see the publication of this book.

Although the authors edited and commented on one another's labors, the work was divided as follows: Nina Perlina wrote the commentaries and provided the footnotes for the documents per se. Cynthia Simmons wrote the Preface (with the exception of Nina Perlina's "Personal Narratives and History") and Introduction; she acknowledges permission to reprint portions of both, which were published previously in a somewhat different form, in "The City of Women: Leningrad (1941–1944)," in *Women and War I: Women's Discourse, War Discourses*, ed. Svetlana Slapšak (Ljubljana: Institutum Studiorum Humanitatis, 2000), 69–99; and "Lifting the Siege: Women's Voices on Leningrad (1941–1944)," *Canadian Slavonic Papers* 1–2 (1998): 43–65.

Most Russian personal and place names and all citations of bibliographical material and words as words are transliterated according to System II of J. Thomas Shaw's *The Transliteration of Modern Russian for English-Language Publications* (the Library of Congress system with the diacritical marks omitted). We have opted for different representations in some cases where Russian personal names are much more pronounceable using Shaw's System I ("Yurii," "Yakubchik") or when, as in the transliteration of "Dostoevsky," another form has become the standard.

22 JUNE 1941	German forces attack the Soviet Union; People's Commissar of Foreign Affairs Molotov's radio announcement
23 JUNE 1941	Workers at the Hermitage Museum begin preparations for the evacuation of the museum's most valuable holdings
27 JUNE 1941	Commission is formed to direct the evacuation of the inhabitants of Leningrad
1 JULY 1941	First special train departs in the evacuation of the holdings of the Hermitage
6 JULY 1941	German forces enter the Leningrad district; by this time 243,833 children have been evacuated from the city
18 JULY 1941	Introduction of a ration-card system for the procurement of foodstuffs and manufactured goods
20 JULY 1941	Order issued to set up barracks facilities for workers in hospitals and other strategic points
4 SEPT 1941	Beginning of systematic artillery attacks
6 SEPT 1941	First massive bombardment of the city; 1,554 killed in first month
8 SEPT 1941	The 872-day-long Siege of Leningrad begins with the fall of Shlissel'burg; this ends the massive evacuation of inhabitants from the city; Badaev warehouses are destroyed by incendiary bombs
1 OCT 1941	Bread ration is reduced for third time, according to category, to either 400 or 200 grams per day for most people
31 OCT 1941	School year resumes for seventh to tenth grades; in 1941–1942, forty high schools remained in session
8 NOV 1941	Germans capture Tikhvin, cutting the last railway link bringing supplies to Leningrad

13 NOV 1941	Bread ration reduced to 300 and 150 grams per day
20 NOV 1941	Bread ration reduced to 250 and 125 grams per day
22 NOV 1941	First column of (sixty) automobiles begins transporting supplies over Lake Ladoga's "Road of Life"
7 DEC 1941	Leningrad Philharmonic performs Tchaikovsky's "1812 Overture"
10 DEC 1941	Red Army liberates Tikhvin
25 DEC 1941	First increase in the bread ration (350 gr., 200 gr., and 400 gr. for the rear army)
1 JAN 1942	Only a two-day supply of flour in reserve; through 13 January inhabitants receive nothing but a bread ration
8 JAN 1942	First convalescent hospital (*statsionar*) opens for the treatment of starvation
25 JAN 1942	Last working hydroelectric power station closes; city left without running water, heat, or electricity; for the only time during the war, the newspaper *Leningrad Truth* (*Leningradskaia pravda*) is not published
31 JAN 1942	By this date 96,694 deaths reported for the month to the register office (ZAGS), although deaths often went unreported in January
2 FEB 1942	Commission formed to fight epidemic illnesses in the city
11 FEB 1942	Second increase in the food ration (factory workers, engineers, and technicians: 500 gr. of bread; office workers: 400 gr.; children and dependents: 300 gr.)
28 FEB 1942	192,766 deaths reported for the months of January and February
11 MAR 1942	State Public Library undertakes to establish a collection of works published during the "heroic defense of Leningrad"
27 MAR 1942	Able-bodied citizens begin the cleanup of streets and courtyards
5 APR 1942	First symphonic concert since the first winter of the Siege held at the Pushkin Theater
15 APR 1942	Tram service resumes along three routes in the city
13 JUNE 1942	*Leningrad Truth* publishes the "Agreement between the Governments of the Soviet Union and the United States on the Principles of Mutual Assistance and Conduct of War against Aggressors"

18 JUNE 1942   Leningrad Branch of the Council of Artists (LOSKh) opens exhibit of works by Leningrad artists

24 DEC 1942   Proclamation of the Presidium of the Supreme Soviet establishing the medal "For the Defense of Leningrad" (and likewise for the defense of Odessa, Sevastopol', and Stalingrad)

18 JAN 1943   As a result of the Soviet offensive "Spark," the first breakthrough in the blockade

5 MAR 1943   Under the auspices of the Leningrad House of Scientists, defense of dissertations resumes

14 SEPT 1943   Classes resume at various institutions of higher learning, including the Leningrad State Pedagogical Institute and the Second School of Art (*Vtoraia Khudozhestvennaia Shkola*)

27 JAN 1944   Complete liberation of Leningrad from the blockade

burzhuika (from *burzhui*—proprietor): a small metal stove that burned fuel economically.

convalescent hospitals (*statsionar*): established from January 1942, to provide supplemental feeding for those suffering from (second-stage) dystrophy.

duranda: made from the ground shells of sunflower seeds, it was used to make pancakes and soups.

gushchaik: pancakes (*olad'i*) made from ersatz coffee grounds.

Mainland (*Bol'shaia zemlia*): Soviet territory that was not occupied by the Germans.

MPVO (*Mestnaia protivovozdushnaia oborona*): Local Anti-Aircraft Defense, to which each building and factory assigned volunteers whose responsibility it was to keep watch on rooftops for incendiary bombs, attempt to extinguish them, and, when possible, call out firefighters.

NKVD (*Narodnyi komissariat vnutrennikh del*): People's Commissariat of Internal Affairs—the secret police; later the Ministry of Internal Affairs.

People's Militia (*Narodnoe opolchenie*): Volunteer civilian defenders of the city who were minimally trained to fight at Leningrad's front lines and guarded strategic sites, such as factories.

"Road of Life": a road over the frozen Lake Ladoga, from Osinovets on the Leningrad side to Kobona on the eastern shore of the lake.

shroty: a byproduct of cooking-oil production, what remains when oil is extracted from seeds; used for cattle feed.

Smol'nyi [Institute]: the residence of the Leningrad City Party Committee.

valenki: tall felt boots.

xli

Daily Bread Rations (in grams)

Date	Workers & engineers	Workers in "hot" workshops	Office workers	Dependents	Children under 12 years
FROM:					
18 July 1941	800	1000	600	400	400
02 Sept 1941	600	800	400	300	300
12 Sept 1941	500	700	300	250	250
01 Oct 1941	400	600	200	200	200
13 Nov 1941	300	450	150	150	150
20 Nov 1941	250	375	125	125	125
25 Dec 1941	350	500	200	200	200
24 Jan 1942	400	575	300	250	250
11 Feb 1942	500	700	400	300	300
22 Mar 1942*	600	700	500	400	400

*Starting 22 February 1943, workers and engineers in defense industries received seven hundred grams of bread per day.

Source: Richard Bidlack, *Workers at War: Factory Workers and Labor Policy in the Siege of Leningrad, The Carl Beck Papers*, No. 902 (University of Pittsburgh Center for Russian and East European Studies, 1991), 44.

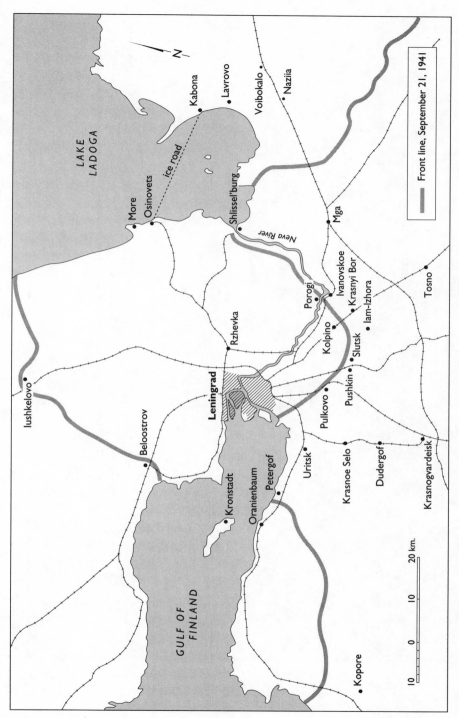

Front Line around Leningrad, 21 September 1941

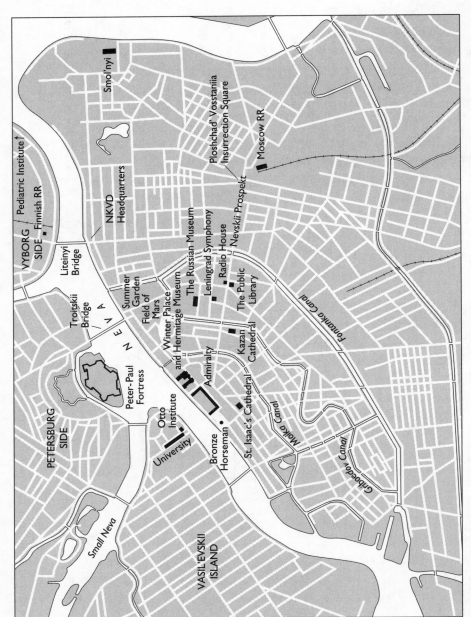

Leningrad, with Points of Interest

VYBORG
SIDE

Pediatric Institute↑
Finnish RR

Smol'nyi

NKVD
Headquarters

Ploshchad' Vosstaniia
Insurrection Square

Moscow RR

Liteinyi
Bridge

Troitskii
Bridge

PETERSBURG
SIDE

Peter-Paul
Fortress

Summer
Garden
Field of
Mars

N E V A

The Russian Museum

Leningrad Symphony

Radio House

Nevskii Prospekt

Winter Palace
and Hermitage Museum

The Public
Library

Kazan
Cathedral

Admiralty

Fontanka Canal

Otto
Institute

University

Bronze
Horseman

St. Isaac's Cathedral

Moika Canal

Griboedov Canal

Small Neva

VASIL'EVSKII
ISLAND

Writing the Siege of Leningrad

OLDER LENINGRADERS STILL REMEMBER THE BRIGHT, WARM SUNDAY when German forces invaded the Soviet Union. Many had already moved to their dachas outside the city in preparation for summer. 22 June 1941. Despite the nonaggression pact that the USSR and Germany had signed in August 1939, Soviet citizens had followed with unease the Nazi expansion into northern and central Europe and northern Africa. Still, it was hard to believe.

22 JUNE 1941. MORNING

I carried Lena out into the garden together with her colored rattles. The sun already ruled the sky completely.

A cry, the sound of broken dishes. The woman who owns our dacha ran past the house.

"Elena Iosifovna, war with the Germans! They just announced it on the radio!" she shouted, crying.

War! I am thirty-four years old. This is the fourth war of my life.

Elena Kochina, *Blockade Diary*

22 JUNE

This morning everything was as peaceful and calm as a still lake. The sun was shining and everything seemed to promise a perfect day. . . .

The fresh morning air, the sunshine streaming through the wide-open windows, and the fact that everything seemed to be going so well combined to give me a wonderful feeling of contentment and joy. . . .

At around nine o'clock, the phone rang. It was my husband calling from work. Though usually calm, he seemed greatly agitated. Without explaining why, he asked me not to go anywhere and to keep Dima at home. . . .

At noon my mother and I heard Molotov speak on the radio. So this was

1

it—war! Germany was already bombing Soviet cities. Molotov's speech was halting, as if he were out of breath. His rallying, spirited appeals seemed out of place. And suddenly I realized that something ominous and oppressive loomed over us.

Elena Skriabina, Siege and Survival

The City of Women

Early in those nine hundred days, the Siege of Leningrad became a woman's experience. Indeed the battlefront was close by—so perilously close that some soldiers attempted to return to the city sporadically at night to bring a portion of their rations to their starving families. Yet the daily tasks of domestic life and labor, and the continual responsibilities of air-raid defense, were left to the women of the city. With the exception of essential military and political personnel, the city was bereft of able-bodied men under the age of fifty-five. Add to this the biological fact that men succumbed more quickly and more often to starvation. In her memoirs of the first and worst winter of the Siege (1941–1942), Ol'ga Grechina writes:

> In November, according to official statistics, deaths of men over draft age (fifty-five) exceeded the normal death rate by 11,000. . . . In comparison with the number of women in the city, there were very few men, and one was immediately struck by their inability to adapt to the tragic conditions of life. They began to fall down in the streets, take to their beds in their apartments, to die and die and die. . . . The long-suffering women of Leningrad suddenly realized that on them lay the fate not only of their family, but of the city, even of the entire country.[1]

Despite the predominance of women in the city, deaths of men far outnumbered those of women even in the first months of 1942. The NKVD reported in January 1942 the deaths of 70,853 men (73.2 percent) and 25,898 women (26.8 percent). In February 1942, 57,990 (60.4 percent) men died and 38,025 (39.6 percent) women. Only in March 1942 did more women (42,842, or 52.6 percent) die than men (38,664, or 47.4 percent).[2] Exact ratios of men to women in the population can never be known. The Siege fell between two national censuses, and no consistent official statistics on inhabitants of

2

"Siege Room." A unique exhibit at the Museum of Bread in St. Petersburg depicts the vitally important and emblematic objects in the circumscribed world of the Siege. From left to right: a water container for hauling water; the children's sled (for hauling); the bread ration (next to the clock); the window taped to keep the glass from shattering; the window blanketed for warmth and to prevent light from attracting enemy fire; the clothes line; the *burzhuika,* a special small stove (on the stool on the right); and the typical Leningrad radio, on the wall, upper right, known as the "plate" (*tarelka*). *The Museum of Bread, St. Petersburg*

the city were kept. Researchers must piece together various reports, such as those of the NKVD above, or figures cited in other Soviet sources, such as reported by A. R. Dzeniskevich, to conclude that by 15 December 1942, 79.9 percent of all factory workers were women.[3] The testimonies that follow corroborate the various statistics that support a characterization of besieged Leningrad as a city of women. Together they highlight the need to study the effect of the Siege on this specific population.

3

Women and War

> Queen Athena—shield of our city—glory of goddesses!
> Now shatter the spear of Diomedes! That wild man—
> hurl him headlong down before the Scaean Gates!
> At once we'll sacrifice twelve heifers in your shrine,
> yearlings never broken, if only you'll pity Troy,
> the Trojan wives and all our helpless children!
>
> THE ILIAD (6.360–66)[4]

In modern warfare, the besieging of a civilian population is considered bar-
baric. Yet the Siege of Leningrad was not the only siege of World War II,
not even on Soviet territory. And the recent tragedies of Sarajevo, Goražde,
and Groznyi remind us that this ancient strategy may still be used in "civi-
lized" Europe. It is not surprising that women and children while under siege
in Leningrad were left to fend as best they could while men (and women)
fought at the nearby front to defend the city.[5] Much has been written about
what was exceptional about the Siege of Leningrad—its duration, its staggering human toll. Yet historians and other analysts have not focused sufficient attention on the realities of the Siege that make it atypical in other
ways. Unlike most sieges in history, the citizens of besieged Leningrad no
longer observed the historic division along gender lines between public
(male front-line) and private (female home-front) reactions to war. Having
embraced the role of public defenders of Leningrad, home-front women
often perceived warfare, and heroism, differently. They inevitably provide
a unique perspective on World War II and the Siege.

In the heroic epics of Greece, and in other prehumanist accounts of
siege warfare, we are inspired to revere the acts of gods, or god-like heroes.
Women's efforts are prescribed, and in the oral and written histories, circumscribed. In *The Iliad*, mortal women play predictable, and usually minor,
roles. The noble women of Troy (as in the epigraph) make sacrifices to the
gods and pray for victory and salvation. Occasionally they may respond, like
Hector's wife, Andromache, with "womanly" timidity:

> "Reckless one,
> my Hector—your own fiery courage will destroy you!
> Have you no pity for him, our helpless son? Or me,
> and the destiny that weighs me down, your widow" (6.482–85).

And they fulfill the woman's role in traditional societies of lamenter or keener:

> So the voice of the king rang out in tears,
> the citizens wailed in answer, and noble Hecuba
> led the wives of Troy in a throbbing chant of sorrow:
> "O my child—my desolation! How can I go on living?
> What agonies must I suffer now, now *you* are dead and gone?
> You were my pride throughout the city night and day—
> a blessing to us all, the men and women of Troy:
> throughout the city they saluted you like a god.
> You, you were their greatest glory while you lived—
> now death and fate have seized you, dragged you down! (22.504–13)

From 1941 to 1944, women in Leningrad also served these traditional functions. Their lamentations, broadcast regularly over the radio and some eventually published, vied with those of the wives of Troy. Yet women's roles during the Siege were more various, and for a number of reasons. In comparison with premodern, if not ancient, times, women by the mid-twentieth century certainly enjoyed greater freedom—and responsibility—in both the public and the private domains. The Soviet woman had in many ways progressed even further than her western counterparts: since the days of reconstruction following the Bolshevik Revolution, Soviet women had often engaged in what had traditionally been considered men's work. Thus women of the Siege of Leningrad, in such roles as doctor, military orderly, civil-defense worker, factory worker, and government official, crossed the boundary from the traditional passive and private role of women under siege to the military and public theater of war. This meant that their deeds, just like those of their sisters serving in combat positions, were *eligible* to be considered heroic.

Hector answers his wife's entreaty to choose peace and private life in the besieged Troy:

> "All this weighs on my mind too, dear woman.
> But I would die of shame to face the men of Troy
> and the Trojan women trailing their long robes
> if I would shrink from battle now, a coward." (6.522–25).

In the Siege of Leningrad, such a response was required of *all* the inhabitants of Leningrad, by the government and in response to the public's highly

5

V. Gushchina. "Portrait of the Guard of the Zhdanov Factory, M. I. Erëmicheva" (*Portret okhrannitsy zavoda imeni A. A. Zhdanova, M. I. Erëmichevoi*), 1943. A woman member of the People's Militia guards the entrance to the Zhdanov Factory. *The Russian National Museum*

developed sense of patriotism. Mostly women and children, they too had to seek the courage of Hector.

It could be said that the "courage of Hector" represents the tenor of all official histories, whose goal is to maintain the social and political order. This is an endeavor that, in a stable society, usually has the support of a nation's heroes and others who gather and disseminate information. Many heroines of the Siege of Leningrad contributed to the writing of its official history. Yet many others did not. Perhaps they simply were not asked. At the time, the private accounts of common people were not considered as significant to history as they are today. Perhaps for some women who had to be simultaneously mother, wife, worker, and "warrior," loyalties became blurred. They could no longer respond as assuredly as Hector: "Fight for your country—that is the best, the only omen" (12.281). Even democratic societies do not welcome into their official histories those with confused loyalties. In the Soviet Union of Stalin, expressing doubt was a dangerous undertaking.

The women of Leningrad had a different relationship to warfare than their matriarchs in besieged Troy or elsewhere in other premodern eras. By undertaking all responsibilities, both public and private, they forged a new kind of courage. It was not simply an amalgam of the courage of Hector, the warrior, and of Andromache, the helpmate and supplicant, for these roles are often antithetical. These recollections of women survivors demonstrate that women warriors affect notions of traditional valor as much as they are affected by them.[6]

6

Women's Lot/*Zhenskaia Dolia* (1941–1944)

During the Siege, the responsibilities of women in Leningrad increased greatly. In addition to caring for family members and, for some, continuing their prewar work outside the home, women were required to contribute in various ways to the defense of the city. As with statistics on mortality, there are no extensive and consistent records of the duties women performed. Information must be extrapolated from numerous sources.

Women responded immediately to the German offensive against Leningrad. Along with children as young as fourteen, they worked digging trenches and building fortifications. Salisbury reports that among the 30,000 Leningraders mobilized to "dig trenches, mine fields and dig gun emplacements, dugouts, and tank traps . . . the brunt was borne by women."[7] Women's work in this arena was assumed. In newly published Communist Party documents delineating work on the Luga line of defense, officials are commanded to mobilize workers and the "local population."[8] However, Zhdanov addresses directly the question of women's involvement in direct military action to defend Leningrad, permitting their voluntary enlistment in the People's Militia (*Narodnoe opolchenie*).[9] In the excerpt from her memoir *A Half Century Ago*, Sof'ia Buriakova provides a statistic. She was among a detachment of 3,000 individuals sent to the Luga line to dig antitank trenches. With the exception of the military leaders, all were women. Women built fortifications within the city as well. They formed workers battalions of 80,000 Leningraders, joining teenagers and old men to construct embrasures in buildings, pillboxes, and firing points.[10]

After the mobilization of eligible male factory workers to the front, tens of thousands of women, along with adolescents and pensioners, volunteered or were assigned to take their places.[11] The first winter of the war proved most devastating for those who were biologically least predisposed to endure starvation—the very young, male adolescents, and the elderly. As a consequence, the vast majority of the positions in industry were then held by women. Among the documents that follow, Valentina Bushueva recounts the hardships of work in the peat bogs and as a member of a coal workers battalion. Mariia Kropacheva reports that women workers at a chocolate factory declined the assistance of male workers at the mixing machines, which required considerable strength. The women were already producing at 300 percent over the norm.

Leningraders gather water on Nevskii Avenue, 25 October 1942. *The Central State Archive of Film, Photographic, and Audio Documentation, St. Petersburg*

Once intense bombing of the city began, women contributed to air-raid defense as well. At the end of the work day and after hours spent hauling water and standing in line to receive the ration, women served the local air-raid defense (MPVO) keeping watch on rooftops for incendiary bombs. Anna Ostroumova-Lebedeva discusses the organization of these watches (*dezhurstvo*) in her diary entry for 2 August 1941, which she writes during her shift on the staircase of her apartment building.

It is usually assumed that in the Soviet Union, women physicians always dominated the field of family-practice medicine. In fact, this situation developed only during World War II and then persisted after the war, when men remained in relatively short supply. The specialty was demanding, including exhausting schedules of home visitations, and did not pay particularly well. As in the West, nursing was considered a woman's profession. During the Siege, primary medical care came to be the province of women. With the mobilization or evacuation of male surgeons and other male specialists, or their death in Leningrad, women physicians took on even greater

responsibilities. Anna Likhacheva chronicles below her research on supplemental nourishment in the clinic of the Red Banner Factory. Yuliia Mendeleva describes her efforts to keep the Leningrad Pediatric Institute operating
and to maintain it as a medical school, as a children's outpatient clinic, and
as a hospital throughout the Siege. The surgeon Valentina Gorokhova provides a detailed description of practicing medicine in primitive conditions
in an evacuation hospital.

Many have noted the immensity of women's work during the Siege.
Some have commented on its variety as well. It is not surprising, however,
that official published documents do not address these parameters. In the
party documents published, for example, in *Leningrad under Siege*, officials
quantify volunteers in the MPVO or workers in factories without regard to
their sex. In the personal documents that follow however, women fill in many
of the details that are absent from official reports, and they often bring a new
perspective to work that in peacetime was done by men.

The Feminine Perspective

Most able-bodied men who remained in Leningrad held higher-level positions in government, law enforcement, the military, or industry, while
women, although they may have held such positions, were still responsible
for "*Kinder, Küche*, and *Kirche*" (children, kitchen, and church).[12] Accordingly they write in their diaries and memoirs, or even recall, aspects of life
that may have been unknown or unimportant to their male comrades under
siege. Yet preserving daily life, above all obtaining food and water, acquired
the utmost strategic significance. The history of the Siege must document
these traditional activities as a "line of defense."

Byt (Kinder, Küche)

Perhaps the most frequent theme of the narratives that follow, "home and
hearth" (the English equivalent of *Kinder* and *Küche*), the Russians call
byt. In *At the Writing Table*, Lidiia Ginzburg notes the inversion of values
during the Siege in the hierarchy of human activity. She recalls that the intellectuals of the 1930s were accustomed to thinking of food in terms of its
psychological attributes. It meant comfort, relaxation, friendly conversation.

N. Petrova. "The Boot-Cleaner," (*U chistil'shchitsy sapog*), 1943. A woman shoe shiner renders her services to a woman soldier in an attempt to "keep up appearances," even in the midst of the Siege. *The Russian National Museum*

They felt, condescendingly, in the 1930s that a dependence on food was characteristic of the "lower order." Later, during the Siege, intellectuals learned to appreciate food as physical nourishment along with the processes of gathering food and preparing it. However, they were often ill fit for life's basic demands. Ginzburg observes that when the intellectuals finally did get involved in the preparation of food, they overdid it. They ruined dishes by their constant "doctoring" of recipes.[13] The ability to maintain the household and feed the family, generally considered to be banal women's work, during the Siege acquired supreme significance. The gathering and preparation of foodstuffs and the transformation of the inedible into the edible constitute the major themes of the documents in this collection. Among them, Tamara Nekliudova's "War-Time Menu" and Vera Miliutina's "Ode to Grass" serve as emblems of this overriding concern.

Although obtaining food overshadowed all other activities of everyday life (*byt*), these women survivors complement official history with the details that consumed their time and energy. A number of them describe the ordeal of transporting a deceased family member to the cemetery and attempting to find and pay someone to dig a grave. Valentina Petrova and Sof'ia Buriakova provide information on working churches during the Siege. Natal'ia Stroganova chronicles the fate of her family members in her housekeeping journal and praises the work of the janitors of her building, who cleared snow and kept watch at night. Many of the *blokadnitsy* (such as Stroganova, Petrova, and Miliutina) provide information on the fate of ordinary individuals whose disappearance during the Siege received no official acknowledgment—a relative arrested by the NKVD or ethnic Germans who were expelled from Leningrad. Against this background of unfounded suspicion, only Avgusta Saraeva-Bondar' encountered a real spy. She recounts her sighting of a *raketchik*, a traitor who signaled to the Germans from within the city. As Nataliia Rogova of the Russian National Library characterized the contribution of these women, they not only preserve the nation's memory, they provide the "small" stories of the Siege. Thus their narratives alter the general historical perspective.

Arbiters of Morality (*Kirche*)

11

In these survivors' narratives, we find a reflection of the third sphere of traditional women's work—the moral upbringing (*vospitanie*) of the family. The responsibility of instilling societal and religious values in the younger

L. Lebedinskaia. A teapot from the tea set "Leningrad in the blockade" (*Chainik iz serviza "Leningrad v blokade"***), 1944. A commemorative tea set produced by the famous Lomonosov Porcelain Factory to celebrate the lifting of the Siege. Pictured on the teapot are the Narvskii Gates, where the Red Army held the front line against the invaders.** *The State Hermitage Museum*

generation must explain in part the revelations of these unofficial histories. These narratives differ dramatically from valorous accounts of the Siege in their narrator's stance as an arbiter of morality. These women often sit in judgment of behavior, their own as well as the government's. Again, we can recall Lidiia Ginzburg's indictment of her own class, the intelligentsia, in the relative inability of its members to cope with the hardships of the Siege. Liubov' Shaporina continues this self-accusation. Despite her ordeals, she does not exempt herself from the alleged spinelessness of the Russian intelligentsia.

Not all the judgments are as sweeping as these. Other Siege survivors confess to relatively lesser failings. Ol'ga Freidenberg writes of the often ruinous effect of the Siege on the human psyche and regrets her ill temper in comparison with her mother's tolerance. And Avgusta Saraeva-Bondar' admits to imitating the sound of an air-raid alarm after the Siege had ended and laments the distress that it caused the inhabitants of the apartment building.

The most outspoken of the *blokadnitsy* in this collection is Ol'ga Freidenberg. She comments on the unfair stigma on those attempting to be
evacuated from Leningrad, the senselessness of not surrendering the city,
the inequities of the ration system, and much more. Liubov' Shaporina
likewise attacks Stalin, his policy on the city, and the continuing arrests on
political grounds of innocent people. Ol'ga Grechina ponders the criminal
act of her friend's mother, who embezzled her patients' money in order to
evacuate her sons, Jews who she feared would perish in a pogrom. Grechina
can understand this crime but cannot accept the evacuation of these two
young men, who should have fought for their country. Kseniia Matus laments
the sacrifice of soldiers sent untrained as "cannon fodder" to the front. These
women also hail contributions that might otherwise have gone unnoticed.
Ol'ga Freidenberg praises the common people who simply carry on during
the Siege.[14] Vera Kostrovitskaia indicts the director of her ballet school for
profiteering and cruelty toward the students and immortalizes a Navy band's
gift of music to their besieged neighbors. As the instruments of official propaganda fell ever more silent in Leningrad, women played their traditional
role of preserving private and familial values with increasing authority. It
is in their role as arbiters of morality that these women make the greatest
contribution to the official history of the Siege.

Until recently, little has been written on the role of religious communities and the practice of faith in besieged Leningrad.[15] However, these documents reveal the significance of faith and organized religion not only during
the war but also in Soviet society in general. The women cite specific events
and concerns that reflect their spiritual yearning. Valentina Petrova still recalls the Russian Orthodox churches that remained operating during the
Siege. Liubov' Shaporina remembers Easter, 1942, celebrated under intense
bombardment and in conditions of extreme starvation. Sof'ia Buriakova
laments her meager offering to relatives who came, as was their family's
tradition, to celebrate Trinity Sunday and their saint's day. Many of the
blokadnitsy reveal the religious and spiritual significance of their extreme
attempts to provide their dead with the proper rites of burial (Èl'za Greinert,
Sof'ia Buriakova, Natal'ia Stroganova). This documentation of their Siege
experience calls into question the commonly held view of Soviet society as
strictly secular. In fact, women in Soviet society, and particularly during the
Siege, supported religious life also in the traditional, formal sense of *Kirche*.

13

Lost Beauty and Youth

During many of the interviews conducted in preparation for this volume, women survivors of the Siege regretted the loss of their girlhood beauty and vitality, of what were potentially the best days of their lives. In the documents that follow, some survivors reveal their most intimate thoughts in response to the Siege as an assault on a woman's body and her potential to experience life as a woman. In *At the Writing Table*, Lidiia Ginzburg addressed this theme as well. She reacted to the process of losing body fat and made an excruciatingly personal observation on the notion of the "front":

> The hostile world, approaching, advances outposts. Its closest outpost suddenly turned out to be one's own body . . . in the winter it had an eternal potential for suffering—with its ever new corners and ribs . . . while people discovered in themselves bone after bone, there occurred an alienation from the body, a splintering of conscious will from the body as a phenomenon of the hostile external world.[16]

Ginzburg despaired at the loss of her femaleness, her identity.[17] Her horror may have resulted also from the recognition of starvation as the final invasion of the body politic at war on her last vestige of privacy and individuality—her own flesh.[18]

Many of our chroniclers remarked on the physical effects of starvation that eventually made it difficult to distinguish males from females and the young from the old. Kseniia Matus, then an eighteen-year-old oboist with the Leningrad Symphony, recalls looking out over the audience during one of the heroic performances during the Siege and being unable to determine the sex of the onlookers. In the excerpt from *Grave Months for the Blockaded City*, Elena Martilla remarks more than once that people called her, a young artist of eighteen, "Grandma." One evening, near to death, Martilla takes a mirror and keeps herself alive through the night by painting her self-portrait: "I'm a young woman and forced to be snuffed out, but I'll die with a paint brush in my hand."

Women speak and write of the effects of the Siege and war on their prospects for a normal life and the difficult choices they were forced to make between their private destiny and that of their country. Kseniia Matus describes a romance with a young man that is experienced in an atmosphere of the relative freedom of war. She eventually rejects her lover, however. The war reveals his self-absorption and cowardice, faults that in ordinary times might have gone unrecognized. Ol'ga Grechina discusses the real shortage of eligible young men during and after the war. She admits her good fortune in being able to find a husband, and a handsome and healthy one at that.

Even before World War II, communist ideology provided for a broader sphere of experience for Soviet women. They had made inroads into masculine realms of work. During the Siege, women of necessity took on even the most traditionally male jobs in heavy industry and defense while maintaining the traditional responsibilities of keeping house and raising children. The personal narratives of women who suffered the Siege of Leningrad shed light on all spheres of existence. Their reminiscences complement official reports of the defense of the city and labor production and provide insight into the day-to-day struggle of the inhabitants to survive. They also reveal the private struggles of women to fulfill the responsibilities and experience the joys of wife and mother, and of girls to survive and fulfill their dreams as women.[19]

Women's Life Writing

> Такими мы счастливыми были;
> Такой свободой бурною дышали
> Что внуки позавидовали б нам.
>
> We felt so exalted,
> We breathed such stormy freedom,
> That our grandchildren would have
> envied us.
>
> OL'GA BERGGOL'TS, "FEBRUARY DIARY"

We are approaching the documents that follow primarily as memoirs. Traditionally, we distinguish memoir from autobiography on the basis of the writer's perceived emphasis on milieu or context over personal life story. In the case of women writers, however, we have been made aware of the nontraditional ways in which women have revealed their lives in writing. That what is easily recognizable as memoir might also serve the function of life writing follows from the reality that large segments of society, among them

15

women, have not had access to the poetics of autobiography. Regenia Gagnier describes the notion of selfhood that underlies the writing of autobiography, narrowly defined:

> a meditative and self-reflective sensibility; faith in writing as a tool of self-expression; an attempt to make sense of life as a narrative progressing in time, with a narrative typically structured upon parent/child relationships and familial development; and a belief in personal creativity, autonomy and freedom for the future.[20]

For much of history, women have lacked (and in some cases, still lack) the sense of "empowerment" that enables the writing of traditional autobiography.

In *Terrible Perfection*, Barbara Heldt studied the Russian tradition of women's autobiography. She observed that women were compelled or permitted themselves to write their lives only when they felt they could contribute to the broader sphere of public life.[21] She categorized the first Russian female autobiographers as revolutionary (Vera Figner, for example), political prisoner (Evgeniia Ginzburg), and cultural conservator (Nadezhda Mandel'shtam). Heldt glimpsed, in these twentieth-century autobiographies, the promise of full-fledged authority, which will recognize the value of recording a woman's private life. Thus we should keep in mind, in reading the documents that follow, not only their significance for the history of the Siege of Leningrad. We must recognize their often muted autobiographical intent and, thereby, their contribution to Russian women's life writing.

Barbara Heldt also observed that in Russia, where women took up their pens later and in fewer numbers than did their counterparts in the West, they are best represented, in the nineteenth century and into the twentieth, in the genres that emanate more from the private sphere—autobiography and poetry. Beth Holmgren later demonstrated that it was this very marginalization of women and their writing that enabled them to serve as cultural conservators during the Stalinist Terror: "despite significant restrictions and deprivations, the domestic sphere under Stalin benefited from this political neglect and women acquired a valuable low profile along with their secondary status."[22] The Siege survivors represented here did not labor to preserve the memory of cultural icons who were victims of the purges, as Nadezhda Mandel'shtam recalled her husband, the poet Osip Mandel'shtam, or as Lidiia Chukovskaia strove to commemorate the life of her friend, the poet Anna Akhmatova. The *blokadnitsy* did on occasion write of the undeserved fate of well-known individuals—for example Ol'ga Grechina deplored the suspicion that fell on the folklorist Vladimir Propp because of his German heritage. However, with respect to Russian "high" culture, their focus was generally more diffuse.

These women, in their own behavior, attempted to preserve a nebulous but keenly sensed Russian culture, and they lament the waning of the customs that revealed it. Saraeva-Bondar' grieves over the loss of Leningraders who embodied the *intelligentnost'* that characterized the city. Stroganova describes her pain at being slapped by her father during the Siege "against old Petersburg tradition." Ol'ga Freidenberg writes disarmingly, in comparison with her often esoteric scholarly prose, of the sacramental quality of setting a festive table in honor of her birthday. The surviving pieces of family china represented "a parade of a home and a spirit that has been preserved; it was my own personal triumph. Only Mama and I could understand the importance of this holiday table." For Natal'ia Rogova, of the Russian National Library, the valiant actions of the *blokadnitsy* represent the preservation not only of the city but also of art and culture. Yet, it is interesting that Rogova, the daughter of Siege survivors, refers to a genderless "people" who saved the city. Typical even of the middle generation of Russian women today, Rogova does not identify the sacrifice of, primarily, women. As Toby Clyman and Diana Greene recognized in their analysis of Lidiia Ginzburg's autobiography from the Siege (Ginzburg intentionally referred to victims of the Siege as "people"), Russian women may not openly reveal or even realize the gendered nature of their experiences: "Her work, like that of many cultural conservators, displays, but does not own, her complex difference."[23]

Although our "cultural conservators" do not qualify as either revolutionaries or political prisoners (Heldt's other categories of women autobiographers), they are impelled to speak and write by a similar sense of injustice. We have referred to their writing previously as testimony. They felt obliged to give witness to what they were experiencing. Yet, their accustomed position on the periphery, in the private realm, emboldened them to write more openly than the men who also bore witness. They not only wrote of the private side of war. They exercised the relative freedom that they had sensed within the home, even at the height of the Terror of the preceding decade. Liubov' Shaporina's and Ol'ga Freidenberg's written indictments of Stalin simply astound the reader.

In many of the documents that follow, women pass judgment not just

17

on their own actions or those of family members—in the tradition of enforcing the moral or religious code within the home—they criticize and condemn acquaintances, the government, and society at large. We can account for their temerity in part as a result of the freedom they enjoyed as low-profile women. Yet they experienced an even greater sense of liberation due to their even more liminal status in war. In Stalin's time, Soviet citizens experienced relative freedom in a limited number of otherwise undesirable places; for instance, the labor camp or the mad house. The chaos of war constituted a similarly liminal and relatively free state.[24] Women at war were thus "doubly" free to write of their convictions and, even if unconsciously, of their lives.

In these letters, diaries, memoirs, and works of documentary prose, we can recognize some traditional impetuses of Russian women autobiographers —the attempt to preserve culture and expose social injustice. Yet, it is often left for the reader to identify the Siege as a *woman*'s experience or the document as a piece of *women*'s life writing. The significance for Russian literature of women's writing on the Siege and women writing their lives during the Siege has escaped the attention, at times, of even the professional Russian reader. The publishing house Soviet Writer (*Sovetskii pisatel'*) rejected Lidiia Razumovskaia's piece of documentary prose, included here, and returned her manuscript with the critique: "All of this is just about herself. There is no background." It is our hope that this volume will draw greater attention to the contributions of the *blokadnitsy*, not only to the history of the Siege, but also to the heritage of Russian women's life writing.

Diaries & Letters

Liubov' Vasil'evna Shaporina (née Yakovleva), artist, stage designer, and organizer of the marionette theater in Petrograd, kept a diary for decades, beginning in 1917. Her diaries, purchased by the manuscript department of the Russian National Library (St. Petersburg), were prepared for publication by the department's senior researcher, Valentina Fedorovna Petrova. When publication of the diaries was delayed, Petrova (herself a Siege survivor) secured for Shaporina's manuscript a place in the anniversary exhibition "The City of Leningrad during the Siege." In 1995, V. F. Petrova generously shared with us cultural and biographical information about L. V. Shaporina and a number of entries from the diaries themselves, which Petrova herself selected. Shaporina's notebooks (March 1935–October 1939) have been published, with no references to the location of the original sources.[1] These fragments are all focused on the ideological "cleansings" of the 1930s: "They interrogated me for five-and-a-half hours," from the diary entry of March 1935. "And everyone in Palekh has been depressed since A. I. Zubkov's arrest."[2] In her last entry, dated 24 October 1939, she states: "It's terribly hard to build, but oh, so easy to destroy."[3]

After September 1941, while continuing to work as a freelance stage designer for Leningrad City Theater (nicknamed "The Siege Theater"), Shaporina was employed as a nurse at the hospital nearby on Liteinyi Avenue. The position of nurse provided her with the second-best food ration (*kartochki vtoroi kategorii*) and an additional meal in the hospital's canteen. In the besieged city, Shaporina created sets for *The Queen of Spades* and *The Marriage of Belugin*. She also wrote an article, "Twenty-Five Years in the History of the Puppet Theater," and was recommended to become a member of the Leningrad Chapter of the Union of Soviet Artists by A. P. Ostroumova-Lebedeva.

In her diaries of the 1940s, however, Shaporina rarely reflected on the life of Leningrad artists; likewise, she did not mention any of her own creative works in the notebooks written during the Siege. For her, the great terror of 1937–1939 evolved, without interruption, into the war of the two Herods—Hitler and Stalin, and the sacrificial lambs in this battle were "we, the philistines, the *quantité négligeable*," Russian common folk whom Stalin had "been grinding to a pulp for the past twenty years." Shaporina treated the ordeals of the Siege as the punishment the intelligentsia and the entire nation deserved. She quoted the nurse Masha Tsvetkova: "They have eliminated the church. There is no God. But He, our Holy

Father, has great patience, yet punishes severely. Now punishment is being inflicted for our iniquities." A dedicated Christian and a true lover of her Motherland, Shaporina prayed to God for mercy. During the second week of the fierce battle that preceded the liberation of Leningrad from the Nazi blockade, she "prayed for every living being who dies here, next to us, on behalf of us, on behalf of Russia."

L. V. Shaporina's diaries are held in the Manuscript Department of the Russian National Library, OR RNB, Fond 1086, No. 7–11 (1941–1945).

4 SEPTEMBER 1941

Leningrad, our former Petersburg, is surrounded on all sides. Word has it the Germans have parachuted tanks and cannons into Terrioki, beyond Kolpino, and now down the Neva into Ivanovskoe.[4] People standing in line say that famine set in immediately; yet for me it set in long ago. Bread rations began to be cut on 1 September: for workers, six hundred grams to four hundred grams per day, for dependents—to three hundred grams. The morning of 2 September, I went out for butter and sugar—they would only sell me one hundred grams of butter, and it took me half an hour to get it. Then it took me two more hours to get two hundred grams of sugar, the limit I was allowed to buy. I ran into Gipsi.[5] The information he passed on to me made me weak in the knees: three days ago they arrested Cherniavskii.[6] They came at night, conducted a lengthy search, found nothing, and took him away. Gipsi walked me home. I went upstairs, entered the apartment, and there was Elena Ivanovna Glen.[7] She looked awful. That morning she had been called in by the police—they are to be deported within twenty-four hours. Where, how, when the trains are not running? "On the 3rd, you'll be loaded onto a barge and taken to Shlissel'burg; after that you are free—go anywhere you want, live in any place you wish, only not in the Leningrad district. You may take with you anything you want." When, instead of Lilly, Vasia[8] came at the appointed time to inform the authorities of her illness, he found about a hundred people there waiting to be exiled; they were mostly women, old women in old-fashioned capes and worn-out plush coats. These are the enemies that our government is capable of fighting. And, it turns out, these are the only ones. The Germans are at the gates, the Izhorsk Works has been partly destroyed, the Germans are just about to enter the city, and we are busy arresting and deporting old women and lonely, defenseless, and harmless people.

7 SEPTEMBER

If today turns out all right for those thousands of people who were sent to dig trenches under German fire for the glory of the Monster, it will be a miracle.

8 SEPTEMBER

G. Popov[9] dropped in on us today and played the piano. He called me into the room and started to play Ravel's "Promenade in auto." At the most bravura place he says: "They're shooting." I tried to calm him down, but he ran to the window. High in the sky there were white balls of explosions—the desperate efforts of the anti-aircraft guns. Suddenly, from behind the roofs a white cloud started to grow; it expanded quickly and other clouds piled on this one. They were all dyed amber in the setting sun. They filled up the entire sky; then the clouds turned bronze, while from below a black stripe started moving upwards. It was so unlike smoke that for a long time I could not comprehend that it was fire. They say it was the oil tanks and Badaev warehouses burning. It was an immense spectacle of stunning beauty.

10 SEPTEMBER

The bombardment of the city has begun. At around 10:00 A.M., an air-raid alarm was sounded, and it was followed immediately by an explosion. A sudden tremor from underneath the floor was followed by an explosion; then another one even more powerful than the first. The explosions continued, but they were now less powerful. . . . Our boulevard is clogged with personal possessions, from the devastated buildings. Building No. 12 on Furshtadtskaia Street had its corner blown off, the one that extends into Druskeninskii Lane—a room and a half, and a kitchen or a hallway. . . . On the upper floors, in the remains of the room there are white tile stoves with fireplaces, an orange shade dangles from the ceiling and sways in the wind, a buffet—blown to bits; on the only wall left standing, which can no longer be reached, there is a peg with two coats on it, a man's and a woman's, and next to it, a suitcase.

12 SEPTEMBER

Evening is approaching. I feel heartsick. We are all on death row; we just don't know who is next. For twenty-three years we have all been on death row in theory, but now we have reached the epoch's grand finale. An inglorious finale.

23

Rations are being cut once again. Now I receive two hundred grams of bread instead of six hundred, and that is certainly not enough. Two hundred grams of bread for an entire fourteen-hour day in the hospital is rather difficult, to say the least.

They say the Germans have dropped leaflets: we're giving you a respite until the 21st; if you do not surrender, we will grind you to a pulp. It's unclear whom they are addressing. We common people are a *quantité négligeable*. As for Stalin, he has been grinding us to a pulp for the past twenty years. He detests Leningrad—no one here has known him or seen him since the Revolution.

Yesterday there were twelve air-raid alerts.

Yesterday I was thinking—Russia has earned her punishment, and the "heavy hammer" [*tiazhkii mlat*][10] must forge in her a true love of nation, of the very land. For a hundred years, and maybe more, intellectuals have reviled their country, their government; they have received Manducus as tsar and have begun basely and hyperbolically to bow down, to offer up incense to him, thinking only of their own skins.[11] It is sickening to think of the apotheosis of "How the Steel Was Tempered" in Radlov's theater with Stalin at the center of the action.[12]
And Alesha Tolstoi!![13]

One should remember the assassination of Alexander II. Now the hour has struck for Nemesis.

Translated by Alla Zeide

ANNA PETROVNA OSTROUMOVA-LEBEDEVA (1871-1957)

Anna Petrovna Ostroumova-Lebedeva was an artist, printmaker, and book il-
lustrator. Her husband (m. 1905) was the chemist Sergei Vasil'evich Lebedev.
Ostroumova began her professional education in Baron Stiglitz's institute of technical drawing. She then studied at the Academy of Art and spent several years in
studios in Paris and Italy. In 1899 she joined the famous Petersburg society of
artists called "The World of Art" (*Mir iskusstva*). City landscapes, especially St.
Petersburg and its environs, figure significantly in Ostroumova's works. Notable
among these are the etchings she created for the book *Petersburg* (1912), written
by the historian of urban culture V. Ya. Kurbatov; a series of etchings for *The
Soul of Petersburg* (Dusha Peterburga, 1920), by N. P. Antsiferov; etchings to illus-
trate the Petersburg cycles of poems by Aleksandr Blok; and an album of lithographs, *Petersburg* (1922). For many years Ostroumova kept notebooks and the
diaries "Paths of My Creation," and on the basis of these she compiled her *Autobiographical Notes*. The latter were published serially: the first volume in 1935;
the second in 1945; and the third in 1951. All these volumes, as well as the reprint
of the *Notes* in 1974, were edited to conform to Soviet ideology.

During Soviet rule, Ostroumova succeeded in preserving her pride, patriotism, independence, and freedom of thought—qualities characteristic of the
best of the Russian intelligentsia before the Revolution. Professionally, she pros-
pered. She was recognized as an artist, and her works were shown in numerous
museum exhibits. She remained in contact professionally with the aesthetic cur-
rents of Russia and Europe, past and present. Thus when Ostroumova visited an
exhibit in the Russian Museum, "The History of Russian Woodcuts," she was especially struck by the seventeenth-century "Archstrategist Michael." The next
day she made herself an impression of the ancient board. In an excerpt from
her diaries that was not published in *Autobiographical Notes*, Ostroumova
wrote of the expressive force of this woodcut: "It has an immense firmness, in-
flexibility, even severity, but not cruelty. I write and speak so much about this
woodcut because, in addition to the fact that I was so struck by its scope, the
strength of its artistic flair, and its beauty, I felt an unusual spiritual affinity and
relation to this unknown woodcutter who lived two hundred years before me. I
feel in myself the line of succession from this unknown master."[14]   25

Only days after Ostroumova visited the museum, Hitler invaded the Soviet
Union. She remained in besieged Leningrad and continued to work. As the city

was under martial law, photographing and sketching on the streets was strictly forbidden. In January 1942, Ostroumova was able to obtain temporary permission to sketch on the streets for her project "Leningrad in the Great Patriotic War." Nonetheless, she was arrested: "I implore you to grant me permission to continue my sketching on the streets of the city," she wrote to Commissioner for the Arts A. A. Bartoshevich. "Today I attempted to make a small sketch, and they arrested me and conveyed me by convoy to the NKVD. There I was subjected to a lengthy interrogation (totally warranted), which concluded with their suggestion that I cease drawing until I receive permission."[15] In such difficult conditions the seventy-year-old artist, suffering from hunger, cold, and the stress of the bombings, created in 1942–1943 a series of artistic envelopes and postcards, "Open Letters to the Front."

In the spring of 1942, Ostroumova was invited to a special session of the City Council [*gorkom*] to discuss the creation of an album in response to a gift from the women of Scotland, who in the winter of 1942 had expressed, in the form of an album, their support and sympathy for the women of besieged Leningrad.[16] Ostroumova, with the help of the architects Yakov Osipovich Rubanchik and Boris Pavlovich Svetlitskii, the artist Vera Vladimirovna Miliutina, and two bookbinders, accomplished this task in five days.

On 1 November 1942, the newspaper *Leningrad Truth* announced that Ostroumova had been named an Honored Artist of the Soviet Union. However, this high award did little to ameliorate the conditions in which Ostroumova lived under siege—she was forced to paint portraits in exchange for bread and wood.[17] Throughout the war, Ostroumova continued to keep her diaries and to prepare for publication the second volume of her *Autobiographical Notes*. She wrote by the light of an oil lamp on a drawing board that she placed over the sink in the bathroom—the sounds of the air attacks were less audible there. The war and siege took a toll on Ostroumova's health, and in 1946 she ceased printmaking. Her last works are entitled "View of the Peter and Paul Fortress at Night" (1946) and "My Epitaph" (1946).

The following unpublished excerpts from Ostroumova's diary would never have made it past the censor. The artist writes openly of the inequities of the food-distribution system during the Siege and the animosity she and her friends felt toward Jews (despite her own cordial relations with Jewish intellectuals— see the excerpt from Ol'ga Freidenberg's diary). Although anti-Semitism was not unknown among Russians at that time, such attitudes were not officially condoned —all Soviet peoples were to live in harmony and to relate to each other without prejudice. As for Ostroumova's complaints of apparent Jewish self-interest, they wither before the courage and selflessness of Soviet Jews documented in these pages and elsewhere. See, for example, *The Book of the Living* (*Kniga zhivykh*) (St. Petersburg: Akropol', 1995).

A. P. Ostroumova-Lebedeva's diaries are held in the Manuscript Department of the Russian National Library, OR RNB Fond 1015, No. 57–60 (1941–1945).

6 JULY 1941

I suffer from constant mental and physical fatigue.

I cannot stop thinking for one minute about our courageous warriors, about our heroic youth, being slaughtered by the thousands by German tanks and planes.

Can it be that the war that has broken out between us and Hitler was brought on by the insidious politics of England? From what they allow us to know about the international situation, and in general about everything that's going on on our front and the European front, it is possible to understand from the officially reported information that the German pressure on the Suez Canal, on Egypt, on the English islands and in the Atlantic has weakened, and possibly, has completely subsided.[18]

Isn't this then the result of the ingenuous politics of the "perfidious Albion"?[19] Wasn't it they who caused Hitler, this raging wild bull, to turn his gaze on our country?

What methods have they used, what promises have they made? Is it possible that Hess himself (apparently insane), having parachuted into England, was able to make a deal with the English, or the other way around, that they were able to make a deal with him, settling accounts with each other using our country and the blood of our people?[20]

Yesterday Istoshina called me and proposed that I give them temporarily, for safe keeping, my archive and my watercolors. I am so tired of sorting and cataloguing my artwork. You can't give everything to the Museum, and it's necessary to select again what is more significant and what is of artistic interest, but what has to do with my family, intimate things, I won't hand over (that is for my archive).

But nonetheless, I gathered together my manuscripts, both those that I had used for the first volume and those for the second, unwritten volume.

The manuscripts are preliminary, with endless corrections, then forty-seven letters from N. I. Romanov to me, my notebooks and account books for various trips and other manuscripts and having sewn them into a canvas with lilac thread, and having sealed them with sealing wax, I took them myself to the Russian Museum.

In the drawing and watercolor department, the professional staff were filled with indignation at the behavior of the Jews working in the Museum. When there was an appeal at a meeting for volunteers, they spoke very fervently and patriotically, but in practice they all managed to find warm and safe places for themselves, all of them without exception. Some of them even took advantage of staff reductions to secure better positions for themselves than they had had before. In a word, my friends said that all of this was insultingly vile and mean.

∞

8 JULY 1941

This morning there were two air-raid warnings. The second one found me on the embankment, and I took shelter in the main building of the army hospital. A large detachment of military medical students also entered, and some people from the street—schoolgirls and little boys who were fishing on the Neva. The vestibule was large with a lot of couches and chairs. The students were forbidden to smoke. Right there in a kiosk they were selling papers. Then someone in charge ordered everyone to a kind of semi-basement. Some went, others didn't. The warning lasted for about a half-hour. One could hear anti-aircraft guns on both sides. The military report is very cautious, but they say nothing about a retreat to new positions. Again, it's difficult without a radio. And there is no loudspeaker in the street near us, so that it is hard to hear when a warning is lifted, not to mention the news from the front.

In the evening Ol'ga Anatol'evna visited. She is surrounded by panic-stricken co-workers, because they're all Jews. In that institution there is a 5 percent quota for Russian workers.[21] Everyone is running around looking for a way to leave. And all this is done on the sly with exceptional cunning and pushiness.

∞

2 AUGUST 1941

Our army is tenaciously holding its own. Today ends the sixth week of the war.

One has to marvel at and respect the courage and determination of our soldiers and their leaders.

And our pilots—the height of great bravery and resourcefulness!

So far not one bomb has fallen near Leningrad, despite frequent attacks by enemy aircraft.

Recently during an air-raid alarm, the radio broadcasters, stricken by panic, started to yell, "Everyone to the gas shelters! Everyone to the gas shelters!"[22]

We didn't hear it, but Elizaveta Martynovna (our neighbor and the temporary house manager) called and shouted for us to run to the gas shelter. Lilia[23] and I didn't go, having decided that if we were to run to the gas shelter every time there was an alarm, we wouldn't survive even a week of such a regime.

Shmidt, the Girgolavs, husband and wife, and everyone in the apartment building, except for the eighty-six-year-old woman at the Gaskeviches, left the building.[24]

There was heavy anti-aircraft fire. And suddenly to our surprise, Ol[impiia] Vl[adimirovna] Girgolav and Eliz[aveta] Mar[tynovna] Shmidt returned during the alarm, having remembered that they were members of the fire squad and were responsible for the safety of the building if there were to be a fire. And they took off and ran back. They were very apologetic and kind.

It turns out that a German plane was flying very persistently over the Military Medical Academy, but it didn't drop any bombs, and apparently it was a reconnaissance aircraft.

In our building an around-the-clock watch has been organized, in which Lilia and I participate. Each person keeps watch two hours on the stairs leading to the attic. It's light there, and one can sew, darn, and read.

Right now I'm sitting on that staircase and writing in my diary.

Yesterday, 1 August, I went to see Aleks[andra] Nik[androvna] Verkhovskaia.[25] They're about to leave. Her son-in-law, the husband of her daughter Asia, Levushka Sazonov, is being evacuated with the Optical Institute and the factory to the former Kazan' province, now the Cheremiss republic, to the town formerly called Tsarevokokshaisk (I don't know its name now. Something clever—Cheremiss).[26]

In my opinion, these hastily organized evacuations are so unnecessary.

They evacuate especially hastily those institutions that are headed up by Jews.

Al[eksandra] Nik[androvna], Asia, and Levushka are very depressed at

29

having to go to an unknown place. They have been warned that there will
be no housing for the new arrivals. They will have to build barracks right
away, and later they will live in dug-out huts [*zemlianki*].

What will they do with their Andriusha, such a spoiled and pampered
little boy? Will Aleksandra Nik[androvna] be able to survive the trip with
her heart condition and her weight?

I'm sorry for them and for me too. I was very close to them.

Vadim Nikonorovich was there too—the ex-husband of Aleks[andra]
Nikandrovna. Several times he started to tell me how tight money is since
the government order not to permit withdrawals from savings accounts for
more than two hundred rubles at a time. And therefore he has been unable
to provide financially as he should for Aleks[andra] Nik[androvna].

8 MARCH 1942

What an immense panorama of fire has engulfed the whole world! The
whole world! No, it seems there is no country whose peoples would not
writhe and die in the flame of this fire. Some kind of mad desire for mutual
extermination has seized everyone.

And our Leningrad, its siege and we its inhabitants, perishing from
hunger (20,000–25,000 per day), and from shells and bombs—we are only
a tiny detail in this entire, horrible, nightmarish, but grandiose and amazing war.

And just think: among the nations of the entire world, especially among
soldiers engaged in combat, how often have we seen manifested the ennobled
feelings of heroism, self-sacrifice, courage, and resourcefulness. What tremendous mental anguish soldiers must experience when they are commanded to kill the enemy—people just like themselves. We might assume,
and I think without error, that three-quarters of the combatants do not
thirst for the blood of their enemies.

But simultaneously along with the valorous actions of our warriors and
of people in general, how often have they demonstrated brutality, cruelty,
often completely unnecessary and senseless. And how much deception and
baseness!

But there is nothing more vile and insidious than those who, preying
on suffering and misfortune, bleeding people, stuff their pockets by means
of speculation and stealing. And there are a good number of them!

Recently I came upon a speech by Churchill, published in our country,
excerpted of course, in *Pravda* on 27 February.[27] It amazed me. He conveys

30

a stark picture of the madness that has gripped the whole world. And I would paint this picture thus: clouds of stinking black smoke have obscured the whole earth and sky. And tongues of fire, with sparks and steam, break through and dance about.

And below people swarm about. Fortresses fly into the air. Cities fall to the ground under the blows of artillery shells and falling bombs. People, like ants, perish under the debris of collapsing houses. Tens, hundreds of thousands of sailors cast themselves into the teeming waters from their fiery ships, all to perish in the sea. The African heat and sands incinerate entire divisions, and the desert is sown with the corpses of the unfortunate ones!

Within a few days corpses are transformed into a pile of white bones under the scorching rays of the sun. In other arenas of the war, soldiers freeze to death in the bitter cold, which it is difficult to survive, especially for the wounded or unconscious.

In several hours they transform into ice-covered corpses. Then, later, it is difficult to find them, since the snow covers them with its white shroud, altering the relief of the terrain.

I return again to Churchill's speech. It was striking for the courage shown in admitting England's seemingly total powerlessness before Germany, Japan, and Italy. He had the courage himself to tell the whole nation and whole world about the surrender to Japan of 673,000 English soldiers, including their commanding officers.

In all this worldwide phantasmagoria, I feel some kind of satanic romanticism, and in addition, grandeur, a head-long irrepressible rush to death and destruction.

Some horrible and violent whirlwind has landed on earth, and everything has gotten mixed up and has started to spin in black smoke, fire, and snowstorm.

And we, we Leningraders, choking in the siege, are microscopic grains of sand in this whole, immense cyclone.

22 MAY 1942   31

Rainy, overcast days. Today there was a fierce battle in the air. Evidently our heroic pilots were trying to keep the enemy planes from flying over the city. And they succeeded! There wasn't even an air-raid alarm.

All last week I was writing my "Autobiographical Notes, Vol. II," a chapter on my trip to Holland and Belgium.[28] I write sluggishly, and with difficulty. I haven't eaten well for the past ten days.

The academic ration I was allotted, and which I received for the first time on 8 April, wasn't distributed in May. And on what they give on the ration cards, it is impossible to survive, without starving, or losing the ability to work, or dying.

Anastasia Osipovna came to see me.[29] She had recently been to the public baths and was completely astounded by the large number of well-fed Rubenesque young women with radiant bodies and glowing physiognomies.

They are all workers in bakeries, cooperatives, soup kitchens, and children's centers.

In bakeries and cooperatives they cheat the unfortunate inhabitants. They divide the best food among themselves; for example, they leave the hind quarters for themselves.

In the soup kitchens and children's centers, they simply steal.

The same thing goes on, I think, at the highest level of the food-distribution system. What happened to two hundred cars of food, brought in as a gift to Leningrad from the collective-farm workers? And many times we received gifts of food from various districts, and what did we see of them? Everything gets lost in the "apparatus."

The organization of the food-ration cards with three categories is very convenient for well-known goals, for example for the "unloading" [razgruzka] of Leningrad.

As it is now, the third category is a disgrace. It is the category of dependents, i.e., people who can't work, pensioners, i.e., old people, and that includes housewives (they work, but privately).

All these old people, dependents, and pensioners are useless and represent superfluous mouths in Leningrad, and in order to get rid of them, the third-category ration is quite reduced, and if not reduced, then quite meager, and it is impossible to survive on it.

Then it remains for those persons in the third category either to die here from "emaciation," or to be evacuated, which for them also means death. In any case, the goal is achieved—people "leave," abandoning Leningrad.

Translated by Cynthia Simmons

ÈL'ZA GREINERT, LETTER TO HER CHILDREN AND GRANDCHILDREN FROM BESIEGED LENINGRAD

The editors received this letter from Èrna Mikhailovna Shusterovich (Èl'za Greinert's granddaughter), a medievalist and translator. Èrna's mother, Ol'ga Ivanovna Greinert, was German, and her father Mikhail Shusterovich, Jewish. During World War II, Mikhail Shusterovich served in the Red Army, which to some degree protected his wife and her family from persecution. In the summer of 1941, Ol'ga Ivanovna Greinert, a kindergarten teacher, was evacuated from Leningrad. Her younger son Arnold (Arnolia) went with her. Her older daughter Èrna was sick and was not permitted to accompany her. Èrna remained in Leningrad with her grandmother and grandfather and only later was able to join her mother in evacuation in the Urals. There Ol'ga Ivanovna Greinert, despite her husband's service as a Red Army officer, experienced persecution. For no apparent reason, she was transferred from one workplace to another, from the better children's homes to ones without a stable supply of food.

Èl'za Greinert's letter was written 23 January 1942. Èl'za Greinert would not have dared to write in her native German, but her Russian is not entirely grammatical. The letter lacks standard punctuation, there are several grammatical errors, and the register of the discourse is often inappropriately formal. Occasionally in the English translation, the grammar and punctuation have been normalized.

My Dear Children Hansi, Olichka, Bubi, Arnolia,

I am writing you all one letter, and you can send it to each other by registered mail. I don't have the strength to write the same thing several times, don't be offended, I hope you'll understand why. On the 13th of January, at 7:00 in the morning, quietly, and without great suffering, your father passed away. This will be a huge shock and loss for you, especially for Bubi, which I wanted to keep from him while he's in the army and feeling poorly, judging from his letter: "The hope of seeing you all alive gives me the strength to keep on going." I'll leave it up to you to decide whether to tell him or not.

For the time being I will not mention Papa in my letters.

33

È'lza Greinert's letter to her children.

As I've already written, your papa was sick and even psychologically disturbed, but for the last two days he was completely normal and especially affectionate toward me, calling me all the time Èl'zunia my dear and agreeing with me about everything and doing everything the way I told him. He sensed his end and talked to me about it, but I kept hoping that my efforts would put him back on his feet again. On the eve of the 12th, I sensed that he wouldn't survive, all night long he prayed, blessed me, you, the grandchildren, Misha, Zina, asked me to live with everyone in peace and harmony, to gather you all together and said, "I pray to the Lord God for you. The Lord has protected us up to now, and He won't leave you. He will hear my dying prayer." Then he fell asleep, coughed strongly, but couldn't clear his throat, phlegm was suffocating him. I raised him up often, he urinated frequently, and he lay uncomfortably all day the 12th. He was very calm, he didn't grumble as he usually did, didn't swear and asked to eat, but there was nothing to eat but one bowl of soup from the cafeteria and a piece of bread, he patiently bore his hunger and grew weaker by the minute and thus he died in my arms covered with my kisses. Two large tears flowed from his eyes, but he said nothing more. I washed and dressed him myself and with Natasha laid him in our room on the bed. While dying he grew more handsome and as he lay dead he looked so quiet and content. Absolutely everyone who came to pay their respects was surprised at how handsome and young he looked, except for the white beard, but that didn't spoil him. All day the 13th, I sat at home not knowing what to do, where to go, what to busy myself with. On the 14th, I went to the clinic to register a [death] certificate, stood in line from 8:30 to 2:00, the 15th I went to the bank, stood in line from 7:00 A.M., on the 16th I went to

34

the registry office [ZAGS], the 17th I went to get a coffin, but I didn't get a coffin since there were fist fights over them and you had to stand in line. I looked for a craftsman and found a fellow in our building who made a coffin out of my material for four hundred grams of bread and fifty rubles cash, the 18th Liusia came for two days, she upholstered the coffin, covered the top with leaves from my flowers, we laid him in the coffin and put it in Hansi's room. The morning of the 19th Liusia, Olia, Marina, Artur, and I set off to bury the coffin. We put it on two children's sleds. Liusia and Olia pulled the sled, Artur and I walked. We arrived at the cemetery to find out that you can no longer bury anyone in ours. Finally the brigade leader promised me to arrange everything by the 20th at 4:00 P.M. We turned the coffin over for storage in the morgue and went home. On the 20th, Olia and I went again to the cemetery, but that crook hadn't done anything and it was even his day off. We were in such despair. We didn't know where to begin. Walking through the cemetery, we saw a man digging a grave and from him we found out that we had to petition Comrade Romanov of the Moscow district municipal office [*raisovet*] for permission. On the 21st I flew to the district municipal office and as you can't get anywhere without lying, I didn't say that I was the wife but said I was from the local trade-union committee of the State Bank [*Gosbank*]. I am petitioning the head treasurer for permission to bury in the Lutheran cemetery in the family plot. In five minutes I had permission. On the 22nd Olia and I set out for the burial even though there was no one there to dig a grave for anyone. We ran around, searched, and in that way found some crook who dug a not very deep grave next to Aunt Vera. While he was digging we went to get the coffin and at 5:00 P.M., after great hardship, worry, and effort, I buried Papa. For what this poor wretched burial cost me, one could in earlier times have buried a prince with a banquet and music, but I'm not at all sorry. I have done my duty before God, before Papa and you, I didn't throw him just anywhere as has become the practice here, and if we're alive, you'll know where your papa is and you'll go and pray at his grave. Although they don't do any burying there, they do steal, mercilessly, all the trees, tear down fences, and crosses too, for there is no firewood, we don't have any crosses either, and the fences, everything has been burned, and all this is done openly. The director of the cemetery was walking with me and didn't even say a word to a lady who had torn down crosses next to us. I must also

35

add that I had to do all of this on foot since in the city we have no means of transportation. So today the 23rd, I will stay home and nurse my feet since they are swollen and hurt terribly. Tomorrow the 24th I have to go to the bank to make a withdrawal, then apply for a pension and then I have to try to get the insurance that Papa transferred to my name in view of the fact that Bubi could not come, but he asked that I not spend this money, but give each of you one thousand rubles at your discretion, do with it what you wish. I think that with the withdrawal, I'll live until 1 May and then all will be clear. Now the question of the apartment. They will take two rooms from me, but I have a month to find a lodger by myself. That is what I'll do. Some pieces of furniture I will sell because I have to buy wood. I don't have even one log. I burn everything I get my hands on. I will keep living in Olia's room, and in the little sewing room. I will have one window glazed, Papa already bought the glass, and we'll move from the kitchen into the room, although it's quieter in the kitchen, you can't hear the firing and howl of shells, but since all the rooms will be occupied by strangers, it will be necessary to clear out of the kitchen. Beyond that I can't imagine what I'll do, what'll I do with Èrnochka, when I myself can barely keep going. I don't know how to be evacuated or where to. I don't have any letters of authorization either from Misha or Bubi so I can't apply through the military registration office [*Voenkomat*]. I can't even get a dinner for Èrnochka, since she doesn't have proof that her father was called up or by whom, horrible carelessness on his part, and we will die of starvation, we have buried one, and the same awaits us. Tell me, what can I do? I can't write any longer for I'm writing under the icon-lamp, it's dark, and my eyes hurt. I kiss you all, my dear ones. Only God knows whether I'll see you again. Write. Your mother

Translated by Cynthia Simmons

The author of this testimony insisted that her name, as well as that of the family she describes, not be revealed. Her persistent fear is another aspect of this painful memory of persecution.

I will speak only about a few people well known to me during that horrible time for the simple reason that they turned out to be doubly unfortunate: first of all as inhabitants of a city surrounded by an enemy; second, by reason of their membership in the same nation as the soldiers of Hitler who held this city in the iron vise of the blockade.

They were just a family. They lived across the way from us, off the same staircase of apartment building No. 11 on Nevskii Avenue. I see all of them as clearly now as I did then. They have remained within me.

There were three kids, two boys and a three-year-old girl. The two older children, twelve and sixteen years old, were sometimes at our place. I had been taking German lessons from their mother and aunt, such beautiful, elegant, and intelligent women. The boys' mother was especially kind and, in addition, highly intellectual. It seemed that the elder of the sons had inherited all the talents of his mother, and of his father too, an engineer who knew several European languages. I can say with certainty that the country lost a future scholar when it lost this young man.

More precisely, it lost them all.

This is how it happened:

    in 1938 they arrested the father

    in 1941 they likewise arrested the mother

    in 1944 she was shot

The sons were left orphans with nothing whatsoever: all their possessions were confiscated. The latter fact led to the death of the older one from starvation (one could exchange things for bread).

The younger son remained with his aunt and her little daughter. They

37

were living shadows: a woman dying from hunger and two dystrophic children. In this condition they were deported from Leningrad—over the ice of Lake Ladoga.

While awaiting the crossing, the woman died, and the children experienced the worst thing that could yet happen to them. Brother and sister,[30] now each other's only remaining relative, were separated forever: they simply tore the three-year-old girl from her brother's arms, they dragged her away by force; the van in which they had been riding started off and the crying boy left for who knows where. . . .

Now about Building No. 11 on Nevskii Avenue, where this family lived. As long ago as 1755, the architect B. Rastrelli built, on the spot where the movie theater "Barricade" now stands, a huge one-story wooden building as a temporary palace for Peter I's daughter, the empress Elizabeth; which extended to today's Gogol Street (or Little Morskaia). And several decades earlier at that same location, Building No. 11, there stood a house which Rastrelli and his son moved into in 1710. At a later date at the site of this building there would be a fashionable shoe store called "Aleksandr." The owner of this store and of the building itself (Nevskii No. 11) was the head of the commercial firm "Aleksandr," Aleksandr Triberg, and one of the founders of this famous firm was in fact an ancestor of the family described here, who perished during the last war with the Germans, but not, strictly speaking, at the hands of the Germans.

Translated by Cynthia Simmons

EVGENIIA VADIMOVNA SHAVROVA (1919–1991)

Introduced by her sister, Elena Vadimovna Fassman

Presenting us with the diary of Evgeniia Vadimovna Shavrova, her younger sister Elena (b. 1946) gave a brief history of their family. Below are excerpts from the interview with Elena Fassman (July 1995), a letter of 26 May 1942, written by Zhenia (Evgeniia) and her mother to Vadim Shavrov, and fragments from Zhenia's diary.

ELENA FASSMAN

Her name was Evgeniia. Mama's married name was Shavrova; Shavrov was a famous aircraft designer. His first hydroplane (as noted in the Museum of the Arctic and Antarctic) was launched in 1929. It was for polar flights. And Mama, when she married him, took his name. Her maiden name was Fassman, a German family. Thanks to Shavrov, they didn't bother our family during the war. But Mama immediately (they were married in 1927) took his name, even then she understood everything.[31] At that time she was studying at the university, and already then she wrote everywhere that she was "Russian" and spoke German only with her sister. Mama was born in 1903, and in her family there was French, German, well, Russian of course. Mama's family is culturally Russian. My sister also studied French, German, and English. And they spoke German among themselves. But I didn't understand anything. I remember in the '50s I would hear the phrase, "*Man muss nichts sagen*" (don't say anything). Everyone kept quiet around me. But I was born in 1946, and you know how awful it was then. And they didn't talk about it. What was worse, my father was himself a German. I didn't know anything about our German ties. I began to learn about my German roots only after I finished school. That was in '65. We had a lot of cousins. They were all exiled, some to Vorkuta, others to the Urals.[32] Their grandfather was shot. They didn't touch our family. In Germany we don't have anyone anymore. I wrote to the magazine *Guten Tag*, but the editor answered that there isn't anyone there. But it turns out that my grandfather on my mother's side and my great-grandmother on my father's side were cousins. That means they, my mother and father, were related. But none of this was documented. No questions arose. All my relatives knew about it. He, my father, didn't suffer any repression. He was in the war, fought, nothing happened to him.

When Mama separated from Shavrov, she kept his name. Memory, love, all that remained. He returned to Moscow to work on all his ideas, and she remained here. He and Evgeniia were very connected to each other emotionally. They corresponded and wrote each other letters almost every day. During the war too. During the war he did military work in his TsKB (Central Design Bureau)—first in the Tupolev Institute [of aircraft engineering], and later, in his own bureau, somewhere in Sverdlovsk, in the Urals. And Mama lived her whole life here in Leningrad with my sister on the Square of the Arts (*Ploshchad' iskusstv*). They lived in a communal apartment there. That's where the "Stray Dog" (*Brodiachaia sobaka*) was.[33] By the way, they're now restoring it. Zhenia went to "Peterschule." During the war Mama was asked to work in the district committee (*Raikom*), and she directed the district plan (*raiplan*) for the Kalinin district. That was a high office. She held that office from 1943 on. It was far away. She walked there on foot, when the trams had stopped running.

∞

In the former Peterschule there is now a museum of the school. The director of this museum managed to find me. And thanks to him I learned some things. He also graduated from that school; now he's quite an old man. Their project is the history of the school. And part of that history concerns the war. Right next to it is Peterkirche. They are now renovating it. They closed the swimming pool that they had built inside it, and now they're renovating it. But it will be many years before they re-open the church. Now the Lutheran service is held in the Annenkirche. The pastor there is from Germany.

∞

40

In February 1995, in the Palace of Pioneers (now the Children's Palace of Creative Art), there was a meeting of "children" who had survived the Siege.

And they invited me to come too, although I came across them totally by chance. I didn't know where to go with Zhenia's diaries. I was walking along Nevskii, and I thought, "Why don't I go into the Palace of Pioneers?" And the director took up a search to find out when she went there and what classes she took. It was mainly singing that she did there. And they took several pages relating to that. I understood that they had to do that. And she [the director] invited me to this meeting. The meeting was amazing, since all of those who came had been schoolchildren during the Siege. Lazar' Magrachev came, it was there [at the Palace of Pioneers] that he began (working as a reporter). There was an actor. They had all gotten their start at the Palace. And I met one of Zhenia's friends there, Lelia, an Armenian woman, who had lived in the same apartment building as she did. Sometimes we run into each other at concerts.

Letter from Evgeniia to her father, 26 May 1942

Papa dear, hello! We haven't received any news from you for a long time. I sent you a letter not long ago. Did you get it? As you can see, we are for now alive and healthy. I go to school every other day and we have three classes a day. In my spare time I embroider and go around to the stores. Somehow I'll send you my drawings. We have air-raid alarms here, and when they happen, we go out into our front hall. If the anti-aircraft guns really start pounding, then we go to the bomb shelter. Life is monotonous. I'm not getting any postcards from you. Write a little more often. Let us have some bit of news from you.

Further on, her mother writes:

Life is so complicated and harsh that this year has aged us by many years. Right now it's much easier. At least it is warm and sunny. This is enough to feel better. And the food situation has improved somewhat. But we are frightened by the prospect of the fall and winter and the possibility of a repetition of all our misfortunes. So that you can have some idea, I'll give you two numbers. Before the war, I weighed eighty kilos. Now I weigh fifty-seven. Zhenia was forty-two. Now she's thirty-one. A short history of our life lately goes like this: From December to January we ate thanks to the

41

Klauses (our acquaintances). December and January were the most agonizing. I could hardly drag my feet, was working more than five kilometers from home, and the trams weren't running. Toward March, sensing the hopelessness of the situation, we decided to be evacuated, especially since the Klauses, the Famsters, and other acquaintances of ours had already left. On 10 March, I arranged a withdrawal. I had packed everything, had sold off two-thirds of the dishes, and almost everything was ready for our departure. But by that time Zhenia was already so weak that on the advice of the doctors the trip had to be postponed, for they predicted that she would die on the road.

A convalescent hospital opened nearby, and Zhenia was admitted for three weeks of supplementary feeding. In addition, I bartered some things for food, and this put Zhenia back on her feet, but we had to put the trip off. I decided to make a radical change in my work, and with the help of friends I managed to get a job as a saleswoman in a bakery. True, it is far away, in Okhta. In March and April I went by foot along the Neva. The conditions are savage. Zhenia got out of the hospital and spent two weeks with friends right in Okhta. For a while I rented a corner there, and Zhenia rested there. But 4 May, classes started up again at school. Zhenia has all her meals there. It's too little, but still better than at home. And she has to study too. Zhenia has gotten somewhat stronger, and I'm able to get her extra food. So that now, physically, we are a little bit better, although we look awful. Clothes hang on us as if on a hanger. All our nicer things have been sold or bartered. So that life isn't very enjoyable. What you write about evacuation is correct —we'll go to a *kolkhoz*, we'll follow our noses. Of course, to be evacuated to big cities and centers is madness. We have nothing to exchange, no money, and you can't survive on a salary. I had another idea—to send Zhenia by herself to you to get fattened up, just for a while, and I could stay here and somehow fight for my life, and nothing more.

Fragments from the diaries and letters of Evgeniia Shavrova

Foreword to the diary of 1942: About the difficult winter past, I am not going to write. First of all, those memories are painful and gloomy. Second, I didn't write anything down then—other things were more important. Of course everything I experienced then I will preserve in my memory forever. It can never be erased. Now that life has returned to being more or less normal, I have resumed writing in my diary. I will only make brief mention of the past. In general, of course, I am writing about what is happening now. I will try to recall and make note of as many of the features and events of our life as I can and to describe them in detail.

Excerpts from Evgeniia Shavrova's "A Schoolgirl's Diary"

10 JULY 1942

I've begun going to the Palace of Pioneers. It's still open. But I haven't been there since February 1941. I've joined the needlework group. There's even a boy who's learning with us. He has fire-red hair and really knows how to choose threads. But he's a big braggart. He even bragged that last winter he went skiing and played. His mother works in the cafeteria. I can't imagine that during the worst days, when everyone was dying and I could hardly drag my legs to the school cafeteria, that someone could run and play!

21 JULY 1942

At the Palace our dance group put on a concert. The kids did a good job performing Dunaevskii's "A Song of Youth," comic dances, and folk dances. The group is led by Arkadii Efimovich Obrant.[34] His ensemble often goes out to perform for the troops at the Leningrad front.

The composers Mikhail Glukh and Nataliia Levi are teaching their new songs to the vocal ensemble.[35]

Some of the children, from various groups, find a way sometimes to eat twice in the buffet, even though they're not supposed to.

18 JANUARY 1943

All of a sudden late one night on the radio we heard about the breakthrough in the siege. Probably no one was sleeping at that time. Nonstop on the radio we heard from workers, soldiers of the Civil Defense (MPVO). Ol'ga Berggol'ts spoke. Mama began right then to write a letter to Taisiia Fedorovna in Novosibirsk. She sent her some poems by Vera Inber that just came out. Now when they start to broadcast "At the Last Moment" (*V poslednii chas*), everyone waits for the news, everyone has cheered up a little bit.

43

This morning at school there was a rally. Lilia Kiseleva was really excited and spoke very well. After school I went to the office of *Leningrad Truth* with an article about the breakthrough in the siege. But no one was there. I left my article with the woman on duty and asked her to give it to the editor. Of course, they never printed my article, and I submitted it to the school (wall) newspaper (*stengazeta*).

1 FEBRUARY 1943

It has somehow become a little more enjoyable to live and study. Now we no longer hear on the radio: "Our soldiers have abandoned the city. . . ." In Russian class Rebecca Efimovna is reading us Vera Inber's *Pulkovo Meridian*.[36] We select examples of points of grammar from there rather than from the textbook. Grigorii Mikhailovich often tells us about the Suvorov campaigns, although it isn't in our curriculum. He's a wonderful teacher, we like him very much. Sometimes we even applaud after an especially interesting story.

We have become the sponsors of a hospital on the corner of the Moika and Dzerzhinskii Street. The hospital is very large; it's located in a former school. Many of the wards are in classrooms. Our class has been assigned wards where some are even seriously wounded. We visit the soldiers almost every day, read books, write letters, fulfill various requests from the Leningraders among them. First of all, of course, we search for relatives and friends. Many of them lost their families in the siege, and how can we console them, how?. . .

28 OCTOBER 1943

Today was a red-letter day. In the assembly hall of School No. 211, we were awarded, along with the boys, medals "For the Defense of Leningrad." We were decorated for our agricultural work. It was the first government award, and we received it at such an early age. It means that we schoolchildren are now considered to be real defenders of the city. . . .

16 JANUARY 1944

Soon, soon we will be free, the siege will be over. Yesterday morning in thick, frosty, clouds of smoke we saw bolts of fire; we could hear from far away an unusually loud roar of cannonades. Everyone was saying: "It's begun!" Now everyone knows that our forces are approaching all along the Leningrad front. But how many shellings have there been only recently, just this month, how many victims? Our classmate Rita Vinogradova's father was killed, Lena Pevzner's mother was wounded. A shell that landed in the courtyard of Nevskii No. 27 killed Sima Pavlova's father and mother (she wasn't home).

28 JANUARY 1944

I just can't realize that the siege is over, that there are no shellings, black-outs, bombardments, that now it will always be *quiet*. Yesterday everyone was at the Field of Mars.[37] They watched the *first* Leningrad salute. Out in the frost it was actually hot. Everyone unbuttoned their coats, no one was afraid of catching cold. It is impossible, of course, to describe the joy. Mainly it is hard to believe that it is now quiet. Wasn't it not so long ago that we pressed ourselves against the walls of the buildings and couldn't lift our heads?

In the morning during our first period in school, we had a general assembly. Nearly all the teachers spoke, and many of the students. From our class I spoke too. On this day, of course, we didn't have to do any work.

Our life must now change, Leningraders have to begin to live in a completely different way. I don't know what it will be, but it will be completely different!

9 JULY 1944

It is very, very difficult for me to write now, but nevertheless I must. Yesterday is a day I will never forget. We finally managed to get to Sestroretsk, where for many years we had a dacha, where I spent most of my childhood.

We came out onto the square by the old railway station (it survived), and immediately we sensed a strange silence. Before the war this little town, no matter what time of day, was always full of people, it was all motion, alive and bustling. And now time stood still. But it wasn't just quiet all around, but some kind of ominous emptiness. We knew that everyone had been evacuated from here in 1942 because of the proximity of the Finnish front, and that only military personnel had remained. But the inhabitants apparently had not begun to return, and that surprised us after the lively streets of Leningrad.

When we turned onto our Liteinaia Street, there appeared before us an unexpected and eerie picture, as if from a book on ancient cities, destroyed and abandoned forever. The entire street was overgrown with tall weeds that reached above our heads. Wild burdock, gigantic goose-foot, nettles, and some completely unknown plants that we had never seen before the war. . . . We made our way through the area, along the dachas, which were just as overgrown. Shutters banged in the wind, doors creaked, something rustled mysteriously. There was no sound from anything living—the cry of a rooster or a dog.

Our dacha also turned out to be half boarded-up. The leg of a piano was sticking out of the door. From the balcony of the neighboring house, a couch was hanging.

On the shore of the little river, which also seemed dead, by one of the dachas, a man was walking. It was the owner, the first to have returned to this street. He recognized us and told us many painful things. He reminded Mama of the miller in Pushkin's Rusalka. . . .[38]

We didn't stay there long. It was sad and simply frightening in this desert of nettles. The whole way back on the train we couldn't talk.

Translated by Cynthia Simmons

Vera S. Kostrovitskaia grew up in a cultured Petersburg family of Polish descent. She was the niece of the French poet Guillaume Apollinaire (Wilhelm Apollinaris de Kostrowitzki). In 1916 she entered the Imperial Theater Academy (*Imperatorskoe teatral'noe uchilishche*) and, on graduation in 1923, was accepted into the Mariinskii (Kirov) Theater of opera and ballet. Until 1936, when her performance career was cut short by tuberculosis, Kostrovitskaia danced with the company, for a time working with George Balanchine. After several years' training, in 1939 she began her career as a teacher.

Kostrovitskaia is remembered by her student Gabriela Komleva in "The Curator of Ballet's Mysteries."[39] Komleva writes that Kostrovitskaia lost friends and loved ones (including her first husband, the theater artist V. V. Dmitriev) to Stalin's purges. She survived the Siege of Leningrad, Komleva claims, thanks to her "rich inner world"—she was a fervent devotee of painting and other art forms. Kostrovitskaia is the author of books and articles on classical ballet and choreography, including "The Methodology of Fluid Movement," "Classical Choreography," and "100 Examples of Classical Dance."

In 1970 Kostrovitskaia traveled to teach in Budapest, Hungary, and from the mid-1970s, she established contacts with the American ballet master and teacher John Barker.

V. S. Kostrovitskaia's diaries are held in the Manuscript Department of the Russian National Library. The following excerpts (OR RNB, Fond 1274, No. 1) vary greatly from the (self-?) censored memoir published in *Neva* 9 (1973) and translated in *Dancing Time*, March 1985, 505–06 and April 1985, 601, 603.

> In a city where there are garbage pits,
> cats, and dogs, a person won't go hungry /
> instead of an epigraph

Lelenka, I am trying to honor your request to record all that I observed and experienced.

We all delicately conceal from our neighbor that we eat cat meat; we refer to it simply as eating "chat."[40]

47

∞

The pressure of death, which rose with the whistle of dropping bombs, penetrated even the pain of hunger, rendered the icy temperature of the air imperceptible, isolated the ear from everything mundane and otherwise audible. And nonetheless I heard it. Incredible! In the dark on the staircase landing of the building in which I lived, where I was standing watch, for a split second there penetrated the sound of wind instruments; then everything was swallowed by a deafening boom.

An aural hallucination—it's possible.

I didn't know why the sailors were here. . . . From the windows of the fifth floor I could clearly see into the windows of the low two-story apartment building across the way. In the room there were cots, an empty table, and dimly gleaming wind instruments. They didn't have the kind of little stove that people were using during the siege [*burzhuika*], and therefore their window wasn't frozen over. . . .

At home they played a lot, sitting in their overcoats on the cots. Usually the clarinet would begin, establishing the melody, then it would be repeated by the two first trumpets, and then the trombone and flute joined in. The "drummer," when he was free, filled the role of conductor.[41]

Every day, to spite the bombing, hunger, and severe cold, they sounded the marches of Dunaevskii, Solov'ev-Sedoi, the songs of Blanter and other Soviet composers. During these hours it seemed that one need only to gather one's strength, endure a week or two, and all would be like it was before the war. Music helped a person then.

In November we lost electricity in our apartments, the pipes froze, newspapers stopped, and mail.

We don't live by the calendar. We become aware of days and dates only by means of small square paper coupons with the number 125. That signifies a small piece of greenish-brown bread, half wood shavings.

Could these musicians really have had reserves of food? . . .—They continued to play.

But the more the city became shrouded in silence, the weaker became the sounds of their music. First the bass fell silent, then the flute could no longer be heard, and, as if paralyzed by the cold, the tempo of the clarinet and trumpets became slower. . . .

∽

At the end of November the bombardments ceased, and in the beginning of December, the radio fell silent.

It became completely dark and still.

Through the icy scab of the windows, crisscrossed with paper strips, there came some cautious sounds. But it was no longer a whole march or song: a lone trumpet uncertainly drew out a piece of the melody and broke off; sometimes they lost the rhythm and mistakenly hit the cymbal. Then it all died down.

At noon, which brought light, you could make out the supine figures. They hardly moved. Sailors' boots were visible from under the gray blankets —they had no *valenki*—and some kind of rags on their necks and shriveled faces.

A lonely teapot stood frozen to the table.

The one who could still play lay on his back, he was so thin that you could only measure his length; not his volume. Alongside him on the cot lay his trumpet. Sometimes he would sit up and bring the instrument to his lips. It was the only thing that he could give to his comrades in place of heat, fire, and bread.—It was nonetheless *courage*.—Several began to stir, were delirious for a while, then again settled down on their cots.

Now they no longer went out. And once while the city was bearing the sharp intensity of a 40-degree freeze [-40°C], two of them came out into the courtyard.

They spent a long time adjusting on a children's sled a tiny figure, swaddled in a Navy greatcoat.

The smallest, the weakest—he died first. Gasping from this light but so heavy burden, two figures bent like old men dragged themselves into the approaching twilight, pulling after themselves a sled.

The snow fell on and on, covering up the last traces of people fading from life.

49

∽

L[idiia] S[emeonova] T[ager] called me into her office and tried to persuade me to move to the school to live, but alone, without Mama. Of course I refused. This is her point of view: if a person has a dependent, then the latter has a responsibility to die, and if he doesn't die because you share your ration with him, then that is not only stupid, it is a *superfluous luxury*. The news that your mother *still* has not died she takes as tactlessness and sentimentality inappropriate to wartime conditions, almost as immorality. That an eighteen-year-old girl (a ballet dancer at the Kirov Theater, Tamara Bogdanova) left her dependent mother in an empty apartment for five days and never once brought her anything to eat (the mother died on the fifth day) did not incite L. S. T.'s indignation. She said that Bogdanova acted correctly, since in the first place, one must think about one's own life. For—a young life is needed by the government, but an old one is not.

∽

FEBRUARY

People are worried and always discussing whether they will give us fifteen or twenty grams of herring, ten or twelve grams of sugar. Neither one nor the other will quiet our stomachs. The portions that the blockade has doomed us to are less than what is customarily given to a nursing infant as a "supplement."

∽

[When the ballet school is ordered to help clean up the city in the spring of 1942, Tager threatens the students with the loss of their ration cards.]

"Hypocrites, sluggards, I'll leave everyone without their bread-ration cards." Rosy and chubby-cheeked, she grabs a shovel to give us an example of how to dig, how to throw, and then she stands and watches us for hours.

APRIL

50   And there, across from the entrance to the Philharmonic, by the square, there is a large lamppost.

With his back to the post, a man sits on the snow, tall, wrapped in rags, over his shoulders a knapsack. He is all huddled up against the post. Apparently he was on his way to the Finland Station, got tired, and sat down. For two weeks while I was going back and forth to the hospital,[42] he "sat"

1. without his knapsack
2. without his rags
3. in his underwear
4. naked
5. a skeleton with ripped-out entrails

They took him away in May.

APRIL

Since in April it became necessary to portray the rebirth of the city at the hands of people half-dead, L. S. T. got the vain idea to give the first public concert on the premises of the Philharmonic through the efforts of our school, or more precisely its remains.

Some of the girls had maintained relative good health, thanks to a fortunate situation at home, but everyone had scurvy. The most talented, Liusia Alekseeva, couldn't dance the "classics." Her legs, covered with the blue spots of scurvy, gave way and wouldn't obey.

I informed L. S. T. of the situation.

In answer there came a furious shout and threats to deny those who refused to dance their food-ration coupons for the following month. . . .

The concert took place. There was even the "dying swan" and other ballet nonsense. Petia, made by me to look like a living person, "danced" two numbers.[43] The girls, in order to keep him going, brought him bread and a dish of kasha. On stage I led him by the arms as he "danced," I tried not to watch, and during the intervals off-stage, he drooped into my arms and vomited the kasha he had eaten.

There was no public audience at the concert, for there was none in the city. The first two rows were taken by the Council for the Arts [*Upravlenie po delam iskusstv*], representatives from Smolnyi and party organizations. With her hair died red and dressed up like a model, L. S. T. shone during the entr'acte, accepting greetings, unnaturally loudly recounting her love for the children and how all winter she had saved their lives.

51

Just imagine, throughout this terrible period this woman, an official and member of the party, appeared almost daily in expensive new dresses, shoes, and hats. In the course of one winter, four new fur coats and countless pieces of expensive jewelry. They had all been acquired in exchange for food— perhaps that puts Petia's death in a different light. After all, rather than four, wouldn't one fur coat have sufficed? Not twenty dresses, but at most, say, five, and so forth. And Petia, with his forelock and rosy face, would still be among us. Lidiia Semenovna Tager—the wife of the head of provisions for the entire Leningrad front.

Translated by Cynthia Simmons

Mariia Viacheslavovna Kropacheva, a history teacher and party member, in 1940 received the title of "Honored Teacher of the Russian Federal Republic of the Soviet Union." During the war she joined the volunteer civil defense and was decorated for her actions. She was twice chosen as a Deputy of the Supreme Soviet. From 1950 she was a Corresponding Member of the Academy of Pedagogical Sciences and Assistant Director of the Leningrad Scientific Research Institute of Pedagogy. Kropacheva's politically correct assessment of events often differs from that found in other documents in this collection. Her diary served her well in her teaching and propagandistic work during World War II. An example of the latter, her "The Children's Voices Call for Revenge" (*Golos detei zovet k mshcheniiu*), was published in the series *For the Homeland, For Leningrad* (*Za Rodinu, za Leningrad*) in 1943.

As a typical example of ideological propaganda, her notes represent "the attempt to transmit social and political values in the hope of affecting peoples' thinking, emotions, and thereby behavior."[44] Comparing her notes with other remembered events in this collection makes clear that the doctrinaire interpretation often takes precedence over the significance of the events themselves. Thus the notes of July 1942 instruct that personal grief be subjugated to hatred for the enemy, devotion to the party, and the selfless struggle against the Fascists. Accordingly, Kropacheva describes a woman who, having learned that the Germans have killed her three brothers and husband, joins a labor brigade and becomes the head of a medical assistants unit. Kropacheva's patriotic pathos commanded "stern vigilance" and hatred of "enemy-foreigners." A rank-and-file Communist, Kropacheva understandably could not know that from 1941 to 1944, "despite the fact that Finland was at war with Russia," Finland remained unwilling to attack the Soviet Union from the northwest, "and in this way Finland actually protected Russia from this direction."[45] But as a party propagandist, Kropacheva knew well what ideas and feelings, with respect to the enemy, she had to instill in her listeners and readers. According to the patriotic "party" version presented by Kropacheva, Finnish peasant women, who are nursing infants, spy for the Fascists, showing them the way to the partisan command post. For the sake of the propaganda of the "science of hate," Kropacheva sacrifices elementary plausibility and sense, filling the pages of her notes with stereotypical political jargon. Kropacheva supposes that a "strengthening of discipline in government and labor" can overcome starvation. She is disturbed that people

53

weakened from malnutrition cannot work quickly. Characteristic of the culture of Stalinism and socialist realism, Kropacheva writes that party members always and everywhere introduce order and discipline, and if people perish or die of hunger, then it is their own fault—the result of greed or the inability to understand the real situation (as in the note of September-October, describing events on the "Road of Life").

From "The way we work: diary notes" (Kak my rabotaem: Dnevnikovye zapisi), 29 July 1942–January 1943, monograph, 9 pp., Russian National Library.

Life in Besieged Leningrad

SECOND YEAR OF THE WAR, 1942

29.VII: At 9:39 the staff gathered in the editor's office. We read Stalin's order —not one step backwards.[46] Our limits and resources are not boundless. There have been great losses of life . . . of raw materials, of territory. The Germans have begun to fight better than they did in the winter due to better discipline. Rostov and Novocherkassk were surrendered without an order from Moscow. The evacuated factories are working splendidly. We can stop and push back the enemy. We need to learn discipline from the Germans. Stalin's daring, righteous revolutionary order is strengthened by truth. Hitler doesn't have that advantage.

Facts

At the forward positions units of women volunteers are camouflaging the trenches artistically, masterfully, femininely (maybe our men will be in these trenches—please don't let the Germans see them).

A delegation of women met before going to the front. "What will we tell the soldiers?" one of them asked. "As for me, I have three brothers. They fought for Sevastopol' to their last breath.[47] They were all killed. My husband died at the front too. I became the head of a medical assistants unit and began to train the young girls."

"The Germans killed my husband, he was a commander. I enlisted in the ranks of the RKKA (The Workers and Peasants Red Army)," a second said.

"There were nine people in our family. Only three remain. The rest died from hunger. I had no time to think about my grief. I had young girls entering the unit, sixteen-, seventeen-, eighteen-year-old schoolgirls, almost

54

all of them had lost their parents. If you could have seen how they worked, how they perished during the shelling of the city," a third said.

"I have had no great personal tragedy," a fourth said, the youngest, who had been awarded a medal "For Bravery" [*Za otvagu*]. "I have nothing to say about myself, but I can talk about our trainees, how they fight and work. They are wonderful girls."

31 JULY

At the chocolate factory, only men worked at the mixing machine, which requires a great deal of strength. Now there aren't enough of them. The directorate assigned one man and gave him two girls as assistants—Zarembo and Dmitrichenko. After working a little while they asked the administration to reassign the man where he might be more needed, because they were able to get by just as well without him. The girls are producing 300 percent over the norm.

The old workman Lukianov's favorite nephew, a pilot, was killed at the front. In order to avenge his nephew, he produced an output unheard of in his section in peacetime, a record 14,000 kg. in one shift. The foremen in the neighboring sections are young engineers. Lukianov's success got under their nails—he's merely a skilled worker, but, they, engineers, couldn't match him. So they got angry and outdid him.

On Nevskii Avenue two starving women are pushing a cart loaded with things packed in bundles. On top of these things sits a little girl, about three years old. A five-year-old boy with a teapot in his hand walks alongside— that's evacuation.

Of 698 people recognized for exemplary work in the Kiubishevskii district, 476 are women.

1 AUGUST

I delivered a speech on the radio for the partisans. At the studio I met the leader of the "Uncle Vania" division.[48] Here is what he told me:

In a village occupied by the Germans, children near a school were making noise. The Germans started shooting at them. They killed nine children. He himself saw their bloody bodies. The Germans raped two thirteen- and fourteen-year-old sisters, daughters of partisan N. They infected them with their venereal disease and then hung them.

They shoved the mother of another partisan into a Russian stove and burned her alive.

55

On the subject of vigilance: Two Finnish women with nursing infants came to the partisans. They complained about the Germans. The partisans fed them, and they left. Suddenly a punitive attack was launched (the Finnish women had shown the Nazis the way). Many of our soldiers were killed.

2 AUGUST

We went to an exhibition of Leningrad artists. There were many paintings entitled "Leningrad under Siege." Pakhomov's "Fetching Water" is quite impressive.[49] Serov's "Battle on the Ice" is interesting.[50] "We Will Never Forget This" is quite expressive—an execution of our people by the Germans. A teenager and his mother, an old woman. "The Enemy Has Been Here" and a girl during a night-time air-raid warning. The portraits are good, especially the one of Orbeli by Vereiskii.[51]

7 AUGUST

In the forty-sixth section of the factory, the workers who took part in the Obukhov Defense are still alive.[52] In these difficult times, Krezov, a toolmaker, became a blacksmith's striker. Briukhov, "Uncle Sasha," sixty years old, is the foreman of a Komsomol youth brigade. His brigade of fourteen-to sixteen-year-olds doesn't know what it is to stop working. They always overfulfill the plan.

The Plan and Reality or Life's Lessons

It was proposed that when evacuating women with two and three children, they would first send out one child for each adult. But they sent out one child for each five adults. The number of places in kindergartens had to be increased, not decreased, as had been supposed—housewives had to go to work. Previously, of three million inhabitants, there were 30,000 children in kindergarten. Now, with a population of 800,000, there are 130,000 children in these centers.

Because of the evacuation, the number of people with two children has declined by half, and the number of children in orphanages has increased almost twofold. In order not to leave Leningrad, relatives who had taken guardianship of a child would give him up to an orphanage.[53] There have been approximately 40,000 such cases in Leningrad.

To turn Leningrad into a military city, military discipline is needed. I was at the Marti [factory].[54] In the sixteenth section, after a serious discussion by the administration, eight workers out on sick leave "got better." All appeared the following day.

SEPTEMBER–OCTOBER

There's been no time to write. I will try to note down here the most striking things I have heard and seen in two months.

The Institute of Party History sent workers to Lake Ladoga to recreate a picture of the evacuation.

The students of the industrial-vocational schools were dying of hunger, but in their pockets they had uneaten chocolate bars.[55] The guys were selling them and storing up money in order, later, to live it up on the Mainland. The head of the evacuation post heard a cry. A young worker was crying because another boy just like himself had snitched his chocolate bar. The man in charge took away the chocolate and gave it back to the one who was crying. The latter hid it in his pocket. "Eat it right now," the man in charge said. "I can't look after you, and they'll take the chocolate from you again." This argument made an impression. The boy began to eat greedily. He held the bar with both hands and asked only, "Comrade, please don't leave me, just please don't go." With difficulty the boy ate the last piece, and died right on the spot.

In wintertime on a bridge a worker for the City Party Committee (*gorkom*) met a dying Leningrader. He led him to a bench, and the man lay down. He was already in a very bad way. He said, "Many of us— Leningraders—will die, but the Germans won't make it into the city." When the city-councilman, after taking care of his business, was returning by way of that bridge, on the bench lay a corpse, covered with snow.

Translated by Cynthia Simmons

ANNA IVANOVNA LIKHACHEVA (B. 1887)

In 1942, Anna Ivanovna Likhacheva was a doctor in the clinic of the Red Banner factory.

The following excerpts from Likhacheva's diary were published in *Oborona Leningrada (1941–1944): Vospominaniia i dnevniki uchastnikov* (The Defense of Leningrad [1941–1944]: Memoirs and diaries of participants). Leningrad: Nauka, 1968, 682–89.

(15 May–7 June 1942)

15 MAY

Since 7 May I have been working on a very interesting assignment—I am to observe and do a study of workers who have been sent to our factory's cafeteria for supplemental nourishment. . . .

Who eats in the cafeteria? The overwhelming majority are factory workers; then office workers (with second-category rations). Many are emaciated (first- and second-degree [of dystrophy from starvation]), and the second-degree prevails.[56] People eat greedily, some very quickly, but most slowly, swallowing small spoonfuls of soup with crumbled bread in it, as the winter bread shortage had taught everyone to eat. Another characteristic—people who eat in public soup-kitchens have gotten into the habit, when they eat soup, of drinking the liquid first, as the first course, and then the thicker part that remains, as the second course, and they apply that method here too, which I am trying to put a stop to.

16 MAY

Yesterday I decided to go to the kitchen as early as possible, by 6:00 in the morning, and observe the activities of the work day from beginning to end. I checked to see how the pots were washed and how the food was loaded in. The people there work under difficult conditions. The kitchen is on the fourth floor, the water does not always get up that far, the plumbing isn't working right, hot water for the dishes is limited. The dishwasher has no

58

water, and the lift is out of order. All heavy objects are carried on people's backs up and down a difficult set of stairs. When people are carrying food, they often trip, slip, and fall; the pots are heavy—copper. . . . In the first days after they had opened the cafeteria for supplemental nourishment, they did not have a prescribed menu, so they just estimated; as a result of which the workers got even weaker.[57] Then they began to put out a standard menu with a description of portions and number of calories. Theoretically, the menu is varied, with a calorie count over 3,100, but in practice, alas, the basic meal does not fulfill the alimentary norm, which impedes the distribution of food and the very effectiveness of the feeding program.

True, fats and sugar are delivered without interruption. As a rule, anyone being fed receives sixty grams of sugar (and sometimes eighty to ninety grams) per day, and up to sixty grams of fats. This produces wonderful results on a starving organism that has gone a long time without normal nourishment. I experienced this personally at the beginning of May, when I received supplemental feedings for six days. Beginning in January (that most horrible time), when I was still suffering from dysentery and was left without fat and sugar, I developed an agonizing vertigo and noise in my ears, such a noise in my head, in the occipital area and my ears, that it kept me from sleeping. And many people are complaining about this symptom, especially those engaged in mental work. From 21 January to 20 February, I lay in the convalescent hospital (*statsionar*). I received sugar and fat, but my condition remained the same, the noise did not cease for a moment. Obviously a month of rest and of being fed regularly was not sufficient. And here, after just six days, I started to notice that the noise had decreased significantly. I have survived all the stages of emaciation, even the transitional state to the fatal third stage. It began simply with wasting, shortness of breath, slowed thought. On 12 December 1941, the dysentery started, brought on by eating a cold aspic made from horse meat in our factory's cafeteria, along with yeast soup, which I ate, or more accurately, forced down with disgust. And then everything went downhill. The darkness, the deadly cold, the hunger, the lack of strength to stand nights in line to receive the daily ticket for the food that was supposed to be given to us—it did me and my whole family in, and led to the loss of my husband and my son. The fatalities began in December, when the lack of food was coupled with the cold and loss of public transportation. Cold starving people, faithfully carrying out their duties before the besieged city, trudged tens of kilometers, often on only 125 grams of ersatz bread per day and soured cabbage leaves (*khriapa*) or yeast soup for dinner.[58]

How does this irreversible situation run its course? Excruciating hunger forces a person to think and talk only about one thing—about food, to share memories of dishes that one loved or disliked. One regrets his or her past capriciousness, all those unfinished and generally untouched simple dishes that were scorned in the good old days. Wherever two or three people meet, at work, at the office, in line, the talk is only of food. What are they giving on the ration cards, how much, what is available, etc.—it is life's most vital question. . . .

∞

7 JUNE

The more nature comes to life, the brighter the sun, the greener it gets, the more depressed one feels. Spring has awakened frozen human emotions and has cruelly reminded us of our private grief. I have somehow come to terms with Volodia's death. . . .[59] His death is like a dull ache. But I feel the death of my dear, beloved son so intensely, it calls up such pain and despair, that I could cry day and night.

My heart cries for him unceasingly. As soon as I am left alone, I see before my eyes his last moments of life. To the end of my, perhaps few, remaining days, I won't forget that dear face, I won't forget how he suffered from starvation, his love for life, his physical exhaustion, and how slowly he died, cell by cell. What an extraordinarily deep grief has struck us all, the mothers of Leningrad. . . .

At that moment of lingering agony, which actually lasted, I think, several days, Oleg began to have spasms in his arms and legs, he lost his voice, became totally debilitated, and developed bedsores and an aversion to food. He had such a craving for something sour and kept wanting to drink vinegar, but I wouldn't let him. But perhaps if he had drunk vinegar, he might still be alive? Unfortunately, in February and in January, they weren't yet making the coniferous vitamin extract, and they weren't giving out hydrochloric acid.[60] Truth be told, they weren't treating dystrophics at all, claiming a lack of medicine, water, and food. It was a terrible time. When I would bring medicinal drops to the hospital, there was no water to take the drops with; there was no water for the hot-water bottles. Everyone was lying around dirty, unwashed, infested with lice.

Now everything has changed dramatically. They have started to treat and feed people, only Oleg and Volodia are no more.

For the past few months, since April, the Germans have been trying their best to frighten us. They have been firing at us with long-range artillery, people say from armored trains. They have been bombing, flying over, but with no success. We, on the other hand, have become some kind of stone beings. Or we have already become accustomed to the thundering of bombs and shells, or we have grown so tired from all the extraordinary experiences of our lives, that we are completely indifferent to everything. During the first months of the war, and especially in the fall, when there were frequent and lengthy air-raid alarms and bombings, we all ran to the anti-gas air-raid shelters, we hid, we somehow worried, wondered how best to hide ourselves, where it was safer, on the lower or the upper floors, and so on. Life during those months made fatalists of us all. We saw all varieties of attacks, shells, and bombs, and we saw the destruction of all floors by a direct hit through the roof, and strikes from the side, and destroyed basements and bomb shelters. . . .

Translated by Cynthia Simmons

An actress or musician, Nekliudova was sent to entertain the troops at the front. Her description of a special ration provided for the entertainers and notes on the death of Volodia back in Leningrad are held in the Museum of the Defense of Leningrad.

From an exhibit at the Museum of the Defense of Leningrad, "War-Time Menu."

Nekliudova—Joined the ensemble on 19 November 1941.

War-Time Menu
BEGUN 12 DECEMBER 1941

Ration:
- 60 grams of macaroni made from rye
- 60 grams of bread
- 33 grams of fat
- 20 grams of sugar
- 60 grams of boiled pearl barley

Breakfast:

First course:	soup with macaroni
Second course:	coffee
	bread with vegetable oil and fat

Lunch:

First course:	soup with macaroni
Second course:	boiled pearl barley with fat
	(not eaten, saved for Leningrad)

Dinner: Banquet to decorate 140 Heroes of the Patriotic War (invitational coupons distributed by Tselikov)

Portion per person:
- 100 grams of grain alcohol (diluted to 35 degrees)
- 2 glasses of beer
- 300 grams of bread
- Sunflower seeds, split in half
- 50 grams of salted pork fat
- 1 white roll
- 2 cutlets with gravy and buckwheat from concentrate
- 1 glass of cocoa with milk
- 1 pack of Belomor cigarettes
- 1 box of matches

In addition, at the Colonel's suggestion, beer in bottles and a kilo of candy was brought for the women. We shared the candy with Liusia and took about 400 grams to Leningrad.

Leningrad encircled by the blockade
The Great Patriotic War

Continued in Leningrad, during days of severe trials by starvation. In the city of death.

I lost Volodia, he died from starvation. I am going on without him.

On 21 December, I returned to Leningrad. Two months later on 20 March, Volodia died.

20 MARCH 1942

Bread ration: Factory workers—500 grams of bread
                       Other workers—400 grams
                       Dependents—300 grams

Breakfast, morning
Volodia: sweetened coffee, a rusk, boiled buckwheat groats. I fed him every two hours. His last day with us. He ate buckwheat, rusks, and drank sweetened coffee from a cup.

The three of us: tea, bread, butter with fat, yesterday's barley
Breakfast, 3:00
L. K. and I had Volodia's remaining buckwheat, oil, boiled water, bread.
Lunch and dinner, 9:00:
Soup from old bones with barley added, boiled barley, oil, tea, bread.

21 MARCH

Today we are without Volodia.

Translated by Arlene Forman

The Race of Life (Probeg zhizni)

Ol'ga Mikhailovna Freidenberg was born in Odessa to a Jewish family of cosmo-politan European orientation. Her father, Mikhail (Moisei Fedorovich Freiden-berg, 1858–1920) was a playwright, a journalist, and an inventor of telephone and telegraph equipment. Her mother, Anna Osipovna (Asia, 1862–1944), a younger sister of the artist Leonid Pasternak, was the only female child in the family privileged with receiving a high-school education. Ol'ga was the youngest of three children and the only daughter in the family. The Freidenbergs and the Pasternaks maintained familial and friendly relations. Ol'ga was only two months younger than her world-renowned cousin, Boris, and they remained close, ex-changing letters for forty-five years.[61] Under the tsarist regime, women of Jewish origin were not accepted by the universities; thus Ol'ga, following in the foot-steps of her father, became a versatile autodidact. By the age of twenty-four, she knew seven foreign languages and was well read in European literatures. During World War I, she volunteered as a hospital nurse. In 1917, after the elim-ination of restrictions in higher education on race, sex, and creed, Freidenberg became a student in the Department of Classical Philology. When Mikhail Frei-denberg died in 1920, Ol'ga took responsibility for her mother and remained with Anna Osipovna until her death in 1944. During her scholarly career, Freiden-berg published one monograph, *The Poetics of Plot and Genre: The Period of Ancient Literature* (Leningrad: GIKhL, 1936) and more than thirty scholarly arti-cles, but three other book-length projects, more than fifty papers, and *The Race of Life* remained unpublished. From 1932 to 1950 she chaired the Department of Classical Languages and Literatures at the Leningrad State University. She died in Leningrad on 6 July 1955.

This outline of the successful career of a woman scholar in the Soviet Union does not reveal the traumatic and tragic history of Freidenberg's life. That tragedy, as Freidenberg stated in *The Race of Life*, was that those who endured Stalinism were not allowed to fulfill their destiny.

Freidenberg kept a diary under the adverse conditions of the Siege. Those often illegible pages formed the basis of the volumes of *The Race of Life* that chronicle that time. Although a hybrid—a "retrospective diary"—Freidenberg's account retains the sense of immediacy that characterized the other diaries and letters in this collection. Freidenberg wanted her memoir (fifteen typewritten volumes), whose central part, volumes 7–10, is entitled "The Siege of the Human Being," to speak for those who were erased from the Book of Life, whose lives did not enter into the eternal Book of the Dead. In Russia, Freidenberg stated, the Siege of the Human Being was declared earlier than World War II, and it was never lifted. On the last page of *The Race of Life* she observed that the most terrible thing she witnessed was, "The Siege, the scalping of a living human being, which not a single soul can endure. . . . I don't know when and how I will die. Yet if I am conscious, two images will stand before my eyes—that of my mother [who died in besieged Leningrad], and that of the Moscow Nuremberg Trial" (XV: 154).

The handwritten text of *Probeg zhizni* (The Race of Life) is deposited in the private collection, Pasternak Trust, Oxford, England. Two typewritten copies are held by the members of the Pasternak family in Moscow and in Oxford. The complete text has not yet been published, however. Elliott Mossman used many revealing fragments from Freidenberg's "retrospective diary" to annotate her correspondence with Boris Pasternak. Mossman's publication was followed by a selection from "The Siege of the Human Being" (vols. 7–8, limited to the events of 1942) that appeared in the Russian émigré press: O. M. Freidenberg, "Osada cheloveka," *Minuvshee* 3 (Paris: Atheneum, 1987): 7–44.

Volume 9, Chapter 123

And the wheel rolled on. Under the pretense of the public's urging, Stalin bestowed upon himself the rank of Marshal.[62] My God! How powerful the magic of words and titles! A man who possesses everything in the world— endless land, endless power, money, adulation, all sorts of ranks and honors, all the epithets of a deity—he still needed the title, the simple combination of sounds, the word "marshal," an innocent acoustical window-dressing! In honor of the occasion, public enthusiasm was appropriately feigned. The fact that Stalin has become a marshal, figureheads said at political rallies, spurs us on to new achievements! Someone else's rank was to inspire servicemen without this rank to achieve new feats!

Meanwhile, the clouds grew even more charged. We, as usual, knew nothing. Requisitions were taken from the people in unheard-of forms and dimensions, but they remained uninformed. From foreign telegrams and some internal disputes we guessed about events, including the deterioration of our relationship with our allies.

There was no end to our boasting. Decency and politeness with regard

65

to our foreign allies was never taken into consideration. Apparently, public opinion in England and America was against us. This could not help but serve as fertile ground for the scandalous speech by Standley, the American ambassador to the USSR. This man, who knew Stalin and the atmosphere of his court personally, said publicly, to the whole world: "The Russian people are not given information about American aid to Russia. I have searched the Russian press carefully for reports that the Russians are receiving material aid from America, but have not found a single genuine acknowledgment of this." This enlightened man, extremely knowledgeable about the given problem, who knew well, better than the rest of us, the true state of affairs in Russia, was right. Our indecency knew no bounds. Nowhere was mention ever made of the significance of foreign aid. The "home-grown technology" of our weapons and manufacturing was underscored deeply, as if these machines, foodstuffs, medicine, and the army's weaponry were neither American nor English. The splendid feats in Africa, which afforded us access to victories, were ignored.[63]

This would have been scandalous had we been possessed of a feeling of public shame. The American press raised such a hue and cry that reverberations even began to reach us, poor dummies. Someone in America, in our defense, said that Standley was wrong, that all reports of aid to Russia made by Roosevelt and Churchill "are published in the Soviet press and the Russians are zealous newspaper readers."[64] The sarcasm of this characterization of the proletarian dictatorship as zealous newspaper readers, learning of affairs in Russia by reading foreign telegrams, could have killed a people more cultured and with a greater sense of dignity than we.

We acted very stupidly and rudely in the Gandhi affair, the Hindu nationalist leader arrested by England for his call for civil disobedience and his declaration of a hunger strike.[65] The protest sent to Churchill was vigorous, demanding the immediate release of Gandhi, whom starvation threatened with death, and whose death would provoke a complete worsening of relations between the peoples of India and England. This protest was signed by leaders of many Indian parties, including the head of the Indian Communist Party. Stalin, who had received compliments and weapons from Churchill, played a doubly abusive game. In general he pretended (for whom?) that the Comintern was not his marionette. But this time he had, as they say, to play the fool. Churchill took a hard line and did not release Gandhi, despite all the plots and intrigues. Great was the prestige of the

English government and great our embarrassment when a note appeared in small print in the paper that Gandhi's three-week hunger strike had ended and he had begun to take food. Gandhi had starved less than we Russians had! His emaciation had been healed by sweet rolls and cream, and nothing would remain from this hunger strike, save farce. How could Stalin not have had enough dignity, diplomacy, or simply brains not to get involved with this puppet show!

After returning several railroad stations, he got swell-headed and immediately replied to Sikorski in a condescending tone about the future borders of Poland. Sikorski, the Polish leader, had recently visited Stalin. Here he formed a Polish army, equipped by America, to aid Russia.

I remember the impression our treaty with Poland had on me—under it we restored liberty to all Poles languishing in our concentration camps and prisons. It was a summer day, I think. It was 22 July 1941. I was walking along Nevskii Avenue. I bought a newspaper. I opened it and began to read along the way. An irresistible excitement flooded my heart, tears began to pour down my face. For me this had to do with the real Poland—it was about . . . real live Poles, innocent victims of a tyrant, who suffered in our torture-chamber. Oh, how happy I was about the release of these people. . . .

I remember Sikorski's arrival in 1942, right before the new year, and his radio speech, monstrously interrupted by German caterwauling. Certain words from his speech flew to me as hope, as great joy for a real person, as the renewal of our future.

I recall an account of a review of the Polish army in Russia, conducted by the very same General Sikorski. I got goose bumps from excitement. It was a demonstration of magnanimity. The Poles forgave Russia and stood shoulder to shoulder with her in her moment of danger.[66]

And suddenly there was no more news. For a long, long time. Apparently, the Polish army had been recalled. Sikorski, speaking in London, publicly asked us about the borders of the future Poland, and Stalin replied, in a manner typical of a "megalomaniac," that Poland's present borders would be plundered. Stalin was already pursuing his idea of pan-Slavism. This Asian, unable to speak Russian, already envisioned himself the unifier of the Slavs. Now, with the square-tapped cap of an insurgent on his head,[67] he demanded for himself Poland's Little Russia and White Russia and bared his claws at the oppressors of the Slavs.

England and America, supporters of Sikorski, were shocked. Churchill unambiguously called our father a fool. American public opinion demanded the creation of a "sanitary cordon" against the Soviet plague. A great cry was raised in the press.[68]

At the same time we began to founder on the military fronts. The Germans went on the attack and pressed us once again in all theaters of the war. We surrendered Khar'kov and the cities in the Ukraine that we had won with such crashes and booms.[69] Instantly changing our tune, we began to pester England again and to send to Churchill for reinforcements for the second front. England, expending all its efforts in Africa, had to be irritated by this stupidity and cowardice. Stalin, this marshal, commander-in-chief, and military leader of genius, had once again completely faded into the background. . . .

It was impossible to calculate the human sacrifice. All our young people had already been killed. All my students of all grades were decaying in the ground. Now there was no idiot who wouldn't know that we had been sending select young men to a blood bath in Tallinn and Kingisepp, that they went unarmed and unprepared, that our weapons were defective, that we fought with the help of braggadocio and political indoctrination, that the entire cream of our Leningrad youth suffered especially, forced to enlist as volunteers and in civilian battalions, driven to slaughter—our best youth, the seeds of our culture and of all our industrial specialties. All the college students had been slain, all the technicians, all the craftsmen and the best workers. Not a professional specialist remained in the city. All had been murdered, all lay dead. There was not a family that did not have a young man killed. I knew no one at the university, in my building, among friends and strangers, who had not lost sons, husbands, or brothers at Kingisepp or Tallinn, at the Finnish or Leningrad fronts. Millions fell outside Stalingrad and Moscow. It was worse when the victims served as pawns.

Our reserves and resources were coming to an end. The tormented country could hardly draw a breath. No end was in sight, no limit to this bloody game. It was land they struggled and fought for, it was land they wanted, and people were not spared. They were numbers, not people. They were governed and counted by cruel, bloody bookkeepers who recorded in the book of others' fates ever greater numbers. The vanity and ambition of the tyrants; the servility and groveling of their henchmen.

In the twenties of March we began an attack near Tsarskoe Selo. Our city shook under horrific cannonades. The Germans responded with a bloody repulse. Our next senseless "blitz" was concluded with a top-secret inundation of wounded and the activation of the German murderers. They sent artillery such as we had never seen before, which now fired not fifteen minutes, but three to four hours in a row. The technique of killing was being perfected. The shells were the shrapnel type. Simultaneously in almost all areas of the city at the height of the work day, the civilian population was drenched with blood. Overcrowded trams were turned into meat grinders. People fell, bloodied, on streets and in courtyards, in apartments and in factories. Air raids at night intensified. We, in our usual irresponsible manner, flew upon Koenigsberg, which, of course, did not allow us to get near, since "our air force suffered no losses." The Germans responded to our bragging with real murders of Leningraders. During one of the March raids, the Germans dropped more than sixty bombs on our city. There was much destruction, which was not mentioned. So again they began night after night to launch terrible air-raid attacks on unarmed citizens asleep in their beds. They occurred with German savage cruelty, vindictiveness, and meticulousness. One bombing run was not enough for them, so they made a four-hour raid at dusk, a second in the middle of the night, and a third at dawn. They wore down the people who were not yet killed, for the most part, women. There were practically no male civilians left in the city. Having no serious targets outside Leningrad, the Germans destroyed and murdered the civilian population as an "item on the daily agenda." It was already being said that they had drawn up eighteen divisions here, that a second Stalingrad awaited us.

People roamed about like shadows. A deep, dark despair, which had reached a state of complete indifference to everything in the world, took possession of devastated and shattered people.

Mama and Nina lived only for my upcoming birthday.[70] They whispered, kept secrets, hid and set aside things behind my back and consulted with each other endlessly. My effusive mother could never keep a secret from me. My petrified heart did not want any joy, but I dared not deprive my two "children" of it. On purpose I would leave the house "on time," leaving them to their buzzing. For my part, I was afraid that Mama might blurt out the secret, and, indeed, she inevitably blabbed and betrayed all of poor Nina's secrets. I was pleased that Mama was involved in some sort of holiday excitement, which served, at least for some time, to distract and refresh her with goals. To give her pleasure, I cleaned and straightened up our rooms

69

just in time. I myself abstained from candy in March in order to save it for the upcoming refreshments. Nina had contributed so much to this "celebration" of the soul (. . . and of food!) that, in the end, we thought mostly about how to make her happy.

Surprisingly, life showed me much kindness. It was as though she [life] drew me to her breast and comforted and supported me with caresses. Everything came off amazingly successfully, in the best possible way, and exceeded even my prewar birthday celebrations. The weather was cloudy, as it always is during the ides of March—there were no raids. I was penniless, but miraculously it turned out that the lamp, which had been, utterly hopelessly, in a consignment shop for four months, had sold, and I received 204 rubles! Not long before the "holiday" I was given my rations. Popkov was itching to celebrate my birthday.[71] He saved up all the rations for the preceding twenty-odd days, and on that very day, the twenty-eighth, presented me with six hundred grams of candies he had accumulated (the chocolate and cocoa, which I had also secreted, had been unavailable for a month already). During these very days he produced fresh meat—after a year's interruption! Besides that, they issued rice, dried fruits (apricots and apples), herring, and beer. Most glorious of all was my successful re-registration for first-category rations, which had cost me much worry; this was also a miracle in its own right, just like the sale of the lamp. Nina ran over and shoved some packages into Mama's hand.

At last it was the twenty-eighth! What a holiday! On the table in the dining room (not the kitchen) lay a white tablecloth; on it a shortbread pie with apricot jam. We had on clean underwear, my hair was washed, and we were wearing clean dresses. We breakfasted haphazardly, waiting for Nina. She was late. We were listless. Finally, a knock on the door, and in runs a rosy young and happy girl, enlivened by joy, who hugs and kisses us. Preparations for the feast begin. But before this, I receive a king's ransom—a liter jar of my adored condensed milk (sweet and tasty as taffy!) and a big, thick bar of Argentine chocolate. . . .

All three of us get busy and triumphantly set the table. In this there is yet another hidden holiday—the parade of our old beloved china service and cutlery, tied to happy days in the past. It is a parade of a home and a spirit that has been preserved; it was my own personal triumph; I had hidden these things in a trunk and left them there forever before departing for my homeless wanderings. To get my daily bread, I had sold the better part of them for next to nothing. And yet there was still enough to adorn the table, and these old members of the family appeared on a white tablecloth in their former luster and coziness. Only Mama and I could understand the importance of this holiday table . . . like us, it lived and existed after terrors, deaths, siege, hunger, and like it, we still were living and could still resuscitate our hopes for our future arrival in real living life. . . .

For some reason this time in the rations I was given a liter of beer. So we even had something to toast with!

Nina brought remarkable things: melted butter, sugar, American cheese, smoked ham (bacon), red caviar, white-bread baguettes and bread, sprats and onions for the meat sauce, rice, and what we hadn't seen for a long time—green beans. There was a little bit of everything, in little piles and pieces, but it was there and formed an aggregate whole. We had butter and "salami" sausage from the rations. The feast was unusual—appetizers, cabbage soup, meat sauce, green beans with rice, cocoa with sweetened condensed milk with Mama's pie and the chocolate, compote, and candies. . . . But by this time our stomachs had forgotten to digest. Even these little portions could not be assimilated. I went to bed ill, and by morning I had vomited. However, having eaten substantially for one day, we were not hungry for a week.

Volume 9, Chapter 140

Spiridonov recommended me for work in the Archives, where he himself had been called to work.[72] I didn't dare refuse. At the end of June [1943] I began to visit the Senate building.[73] Nothing related to archives was being produced in the Archives, and I was immediately encouraged by this. They were publishing there collections on the military and political evils of the day. They started trying to persuade me to compile a volume on the reactionary role of the Germans in Russia. . . . But I was in terrible torment. The theme depressed me, with its falseness, pseudo-science, tendentiousness, and political mustiness. Was it my job to organize this nasty falsification of history? Outside my specialty, making me out to be a hack, and serving a shameful political function? No, no! But then my mother's emaciated face would rise before me, a horrible symbol of our suffering and loss of rights, which threatened to suffocate us with starvation. I suffered, vacillated, made contradictory decisions. However, the voice that refused the [theme of]

71

"Germans" overpowered all other considerations, and with a feeling of relief I went and refused categorically. Then they offered me the theme of the
heroism of Leningrad women. This was cleaner and did not reek of bom-
bastic scholarship. For my part, I liked the idea of showing how those in the
intellectual professions were managing to work in blockaded Leningrad. It
was accepted. Thus I came to lead a for me new, unexpected, and somewhat
amorphous project. I was given a collective of workers, 1,500 rubles a month,
a secretary, all the amenities and all the opportunities—a publisher, paper,
a typist, a photographer, almost pigeon's milk. I found an explanation for
all of it on the forms for the work permit and in the work agreement, covering the period up to 1 November. "You know where I ended up thanks to
your recommendation?" I told Spiridonov. "At the NKVD."[74]

Volume 10, Chapter 153

The Party Secretary in the archive was Melamedova, a small, young Jewish
woman. This youthful, diminutive being had a lifeless, dogmatic mind and
a vain, envious soul. Half child, she ruled the whole archive and pressured
our "chief," Tsivlina. My group, which I supposedly directed, consisted of
this Melamedova, the secretary, Tsvibak, and two or three other young
Jewish women.[75] All of them had been security officers of the Cheka and
friends from the University's History Department, from which they had
graduated together. However, Tsivlina and Melamedova kept their distance
from these girls; with them and with me they behaved pompously, driving
out any human warmth from their dealings and fearing unpretentiousness
more than anything. Amazing! Those who imitate great people adopt from
them everything save that which makes them great.

Under Melamedova's influence, Tsivlina, contrary to our agreement,
demanded not only that I direct the work of my junior, but that I also travel
to other institutions and expedite all the work of the group, right down to
being a delivery person. There was no end to their tactlessness and nerve,
their presumptuousness and pomposity. But I treated it all with humor, not
deigning to try and balance the scales with them.

72   My acquaintance with Leningrad heroines was of little interest. It
was the common people, rather than the great, that attracted me. The wise
Michurina turned out to be more charming and simpler than I had expected.
And she really was pleasant. She lived like a queen. Already deaf, she had a

personal secretary, Muromtseva, and a maid. Although I had done all I could not to avail myself of the invitation to her home, Ostroumova-Lebedeva interested me. She lived picturesquely, in an old-fashioned style, in a little cottage overgrown with grass on the outskirts of the city. She received me well, she had asked me to visit. She herself and everything she had were simple, genuine, and modest. She gave the impression of a cultured person, but as an individual, she was ordinary. In her home my soul could get a rest from Stalinism. Streshneva, an intelligent, powerful, and sly woman, had the suggestion of the poseur and toady about her.[76]

Ordinary people simply reeked of Soviet heroism, a heroism surprisingly impersonal. They were modest, frightened, and, as if being tested in an exam, they knew by heart how one needs to learn modesty and patriotism. Everything living, everything truthful was inadmissible. Uncensored tragedy wafted through several lives. In her interview, Petrova made it clear that Pavlov used her talent, thoughts, and labors, and before me arose a familiar picture of love, in which a prominent male mind has taken hold of a female heart and female talent, forcing the woman to get ahead not on her scholarship, but on the "casting couch."[77]

I learned the terrible truth about the work of women lawyers during the siege. The tale of lawyers walking along the Neva's slippery ice to prisons where their clients were dying by the hundreds, this terrible tale of human suffering numbed the soul. However, no one dared to write down the truth; much that was unbelievably tragic was conveyed to me orally. Instead, a procession filed past—women like Kropacheva, people without conscience or honor, the favorites and pets of the authorities.[78] A curious tirade was uttered by Tesakova, a Chekist from the Meteorological Institute: "Everything's fine, but why not tell the truth about Leningrad? The heroism of our women would have become apparent then only if it had been possible to speak about the cannibalism, the twenty days spent in the same apartment with five or six corpses, about the arms and legs that dug out of the snow, of the dead children on garbage heaps, about everything we experienced and that killed our souls forever. . . . Now those in Leningrad who survived are considered heroes. But remember how they were persecuted because they would not leave? For some reason it is impossible to tell the whole truth. . . ."

Yes, nowadays, all around, glory is sung, with false pathos, to those who in their day did not want to abandon their city, but was it so very long ago that a person was threatened with prison and dishonor for this very decision?

73

I have remembered. I have recalled.

Several institutions could not provide "heroines," because they played down the real ones and advanced their protégées, but I discovered this in time. That's how it was at the Public Library with its system of barbarous treatment of its workers and its books. The director was a Soviet, ill-mannered woman.

I discovered a staggering picture of human heroism in the Institute of the Party. During an air raid a worker had her leg torn off. Berdnikova and Sokolova, two wonderful women, simple people, resolute party members, would carry their meager portions of cold soup from a cafeteria located at one end of the city to their comrade at the other end. Hungry, with scurvy, they shuffled on swollen feet in terrible freezing weather. Next Berdnikova collapsed. Sokolova then took her in. She put her in her own bed and warmed her with her own body. This was genuine, splendid heroism, this humane feeling amidst a general moral collapse.

∞

I remember that day, 5 October. During the day there had been an air-raid alert. In the evening Yudina came to visit.[79] Mama rushed at her with complaints about some scoundrel who had (in her opinion) improperly played some piece of Beethoven, broadcast in the morning over the radio. It turned out that this scoundrel was Yudina, and both of them, one passionately, the other tersely, discussed this issue. Then we sat down in my room. Yudina was pre-war; I was out-and-out a person of the siege. She talked and revealed herself, while I kept silent. I could not find the words. Yudina said that she accepted evil as an inevitability demanded by life. She was rereading *The Idiot*, lived in the world of aesthetics, understood and accepted heroism. I felt the desecrated soul within me, dying desires, my appreciation of life humiliated and destroyed forever.

Toward evening Mama and I had a quarrel. We could neither talk it out nor understand each other. We did everything one for the other, and all apart from each other, and our efforts to overcome the force that stood above us led to even worse results. The misunderstanding oppressed us, the discord. We were doomed to every kind of "dis" and "mis."

74   Later all would be forgotten. People quarreled and made up. Life's humiliation lay in the fact that after the fighting and cursing, people would completely spontaneously chat peacefully with one another, kiss and caress

each other. Many, coming to themselves, would beat their chests, praying for forgiveness and pity. Lifshits's husband, Fima, was that sort. Once painfully delicate and affectionate, he once got so enraged that he struck Lifshits across the face.[80] She bore it all. But one fine day, unable to endure his curses and abuse, she trampled him under her feet and beat him unmercifully. That is how cultured and loving people behaved themselves.

Mother never uttered a word and never complained to anyone about me. In her most extreme neurasthenia, she did not lose her basic quality, her noble spirit. I was the one who complained about her to everyone.

∞

October [1943] was coming to a close. The night of the 29th there was a sudden thunderstorm. After the shelling, its peals seemed pitiful. Each night our windows were lit up by more fearful lightning, and the thunder of artillery explosions shook much more strongly.

The Germans shelled tram stops and all the places where people gathered, the peaceful, unarmed public, which our tyrant had forced to live and work on the front lines. The trams were transformed into bloody mash.

As a safety measure they decided to move the tram stops. It then became even more difficult to move about. The people found comfort, however, in vodka. Instead of bread and food, the state began every month to distribute vodka. The emaciated got drunk quickly. This was the beginning of the organized poisoning of the people, a most insidious type of tax. Instead of five rubles, vodka cost sixty rubles and sixty kopecks, and people were required to bring in two or three empties each time they wanted to buy a bottle. An empty bottle sold at the market for five to eight rubles. Money, meanwhile, was already very expensive. It was obtained by slave labor, the kind of labor that was used only under serfdom and slavery. A person did not have the right to leave his job voluntarily. Moreover, he dared not switch jobs from one district to another. Living in one part of the city, he wound up assigned to another and didn't have the right to free himself from there. Under fire, in the dark of night, along dark streets, people dragged themselves home from one end of town to another—if they were permitted to spend the night at home. Everything was arranged so that people would not live at home. They were kept at work until late at night. The sick got no care at home. Sick-leave certificates were given only for high temperatures. There were common cases when a cold turned into a serious ailment or death

75

only because the outpatient doctor refused to grant the person prophylactic bed rest. In each and every way the basic principle of Asiatic forms of despotism was sustained—impunity for the guilty, persecution of the innocent.

∞

A meeting was arranged in the Archives with Zel'man (Mikhailovich), the head of all Leningrad archives. It was a remarkable meeting. I was summoned for an answer.

"I can say, like Calchas in 'La Belle Hélene,' I began, 'there are too many flowers.'[81] Too many meetings and reports, more than there is work."

Mikhailovich was offended. Bende started to reproach me, saying that I wanted to set up a market for brides. He demanded that only those "approved" appear in the collection—Vera Inber, Preobrazhenskaia, and Kropacheva.[82] I insisted on a "portrayal of the heroism of the masses" and protested against catholic canonization. The meeting was stormy. I ridiculed Bende. Tsivlina and the whole collective were on my side. Everyone's ears burned. Mikhailovich was cold, cruel, and malicious.

By this time the collection was ready. I was compiling it for about two months. It consisted of documents, autobiographical stories, interviews, and articles. All the women artists, composers, sculptors, writers, scholars, performers, educators, and high-school teachers were included there. I strove for breadth, in order to show the humble toiler, to lead her into the spotlight, so as to give her joy and a holiday. Bende cursed me. He needed to trace the background of every woman, to expose the gender behind every name. In my heart I felt pity for him.

I had long dreamt about leaving this pleasant institution and removing my name from this volume. The introductory article that I had to write embarrassed me. I willingly and zealously would have participated in a truthful collection. But I couldn't imagine how I could write a hackneyed political article in the Chekist-Stalinist manner. I just could not imagine this.

Our government not only profiteered in vodka and foodstuffs. It profiteered in people. The most difficult thing of all was to obtain acknowledgment of the value of one person or another.

Translated by Arlene Forman

Memoirs & Oral Histories

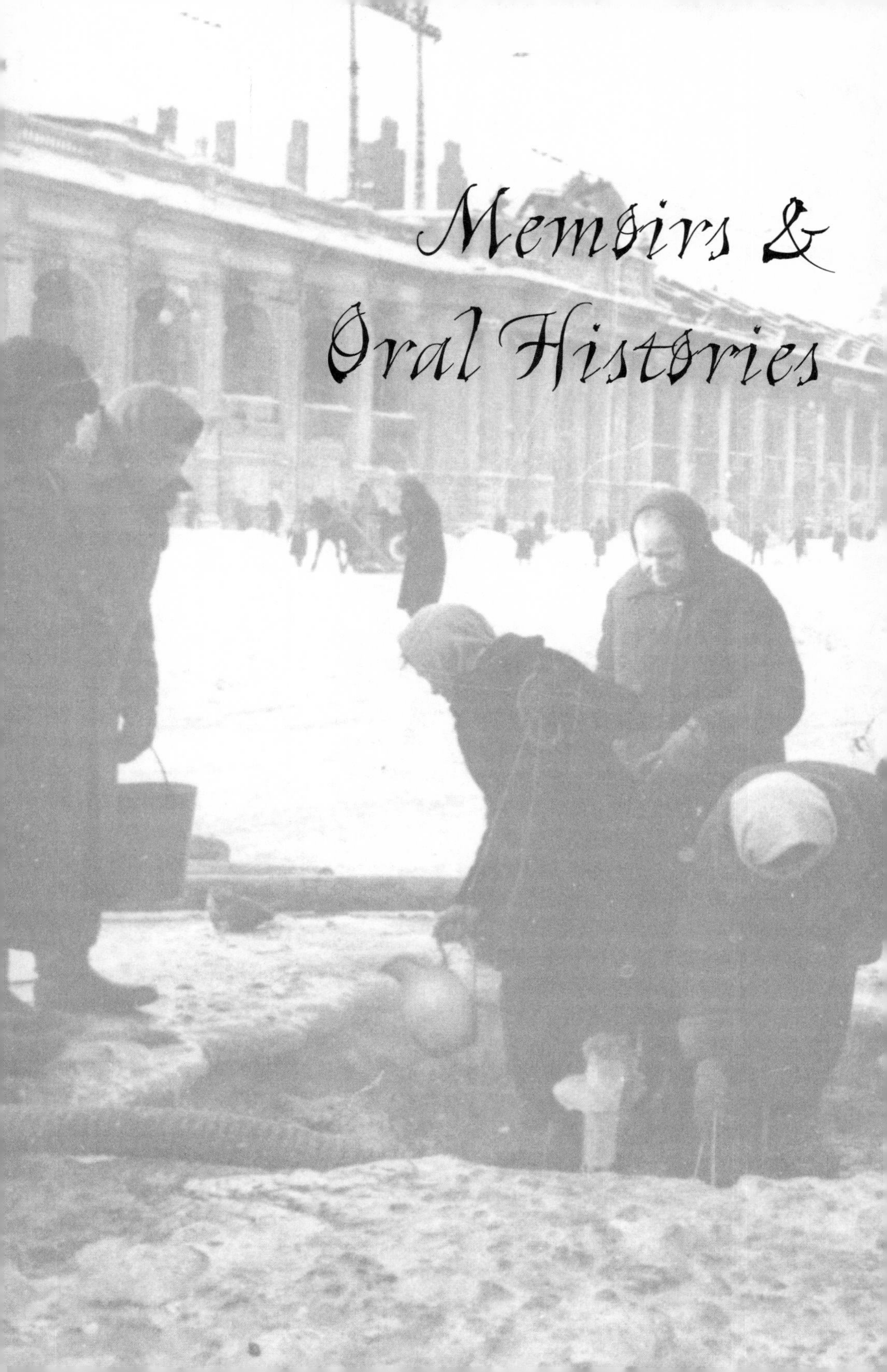

EVACUATION and THE SCOTTISH ALBUM

Vera Vladimirovna Miliutina, graphic designer and theater artist, was born and lived her entire life in Leningrad. Her father was a professor of biology, and her mother was a physician. In the 1960s–1970s and during the last years of her life, Miliutina worked on her memoirs *What Is Remembered* (*To, chto vspomnilos'*). After her death, her husband, A. S. Rozanov, and her friends compiled a small book, *By and about Vera Miliutina*.[1] This book provides vital information on Miliutina's life and is the source of the fragments from her memoirs that follow.

Miliutina began her professional training at the State School of Technical and Industrial Designers; then later studied at the Academy of Fine Arts in the Theater Department. After graduation, she began work as an artist and set designer at the museum of the Leningrad Opera House (1932–1940). In 1942 she became a costume designer for the Leningrad State Variety Theater and designed the costumes for the performers of various dance ensembles. From the very beginning of the war, she sketched illustrations for TASS (Telegraph Agency of the Soviet Union), and with a group of Leningrad artists she produced a series of drawings, "The Hermitage under Siege," whose purpose was "to document damage done to the buildings of the Hermitage by bombs and artillery fire."[2] After the war Miliutina displayed these drawings at numerous exhibitions dedicated to the history of the city under siege (in 1965, 1977, 1984, and 1985). They were eventually purchased by the Russian National Museum. In June 1942, Miliutina assisted A. P. Ostroumova-Lebedeva in the compilation of *The Scottish Album* (see Ostroumova's diary and the chapter "The Summer of 1942" in Miliutina's memoirs). The history of this album and the exchange of sympathetic letters and artwork between Scottish and Soviet women were made known in the West thanks to articles by Tamara Talbot-Rice and Kira Ingal.[3] In 1943 Miliutina began work as a costume artist and set designer for children's dance ensembles at the Palace of Pioneers. After the war she worked a great deal with children, teaching drawing at the Palace of Pioneers and House of Culture and designing costumes and sets for children's performances.

From *Evacuation* (1960)

We lived a stone's throw from the Finland Station, and it was precisely via the Finland Station that the evacuation took place. Having dragged sleds to the station, piled with their possessions tied up in bundles, people would settle down in small packs in the cold, shabby, unheated little station, or on the platform out in the open, if there wasn't a shelling going on. They would sit down and wait. They waited to leave and to get some food before the trip. They were given food, but that happened later, closer to spring. However, their departure was still a long way off. There were thousands of obstacles that constantly prevented people from leaving, but they waited. They waited for a long time, sometimes for several days, and sometimes they never even managed to leave. Or even worse, having squeezed themselves into an overcrowded railway car, they would die there, never having made it even to the "Road of Life."

There were other obstacles. At the last minute someone might be killed during a bomb or artillery attack and without that member of the family, there was no energy left to do anything at all—"does it really matter now where we die?" Documents would get lost. And one had to conceal starvation-induced dysentery, because they avoided taking people who were seriously ill. And then upon examination they might discover lice. A person infested with lice, due to hunger and the lack of water, soap, and heat, would be left behind, despite all pleas and tears.

Just think, we lived right by the Finland Station, right in the middle of this pandemonium. We ourselves had been bombed out and relocated, and yet we always had on our hands relatives and friends, and often complete strangers, who were even more miserable than we were. These people are going to the Mainland! There they will recover. They will live and have bread to eat. They invite us to come along with them; they will write to us from there, from that land of plenty, and Grandfather Serezha and I will follow them there to eat fried potatoes. . . . It's so sad to reckon now who made it where and what happened to so many who left—defenseless, emaciated, precious people. . . . But at that time they believed that the worst was already behind them; that there, there it would be easy, in any case easier than it was here. If only because there wouldn't be any shells or bombs exploding.

There was yet another tragic category of people—those who were or-

V. Miliutina. "The Hermitage, A Shattered Window" (*Èrmitazh, Razbitoe okno*), 1942. A view from within the Hermitage Museum onto Palace Square. This sketch represents Miliutina's work, which was commissioned by government officials at Smolnyi to document the destruction to Leningrad during the Siege. *The State Hermitage Museum*

dered to leave the city in three days. They, you see, happened to have non-Russian last names. But they and their parents had lived their whole lives in Petersburg-Petrograd-Leningrad. They didn't leave of their own free will —they were forced to leave. True, it was difficult to understand anything in that chaos, but you so wanted to do at least something for these unfortunate people, weakened by interrogations and hunger, who had already lost their home, their *burzhuika*, and who had abandoned the walls that had sheltered several generations of their ancestors.

Taking a kettle with boiling water and wrapping a blanket around it, I would set out into this gray mass of swaddled people and blankets to look for those I might help with at least a glass of hot water, and above all, for my cousins the Greunfelds. People in the crowd were lying on their possessions, and it was difficult to make my way through all of this, trying not to step here on a bundle, there on a human being wrapped in a sack. Under the headscarves all you could see were eyes with identical expressions of hope on identical gray faces. What was identical about them was probably not their faces, but an eternal image of Hunger and Misfortune, repeated in a thousand faces.

There were men among the women as well, but their heads were wrapped up too, over their hats.

And they all looked at me as though I were bringing them two hundred grams of bread on a tray, poor things. The kettle with hot water hypnotized everyone. Its contents were divided into a multitude of gulps, and I was on my way back to boil the next one. As long as the harsh cold persisted, I would go to the station whenever I could. Grandfather Serezha would boil water, fueling the *burzhuika* with broken-up chairs. It was a drop in the ocean, but even this drop warmed people up.

I would try to get some of the people up who had fallen in the street. But almost always my efforts were in vain. There was no choice for me but to keep on walking. And I walked on, or rather, crawled as well, because I myself didn't have any strength left. Oh, how these poor people could have used a syringe of camphor or a cup of coffee! But even a glass of hot water was not always available.

And everyone at the station had the same question: "When will the train come? Will it be soon?" But it didn't run according to any schedule. And the answer was always the same: "When it becomes possible to travel."

With a naive belief, they all strove to leave—to save themselves, to become human beings again. And all this despite the fact that few of them were "villagers" heading "home," but Leningraders setting out into a vague and troubling unknown. . . .

From *The Scottish Album*

In the summer of 1942, when exhausted Leningraders had suffered under siege a horrible autumn, a fierce, dark winter, and a difficult, tense spring; could hardly recognize their former acquaintances when they met them in the bomb shelters, on the street, or in the cafeteria; when it was impossible to get warm, even in the sun; when their legs seemed as though they were made of cotton wool, their joints ached from scurvy, and their minds, no matter where consciousness attempted to direct them, inevitably returned to one and the same thought: When can I eat? . . . Will I be able to eat soon? . . .

It was at this time that a plane left Leningrad for Moscow, carrying a heavy package that had been masterfully wrapped at Smolnyi.[4] The plane remained there for a short while and then flew further. Its final destination was far, far away, "beyond the deep blue sea"—in Scotland. I would like to relate what I know about the parcel that it delivered.

13 June 1942, during one of the most difficult periods of the siege— bombings were followed by artillery attacks that gave way to incendiary bombs and then a new round of bombing—I received an unexpected visit from A[ndrei] A[ndreevich] Bartashevich from the city's Council for the Arts (*Upravlenie po delam iskusstv*). He informed me that at the end of the previous year women in Scotland, distressed by the desperate situation of the women of Leningrad, had gotten the idea to encourage them with an expression of sympathy. On the initiative of Miss Plant, Agnes Maxwell, and other parishioners of churches in Coatbridge, Airdrie, and Woodside, they put together a beautiful album of greetings. (The artistry was not of professional caliber, but those touching sketches had been done with great care and love. On a silk plaid binding, against a traditional background of orange, white, black, and yellow flowers, there was a long thistle, the emblem of Scotland. "Your fight is our fight and we shall not fail you or be unworthy of your great sacrifice"—that appeared in the text of the greeting to the women of Leningrad, beneath the lines of a poem by R[obert] Burns, dedicated to the brotherhood of all people.)[5]

In conclusion Andrei Andreevich asked me whether I had the strength to take part in an urgent and crucial undertaking—the creation of an album by way of reply from the women who were defending Leningrad. For this purpose, on the order of the City Party Committee, a team of artists had already been assembled under the direction of A[nna] P[etrovna] Ostroumova-Lebedeva.

I lived on the same street as she did, then it was Nizhegorodskaia, but later it was renamed Lebedev Street, in memory of S. V. Lebedev (the inventor of synthetic rubber), Anna Petrovna's husband. She and her constant companion, Anna Matveevna, had remained in their apartment in a two-story building, practically unscathed by shells, across from the Medical-Military Academy. The road was overgrown with grass and blossoms of chamomile; not all the obstructions had been removed, nor all the craters filled in. Above the building there hung the menacing ruins of a gaping six-story building with its mangled bathrooms and pipes now visible, sheets of metal flapping in the wind.

"My" building, in the next block, had also been bombed out, in the fall of 1941. The next place Grandfather and I lived burned down when it was hit by an incendiary bomb, and we were unable to provide ourselves with even the smallest degree of comfort; art was something I could think about only when I was sitting in the bomb shelter of a neighboring building. My hands had grown coarse from daily hard manual labor, I rarely managed to draw. And all of a sudden I had the chance to practice my art, and under the direction of no less than Ostroumova-Lebedeva herself, and on a team of people I had never met.

꩜

It turned out that it wasn't as difficult to work as at first it seemed it would be. Despite our haste, everything was clear and certain, we all knew what we had to do. Anna Petrovna, with consideration and goodwill, followed our work carefully, especially mine. She showed me, a young artist unknown to her, so much respect as a professional, so much trust—so valued coming from such a great master—that all my doubts disappeared. I knew I had to cope, and that I would. She carefully chose among her large portfolio her most representative prints—landscapes of Leningrad, her hometown, from which she refused to be evacuated, whose grandeur and beauty she wanted to show to our Scottish friends. Her respect for us and our work was striking, her bright optimism, her faith in the resilience of Leningraders, in Victory.

∞

It was my job to compose a unifying design for each page [of the album], to create a composite of the combined insignia of the Soviet Union and Great Britain for the fly-leaves, to make several compositions of the national flags of both countries, and to execute graphic "accents" on individual pages. The required embellishments had to be gotten hold of at the libraries. Thus once it fell to me to go to the Library of the Academy of Sciences (BAN), on Vasil'evskii Island, in search of color representations of the insignia and flags. Along the way I often sat down upon the ruins, nibbled buds from acacia bushes. But when I finally arrived at the Library, it turned out that the women who were lugging packs of books back and forth on sheets of plywood had already gone up to the second floor that day, and they had no strength to do it again. No pleas or arguments helped. The following morning I had to trudge there again.

∞

Five days, more precisely, five days and nights of intense, closed-mouth work —and our worn-out team accomplished its task. On 19 June the completed album lay on the table!

Thick, elegant, in a binding of ancient Russian embroidery, in a matte gold brocade case, it was professionally and beautifully compiled and executed. Watercolors, black-and-white and colored prints by Ostroumova-Lebedeva, drawings by other artists (I don't remember their names) decorated the pages. Reproduced exactly in terms of proportion, color, and detail— the insignia of the Soviet Union and Great Britain (also beautiful, in the elegant style of the baroque, decorated in gold and silver, with a multitude of lions, unicorns, leopards, crowns, knights' shields on interwoven light-blue ribbons, with the English rose and the Scottish thistle). ". . . We are proud that we have such a worthy ally as the people of Great Britain. The treaty concluded by our countries on 26 May 1942 will give us new strength in the battle with the German aggressors. . . . Dear allies, there are many of us! Women are a mighty force!" This is what appeared in the greeting to the women of Scotland on the first two sheets of the album.

On the back of each sheet a large envelope was glued, into which after-

85

wards there were placed sheets of paper with signatures of the women of Leningrad: factory workers, nurses, doctors, office workers, writers. Later A. F. Volkova told me that news that wishes had been received from Scotland for victory over the Fascists and that we were preparing an album of greetings in response had hardly had a chance to spread through Leningrad before all women, and most of all female workers, wanted to sign.[6] Their fathers, husbands, and children were fighting at the front, they had replaced them at the work benches, and each of them wanted to say "Thank you!" for the thoughtful keepsake and warm greeting from our distant Scottish (women) friends. As a result, there ended up being more sheets of signatures than had been foreseen, and the album had trouble fitting into its elegant case, but no one who wished to sign was refused. Shortly thereafter, the album "took off" for Moscow.

A year or so later I learned that our album apparently was exhibited in turn in the churches of Coatbridge, Airdrie, and Woodside.[7] That it lay on the lectern, and every day the minister would turn one page so that each day visitors could see a new page with a new image and text.

About thirty years passed. In 1969 a book appeared in print, *Victory of the Century* (*Podvig veka*), in which the author and compiler, N. N. Papernaia, included my essay on the creation of the "Leningrad" album. And early the following year the English arts critic T. Talbot-Rice sent me (by way of the staff of the Hermitage) a news clipping from the paper *The Weekend Scotsman*, where there had appeared a sizable excerpt from my memoirs, translated by her, preceded by a short introductory article.[8] When this came to their attention, the USSR–Great Britain Society wished to learn about my subsequent fate. Having ascertained, thanks to the Leningrad House of Friendship, that I was alive and continued to work as an artist, the directors of the society sent me, along with warm greetings, touching mementos: a doll dressed in the Scottish national costume, and a towel with a picture of a Scotsman with bagpipes.[9]

Translated by Alla Zeide

THE WAR, THE BLOCKADE,
THE MILITARY HOSPITAL

The following excerpts are taken from the memoir of the surgeon Valentina
Nikolaeva Gorokhova, which is preserved in the Museum of the Defense of
Leningrad. They appear in Part I, which is entitled "The Eve of War and ÈG
[evacuation hospital] 1012" and covers events from the end of May 1941 to the
middle of November 1944. The first page of the memoir conveys a sense of im-
pending catastrophe: Over a cup of tea "with a nurse from our clinic, [we]
heatedly discussed the question that was troubling all of us. Will there be war?
When?" From June 1941 until 19 November 1944, Gorokhova directed the seventh
surgical unit of Evacuation Hospital 1012, located in the Otto Gynecological Institute. Also working at this facility were numerous relatives and acquaintances
of other memoirists in this collection, including a cousin of Valentina Petrova
(excerpts of whose memoir are included here). The final pages of the memoir
describe the fall of 1944, when, having left Leningrad behind—"half-starved,
still not very populous, all in ruins, liberated from the blockade"—Gorokhova
was transferred to the Belorussian third front. Together with Red Army forces,
she spent the remainder of the war in the West, beyond the borders of the Soviet Union.[10]

Gorokhova's memoir differs significantly from most other memoirs of the
war. First, she never loses sight of her professional responsibilities and per-
ceives all events from the overriding perspective of a doctor and surgeon. She
never forgets that she is surrounded by bodies wounded and maimed by the
war; she and her colleagues never cease to wage war with death. Second, she always keenly senses that she is a woman, and that the war is killing the feminine
within her, that all the horrors of war constitute a continual assault on the female nature. She cannot forget that to put a cast on and transfer the wounded
from the operating table to a stretcher, they needed six "stretcher-bearers"—
six women, nurses, exhausted from hunger. She recalls that during the blockade: "Workers from the administrative and economic-executive offices paraded
around in elegant suits of fine wool," while in 1944 she was issued an ill-fitting
man's uniform—a "gift from Mrs. Roosevelt."[11] She observed the effect of hunger
on the female psyche: "All instincts died. Men and women washed together in

87

the bath. Here too, in two adjacent and open shower stalls, a wounded soldier showered with two nurses."[12] As a doctor in an evacuation hospital, Gorokhova had to live in a temporary barracks, while at home her sixty-five-year-old mother was starving. Likewise, her colleague had her mother and five-year-old daughter at home. Suffering themselves from dystrophy, the women wanted to share their military ration with those at home, but they would be detained as they left the hospital, the contents of their briefcases would be checked, and they would be forced to return to work. "I returned to the department defeated and distraught. The next day and the day after that I didn't go to the cafeteria, I starved myself. And a woman orderly took my briefcase to my mother. I was ordered to report to the commissar, and he attempted to persuade me that I didn't have the right to undermine my health, to deny myself food. I agreed, didn't protest, but I informed [him] that I couldn't do otherwise, that my sacred responsibility was to save my mother."[13]

In the chapter on the evacuation hospital, Gorokhova addresses the following topics: "1941"; "Our Seventh Section and Our Work"; "The Staff of the Seventh Section and the Volunteers"; "Our Nourishment?"; "Study and Scientific Work"; "Our Joys"; "Our Rest and Relaxation." Thus Gorokhova's memory leads her from the horrors and death of 1941 to victory and life.

The first director of the hospital, during the most difficult period of the blockade, was Professor Sergei Alekseevich Yagunov from the Otto Institute. Of average height, solidly built, with a fluffy reddish moustache, the "barometer of his mood." Very hot-tempered and a very good person. Professor Yagunov, with his assistants and Commissar Lukanin, Zykov, and others, within five days created a hospital where before there had been nothing.

It was they, our supervisors, using Doctor Grachev's connections and other possibilities, who saved the wounded, the staff, and the entire hospital from freezing. They secured, through superhuman strength, in January 1942 the delivery of electric power, and that meant light, a supply of water, and steam heat.

∾

Conditions in the hospital gradually improved. At the end of 1942 or the beginning of 1943, we received new beds in all the wards—new, nickel-plated, standard twin-sized beds. Bedside tables, stools. They managed to find good pillows. But all of this was considerably later. In the meantime, the

Orderlies run to the wounded during an artillery attack, 19 December 1943.
The Central State Archive of Film, Photographic, and Audio Documentation,
St. Petersburg

winter of 1941–1942 was approaching—unusually severe, frigid, and hungry.

The hospital was not ready for this. The temperature in the wards was below zero. The medicine froze, and the wounded, and the staff. The wounded were put two to a bed. They were covered with thick mats. They were carried in blankets to have their dressings changed.

The staff and doctors worked in their winter coats, in hats, in boots. The fortunate owners of *valenki* wore those. There were no lab coats. Instead [we] put a sheet on over a coat and secured it at the back, on the arms, and at the wrist with surgical instruments.

The critical problem of heating the hospital, as well as the apartments of Leningrad, was solved in an old-fashioned way. We resorted to the life-saving *burzhuika*, which required little fuel, but provided heat quickly. But where was one to find brick and iron for the exhaust pipe in the blockaded city? We gathered bricks and sand for the ovens from the ruins of apartment buildings. A supply of iron was found right here, on the walls of the hospital.

89

We pulled down the drainpipes, with the help, of course, of the doctors, political instructors,[14] the lightly wounded. And the brick *burzhuika*s, the dream of frozen Leningraders, constructed by stove-setters from the ranks of the lightly wounded, took their place of honor in the wards, the dressing station, and in other locations.

Cold was not the only scourge of the long-suffering city. In Leningrad there was no electrical power, transportation, water, food products.

The city. Institutions, hospitals, and private dwellings plunged into darkness.

Lighting—old-fashioned oil lamps; in the best case, a kerosene lamp. The hospitals were lighted by torches also. I recall those night rounds made by the head of the department—the ones that I made.

The long corridor of our seventh department is sunk in darkness. The moans of the wounded can be heard, cries: "Nurse, give me something to drink!" "The can!" (instead of a bedpan). At the end of the corridor by a table, wrapped in coats and blankets, sit two nurses on duty. Both are diligently embroidering, by the light of an oil lamp. In hungry, cold, and dark Leningrad, to the roar of shelling and air-raid alarms, many Leningraders entertain themselves, if you can call it that, with cross-stitching. This activity distracted them from painful thoughts, worries, it soothed them a bit.

The nurse lit the torch, and with a torch I made my rounds of ten wards with 120–160 wounded. You stick your hand under the mat, not to take a pulse, but to reassure yourself that the wounded soldier is alive. This picture —a doctor by now wearing a lab coat and a nurse with a torch—is worthy of the painter's brush.

Under such conditions—cold, hunger, and darkness—one needed not only to survive, but to work, to accept the arriving wounded, make a diagnosis, dress them, take x-rays, perform minor and major operations, apply casts. And write up a brief, yet exhaustive, chart. When military action intensified, the flow of the wounded increased. The team on duty in the reception area of the dressing station sometimes didn't leave for days. And there was such an effort, such a recognition of duty, of the necessity of superhuman labor, that no one complained. Everyone knew that our work would return the wounded to action, would help us achieve victory over the enemy.

We were given moral support by the director of the hospital, by Commissar F. G. Lukanin, and the political instructor of our department, A. P. Kul'kova. She nursed us with sweetened tea that she brought to us in the dressing station.

During the most difficult time for the hospital, in 1941, in cold and darkness, we had to perform our first amputation at the thigh. The artist Osipov had been wounded in the thigh. Not a large wound, the bone was whole, but a major blood vessel was damaged. His foot was gangrenous. In order to save the patient's life, it was necessary to sacrifice the leg.

In a small, cold ward, on a trestle-bed instead of an operating table, by the light of two "bat" lanterns—only in the most decisive moment did we switch on the emergency lamp. The surgeons, with quilted jackets under their lab-coats, emaciated, had great difficulty sawing through the bone. Osipov's life was saved. He slowly got better. After a considerable improvement in his condition, he was flown out to the rear. Unfortunately I know nothing of his eventual fate.

⬯

During the war many thousands of wounded passed through our department. In Leningrad there were 120–195 soldiers in the surgery department. In Kaunas, after the relocation of our hospital to the third Belorussian front, we treated up to 465 wounded a day. The injured came in waves, depending on the intensity of the battles. We were even able now and then to catch our breath.

The injured ranged in age from eighteen to fifty. Some seemed to be little boys; others old men. There were various nationalities: Russians, Ukranians, Belorussians. Inhabitants of Central Asia and the Far North. There were some who spoke Russian poorly. Each had his own personality. But the war united them all. It tore them from home and family, threw them into the fire of war, igniting everything in its path. They were united also by suffering. Wounds that some recovered from quickly and that crippled others and rendered them invalids for life. And how many gave their lives in battles with the enemy! They all, some sooner, some later, thawed out from the horrors of battle and struggle with the enemy. From the cold in the trenches, where they were drenched by rain and covered with snow, and where the enemy's bullets and shells still managed to reach them. And slowly life, and the desire to live, returned to them.

91

A more detailed account of wounds and care of the wounded.

In the reception area on the first floor, the first stage of treatment was the taking of medical histories. This was also the point for preliminary disinfecting. Until the end of January 1942, this was very difficult due to the absence of water and heat. But even with access to both, it was not always easy to wash the wounded. Many arrived in extensive bandages, in transport splints that sometimes covered half or even more of the body's surface. And the bandages and splints could be removed only in the triage bandaging station on the order of the attending physician.

Sometimes the wounded arrived infested with lice. We took precautions to avoid an epidemic, but when an outbreak of pediculosis (lice) occurred, the department waged an all-out war. Both bandages and casts were changed. When possible, the wounded were bathed. And under bandages and casts *peretrum* was liberally sprinkled. Such wounded were put under strict observation. Under casts that had been applied to the severely wounded many days prior to their transfer from the MASH unit (medical sanitary battalion —MSB), wounds had begun to suppurate and gave off a stifling odor. At times when we took off the cast, we discovered a mass of large, white worms. Some thought that by feeding on the putrefaction, the worms cleaned the wound. But how did our staff manage to breathe the stench of putrefaction or observe wounds swarming with worms!

The equipment in the triage bandaging station, the instruments, the anesthesia—everything was primitive. But it was imperative to work, treat, and operate on the wounded. And we worked.

The Seventh Section

The staff for 120–195 wounded is quite limited. In the difficult conditions of the blockaded city, with frequent debilitating air raids, shellings, and bombings, the personnel did not only have to survive; they had to give their work their last ounce of strength.

Medical personnel did not only have to admit, cure, and look after the wounded, but just as important, they had to keep up [the patients'] morale. To bolster their will to live, to get well. And how difficult it was for the weary youth and not-so-young women who were starving and in need of sleep! It was necessary not only to cure, but to maintain the cleanliness of the department, to keep discipline among the wounded and the staff. To see that no one in the ward smoked, they would clean out night stands. [To see that] no one hoarded things under the mattresses or broke up the slats from the beds to use instead of matches. That no one hid or put on uniforms that could be worn for organized escapes and unwarranted absences, and so on and so forth.

There were more than a few violations, of course. For example, we were supposed to shave the heads of the soldiers and the officers. Once a sergeant-major arrived who had a magnificent head of hair—he had been transferred from the casualty ward. We approach him to take care of his hair, and he screams: "Better you cut off my head than my hair!"

A wounded soldier saw a woman's name on the label of some donated blood and he exploded: "I won't let anyone pour a woman's blood into me!"

And there were numerous infractions of all kinds, for which the head of the department would be reprimanded.

෴

In addition to the recuperating wounded, we had as helpers volunteers from the university. They looked after the wounded, fed them. They read newspapers and books. They wrote letters.

Ekaterina Nikolaevna Donova comes to mind, the wife of Professor Donov. Before the war, she was a patroness of the university clinic. She decorated it and made it cozy. A small woman, no longer young, totally emaciated, she gave her last ounce of strength to serving the wounded. In 1941 Professor Donov died of starvation, and Ekaterina Nikolaevna did not outlive him for very long.

Mariia Fedorovna Khosheva worked at the Geography or Geology Department at the University. In 1942 she was planning to be evacuated with her child. The state of her health indicated that she wouldn't make it to the rear. Unknown to the Head of the Medical Services Department, which was in violation of the rules, I twice transfused her with one hundred cc. of blood. It kept her going. She was successfully evacuated, and after the war she returned to Leningrad and to her work.

There were quite a few other volunteers. Among them was my mother, sixty-five years old. When she recovered from severe dystrophy, she com-

93

plained that, "I have no one to look after, no one to worry about." She also read to the wounded, wrote and carried their letters to the post office. On her own initiative, she brought a copper samovar to the ward, so that there would always be boiling water for the wounded.

∞

On 31 December 1942, the doctors put on a New Year's celebration in Dr. I. I. Shafer's office. The senior surgeon, F. A. Kopylov, was at the celebration, along with his wife, Sofiia Vladimirovna, also a doctor. His office was the same size as our surgeons' lounge. But since just one person lived there, it looked spacious. There was a Christmas tree; this time with electric lights from home. They brought crystal goblets from home.

The hors d'oeuvres: herring, canned goods, brisket (from the market), cabbage, potatoes (also from the market). We had only vodka. Whoever didn't drink vodka toasted with a goblet of kissel.

There was a little dancing. The celebration ended at 3:30 A.M. Then in my room in the surgeons' area we were busy until 5:00 wrapping gifts for the wounded and hanging them on the trees in the two wards. Toys, candy, little bags and baskets. We wrote greeting cards for the wounded.

The patient Grinberg played Santa Claus. The nurses and doctors ran to have a look at him. As he walked he was losing the padding from his fur coat and *valenki*, and that made it even funnier when he passed out the gifts from the tree.

On 31 December 1942 and 1 January 1943, all the wounded received fifty grams of vodka. On 2 January 1943 there was dancing in the club for the patients and the doctors.

Life, despite the inhuman grief, suffering, deprivation, came into its own, was revived, even in the blockaded city.

Translated by Cynthia Simmons

A HALF-CENTURY AGO

Before the war, Sof'ia Nikolaevna Buriakova (née Morozova) was a housewife. Her husband, Aleksei Ivanovich (1895–1942), was an accountant; her son, Viktor, a student in the History Department at Leningrad State University. Sof'ia Nikolaevna was born in the village of Troitskoe, in the Yaroslav Region, where until the war, her oldest sister, Mariia, still lived. Sof'ia Nikolaevna's family—her mother, Aleksandra Petrovna, and her father, Nikolai Ivanovich Morozov, and their children—though living in Leningrad, kept up their connections to their native village. As Buriakova recalls, in the summer of 1941, they were preparing to spend the summer in Troitskoe. They had already bought their tickets for the train for 25 June, but the beginning of the war put an end to those plans. Buriakova had nine siblings, six brothers and three sisters. She and her parents lived in the same apartment building, and her father, an elderly worker, continued during the war to work in a factory in the city.

Throughout the terrible ordeal of the Siege, Buriakova and her relatives remained convinced that the Russian people would emerge from the horrible war victorious. On the evening of 21 June, she recalls, she and all her siblings living in Leningrad gathered in their father's room: the sons Nikolai, Aleksei, Ivan, Pavel, Mikhail, and the daughters Aleksandra and Sonia. "Papasha, being a well-read person, told us many stories from Russian military history. And he repeated then the words of the famous Russian military commander A. V. Suvorov: "The Russians have always smashed the Prussians." As Buriakova writes, Germany's sudden attack on the Soviet Union was not an entirely unexpected event: "In 1941, Soviet radio and newspapers encouraged us to believe that Germany was our friend. In the spring of 1941, rumors were circulating that the Germans would more likely attack England, where they would get bogged down." But before 1939, she remembers, the newspapers often carried cartoons that caricatured the Germans. They were depicted in military helmets with horns. Then the cartoons ceased. Buriakova writes that of course one could never express this out loud, but "in your soul, you had the feeling that you could not expect anything good from these horned Germans. And that's what happened."

In the very first days of the war, her brothers were mobilized for active duty. Her son, Viktor, voluntarily enlisted in a special Komsomol detachment,

95

and in 1942 was sent to a military engineering school in Arkhangelsk. Ineligible because of his age for mobilization to the front, her husband was called to serve in the MPVO of the Dzerzhinskii district. While he lived in the barracks, Buriakova was sent at the beginning of July to build fortifications on the Luga line.[15] Her workers' brigade comprised three thousand persons, all women except section commanders and administrators. Buriakova spent more than a month digging antitank trenches. Torn from her family, she received no letters or information from home. Only with great difficulty did her detachment manage to escape from the advancing German army and return to Leningrad.

During the most difficult time of the war and the Siege, Buriakova continued to believe in the leader of the Soviet people and commander of the Red Army, Joseph Stalin. At the same time, as she reminds the reader, she was always a devout Christian. In the course of the war, Buriakova lost all her relatives. Only her son, Viktor, remained alive. The following excerpts are from three sections of Buriakova's vast memoir, which she dedicated to her brother Nikolai, her father, and her husband. She writes of their last days, illness, death, and recalls in detail how she buried her dear ones.

S. N. Buriakova's memoir was recorded by her son, Viktor Andreevich Buriakov, Ph.D. (History), and is held in the Museum of the Defense of Leningrad.

> To the memory of the Leningraders, my kith and
> kin, who fell in the defense of Leningrad.

The bombing and shelling did not cease. The Fascist command intended in that way to break the spirit of the defenders of the city, to incite fear, and to engender a movement among the inhabitants to declare Leningrad an open city and to surrender it to the Germans. Air-raid warnings sounded daily, long and drawn-out. . . .

Our home, our beautiful apartment building in the center of the city on the Moika embankment, for a number of years after the war stood half-destroyed as the result of an enemy bombardment. I think there are now not many left who witnessed the enemy's crime. On 22 December 1941 I was, as always, at my [civil defense] post. They had sounded an air-raid alarm with the late dawn of a day in December. I was in the attic, frozen to the bone and, as always, hungry. My partner, Tat'iana Novikova, and I had agreed to take turns running home to get warmed up and have a bite to eat. I hadn't managed to enter my room and get as far as the warm stove before some gigantic power silently lifted the building, which then settled ponderously with a heavy thud. The floor underneath me began to sway, and I only barely managed to stay on my feet. A horrible crash followed, the glass in the windows blew out, the doors flew wide open. In a state of utter terror, I ran out into the courtyard. The yard was filled with an impenetrable column of dust that was swirling upward. It was impossible to see what was happening. Only here and there columns of red flame shone through, which, as it later became clear, turned out to be columns of brick dust. From those around I learned that two bombs had fallen on our building, on the southern and eastern sides. . . .

Moans could be heard, and cries for help. Very soon a group of MPVO soldiers arrived, and the work began to save the injured residents who had ended up under the ruins. I helped out. How many people perished under the ruins I never found out. I know that many people perished in the bomb shelter, located at the southern side of the building. A grandmother and granddaughter died who had come down from the upper floor to an apartment down below, thinking that it would be safer there. A maid who lived in that apartment, Nastia, was thrown out onto the pavement by the blast and spent a long time in the hospital. In a neighboring apartment, part of the collapsed ceiling crushed the legs of a man who was sitting at the table. In another apartment the Dulovs, brother and sister, both musicians, were that day holding a wake to honor their brother, a pianist, who had died. The explosion occurred at just the moment when Dulov was in the kitchen preparing coffee for the guests. The guests, who were in another room, suffered injuries, but Dulov himself received only bruises. Another incident occurred that could only be called a miracle. A little girl on an upper floor was picked up by a gust of air and thrown out onto the pavement, but was unhurt! . . .

That winter many of us were sent to clear away obstructions caused by debris from destroyed apartment buildings. All my life I have never forgotten one horrendous sight—on the ruins of a destroyed building on the odd-numbered side of Zheliabov Street there lay a dismembered human hand. This person's corpse was covered up, apparently, by debris from the destroyed wall.

To all of these misfortunes there was added, at the end of December, the closing of the bread factories. Wrapped up in blankets, rugs, drapes from the windows, people gathered for a long time at the doors of the closed bakeries. After several hours the boss arrived and announced that there would be no bread, that the bread factory was closed. People listened submissively to these fatal words, and just as submissively dispersed and went home, so that in their unheated apartments they could await the arrival of the following day, when the bakery would still be closed. There was no bread that day either. Only on the third day, in exchange for coupons, they distributed instead of bread eighty grams of flour, or, more precisely, ersatz flour. Starving Leningraders sprinkled this flour into warm water and drank it. Incidents of dysentery increased, which usually were fatal.

Hunger, the constant thought of food, deformed the souls of weak and unstable people, pushed them, especially teenagers, to various crimes. I myself was a witness when a teenager tore a piece of bread from the hands of a weakened old woman, quickly shoved it into his mouth, and then fell onto the floor with his face to the ground and started to chew it feverishly. No matter how much they hit and kicked him, trying to take the bread away, he chewed and swallowed it all. There was a considerable number of such incidents in Leningrad. The usual outcome was that the thief was taken to the local police station and then released to his parents.

A group of teenagers from our apartment building got together to steal things from abandoned apartments. They got into the vegetable storehouse in our yard. They were petty thieves, not professionals, and, of course, they soon fell into the hands of the authorities. Each received a sentence of several years in the camps, where they fell into the hands of the adult criminals. Released and returning home after the war, the majority of them renewed their criminal activities, and then, as might be expected, they ended up again in prison. . . .

Toward the end of the first winter of the blockade, there was a sharp decline in the population of Leningrad. A particular example of this would be building No. 1/7 on the Moika embankment, where I was then living. Before the war there were 560 people living in our building; toward the summer of '42, there were only sixty-five. Of the sixteen people who had been living in apartment No. 43, only I remained. The main reasons for the reduction in population were death from starvation, bombardment, evacuation, and the mobilization of men into the army.

In the years following the war, and even now, in old age, I have asked myself many times—where did I find the spiritual and physical strength to endure all the hardships that fell to my lot? The answer is simple. What played the decisive role was the feeling of civic patriotism, the realization of a patriotic duty—at the cost of lives and deprivations to defend the freedom and independence of our fatherland. During the most difficult days of the blockade, listening to the gloomy reports of the Soviet Information Bureau [*Sovinformbiuro*], we didn't lose faith in our victory. This faith was maintained by the knowledge that at the head of our people and the Red Army stood I. V. Stalin. We recalled his speech in November 1941 at the special meeting and military parade commemorating the twenty-fourth anniversary of the October Revolution. This gave us strength.

The first in our family to fall victim to the blockade was my brother Nikolai Nikolaevich, a skilled shipwright at the Marti shipyard. On 1 or 2 January, he caught a cold, took to bed, and sent a neighbor woman for me. When I arrived, he said, "I'm dying, come, together we'll read the prayer for the dying." And he started to cry. His condition was truly very serious. For a month I visited my brother daily, made tea, fed him. I saw him for the last time on 30 January 1942. His condition was much improved—he could already get out of bed by himself. Before I left, he said to me, "Even though my condition has improved, Sonia, do come tomorrow." I promised, but I was not able to fulfill my promise. On 31 January my son, Viktor, arrived unexpectedly. He had been released for several hours from his military unit. My husband, Aleksei Ivanovich, arrived home as well—he had learned of the arrival of our son. As a result of such a coincidence, I did not have time to go to my brother's.

When I arrived there the following morning, his door was locked. A neighbor woman, coming out to meet me, said, "Something terrible has happened. On 31 January Nikolai Nikolaevich died." I was crushed and cried bitterly. When I asked her to open the room, she said that the supervisor had the key. I waited in vain—he didn't come. I thought, "Why, after all he was getting better?" The thought crept into my mind that a crime had been committed. Not long before his death my brother had told me that he had entrusted to his neighbors the right to receive his ration cards. Those cards meant an extra six hundred grams of bread. For that, apparently, they took his life. In tears I begged them to find the key so that I could give him a Christian burial. My pleading didn't help. No doubt they were afraid that on entering I would see traces of a violent death. A week later they told me that I shouldn't come anymore—they had taken the body away in a hearse and the key had been turned over to *zhakt* [the house-management office]. We have no idea where my brother is buried.

Our parents took his death very hard, especially Papasha. As far as I can recall, he was working at that time at a small leather factory, hemming *valenki* and manufacturing ammunition belts for the front. The factory was

99

located far from home, on Rostannaia Street. Despite his advanced age (he had turned sixty-nine), he walked on foot each day to work, and in the evening, he would walk home again. A great toiler and patriot of our fatherland, Papasha, even then, during the bleakest days, did not doubt the final victory of the Russian people. . . .

Hunger and the bitter cold exhausted his strength. Once, on 6 February 1942, having expended his last bit of strength, he fell down not far from home, on Sadovaia Street, and couldn't get up. Someone saw him and told the yardmen. With what strength I had I went after him and saw from a distance that he was sitting, leaning against the wall of a building. Passersby helped me sit him on a sled and pull him home. The doctor, who was called out the next day, gave him a medical release from work for a month. Staying at home, he got noticeably stronger. Within a month he returned to work, in order to get a worker's ration card. He worked two days and again collapsed. That was his last, mortal illness. . . .

In tears, Mama entered the room and said, "Your papa's dead." It was 5:00 A.M. on 15 March 1942. We cried over the body for a while and then got down to the urgent work at hand. We lit the stove, heated water, prepared the linen. We had to undress the body, take it off the bed, lay it on the floor, and bathe it. Several times we tried to do this, but we couldn't. We didn't have enough strength. Then my sister Aleksandra, a weaver, arrived from the Red October Factory. Together we got the body off the bed, bathed it, dressed it in clean linen, and laid it on the table. Then we decided to put together a coffin. We gathered some boards from the ruins of our apartment building and rather quickly made a coffin. All the relatives agreed that the next day we would take the coffin and the body to the Serafimovskoe Cemetery to be buried. Mama and Shura refused to go with the coffin, because they were too weak. I simply couldn't refuse—after all it was my father. We made an agreement with the carpenter Ivanov that he would transport the coffin, and that Kolia [son of Buriakova's sister Shura] and I would help. Aleksei Ivanovich accompanied the coffin as far as Troitskii Bridge and returned home—it was necessary for him to report to his post. So the three of us—Kolia, the carpenter, and I—transported the coffin to the Serafimovskoe Cemetery, but I wasn't able to bury the body in a separate grave. I succeeded in making a deal with the workers, after I had given them twenty-five rubles, to place the body at the edge of a communal grave. They warned that they would have to remove Papa's body from the coffin and wrap it in a sheet. I had to agree to that. I accompanied the body to the spot where it would be buried, stood there a while, and then, with a sob, walked off toward the exit. On my way out, I turned around several times, and it seemed to me that Papa's face, not covered by the sheet, looked at me in silent reproach. I recalled the request he had made of me while still alive not to bury him in a communal grave. All my life I have suffered pangs of remorse that I was unable to fulfill this single request that my father made of me. Before I left I tried, by orienting myself to the church, to remember the location of the communal grave. In the postwar years, whenever I had the strength, on Papa's birthday and V-Day, I would go to the communal grave and leave flowers.

On the way back from the cemetery, having left Papa in a communal grave, I had the opportunity to look around. On each side of the road there were one or more bodies. On the opposite side of the church an awning had been built, and it was filled almost to the top with bodies. From there the gravediggers would carry them on stretchers over to the communal grave, stepping over and on the corpses that had been placed there earlier. According to what they said, in each trench-grave the corpses were placed in three rows, and in each row there were as many as two hundred corpses.

Having grown numb from work, having lost a sense of what was permissible, the gravediggers stooped to all sorts of disgusting jokes, even blatantly violating the deceased. On the road leading to the communal grave a tall corpse had been stood with a cigarette sticking out of his mouth. His frozen, iced-over arm pointed the way to the trench-graves.

After Papa's death, Mama was afraid to stay in their room and moved to our room. Soon she decided to leave for Troitskoe, having persuaded her younger daughter Aleksandra and her son to go with her. Mama took care of all the expenses for the trip, since Aleksandra had no money. They quickly found a driver who agreed to take them to Tikhvin. On 26 March, with sadness and trepidation, I saw Mama and Aleksandra and her son off. I was left in the apartment essentially alone. My husband, Aleksei Ivanovich, was living in the barracks and would only come home for short periods of time. . . .

In the first months of spring I never stopped feeling anxious about my husband, Aleksei Ivanovich, who was suffering from severe dystrophy. He had gotten a medical work release, which had freed him from service in the local division of the MPVO. While he was recovering, he was allowed to live at home. However, he was not relieved of his military allowance,[16] and every day I went to the cafeteria on Mayakovsky Street for his dinner. My assumption that being at home with family and strolls on sunny days would lead to an improvement in my husband's condition was not justified. A. I.'s health left much to be desired. At the military headquarters of the MPVO, they raised the question of his demobilization for health reasons.

24 May 1942 was Trinity Sunday, our patron saint's day. In the morning we had breakfast, as always very meager.... On the second day of the Trinity, Whit Monday, relatives of my husband came to visit—his cousin Mikhail Dmitrievich Okulov and his sister's husband, Kisin. On the table I set out our meager fare. A. I. said, "Before you would come to the table with pies, but today what?" I answered him, "We'll entertain with whatever God has given." The four of us sat for a while, talked of those who had died, felt a little nostalgic remembering how, before, all our guests would gather for the Trinity in an atmosphere of respect and goodwill, and the festive table would be covered with food. Before our guests left, we agreed to remain in continual contact. Unfortunately, the agreement wasn't kept. They were mobilized into the army and fell victim to the bitter battles for Leningrad.

After the relatives left, A. I. decided to go to the clinic. I tried to dissuade him, but he insisted on having his way, saying, "It seems they're demobilizing me because of my health, and they'll take me off my military allowance. So I have to prepare the documents ahead of time for a food-ration card."

Having gotten dressed, A. I. set out for the Sof'ia Perovskaia Clinic on the Griboedov Canal. I went with him. In front of the window where they gave out referrals to doctors, there was a large crowd of people. They were pushing, shouting, moaning, swearing. With great difficulty he got a referral to a doctor. After the doctors examined him, he got permission to receive a food-ration card. Leaving the doctors' office, he slapped me on the shoulder and said, "Well, that's that! And you tried to talk me out of it."

We returned home by way of the Griboedov Canal. I led him by the arm, and with his other arm he leaned on a cane. At first he walked steadily; then his steps began to slow. I said to him, "Of course, you are tired. Let's rest." When I looked at him, I grew frightened. His face had paled, his nose had turned blue and looked longer, and his eyes were sunken and unrecognizable. This happened across from the Church of the Resurrection . . . near home. . . . Near the apartment building lay sacks of sand. I led him there and sat him down. For some time he breathed with difficulty; then seemed to settle down. I was already frantically thinking about how I would get him home, even though we only had several hundred meters to go. He sat for more than an hour and gathered his strength. I didn't hurry him. When he said it was all right to go, we started. We crossed over the tram tracks and came out on the Moika. Here he stopped again. Seeing that he wasn't well, I told him, "Grab on to the railing and let's rest." But his strength began to fade, and his knees gave out beneath him. Grabbing his back from behind, I tried to support him, but he continued to sink down. First he fell to his knees, and then he collapsed onto his back and lay on the pavement. I was terrified. I started to beg the passersby to help get him home, I promised them bread, but the people passed by, unconcerned, not glancing at him.

Just then a unit of soldiers came down the street. I went up to the commander, crying, and asked for help to carry home A. I., who, I explained, had been a soldier in the MPVO. The commander singled out some soldiers who carried A. I. home and laid him on the bed. He was still unconscious. I tried to give him medicine, but it just ran out of his mouth. I had the impression that he was sleeping. I sat with A. I., waiting for him to come to. Suddenly he sighed rather loudly, and then his breathing stopped. He died.

Dressed in his winter coat, he lay on the bed. No matter how difficult and terrible it was, I had to get to work. I needed to take off his clothes, bathe him, and dress him in clean linen. No matter how hard I tried, I couldn't take off his coat. I didn't have the strength. It became clear that I had to find someone to help. Several times I went out into the courtyard. The yard was deserted. There were no tenants anywhere. I was exhausted from going up and down the stairs. Night fell. There was no light in the room. I grew afraid of staying with the body. I was frightened, not knowing how I would get through the night. Around midnight I went out in the street and stood leaning my head against the wall. It's difficult to say how long I stood there. Suddenly I heard footsteps, and a woman passed by. It was Zhenia Ivanova. She recognized me first and asked me why I was standing there. I started crying bitterly and told her that my husband had died and there was no one to help me prepare him for burial. She tried to convince me that it wasn't so and said that in a half hour she would come to help. And, in fact, she did come, and the two of us did everything that is supposed to be done according to Christian custom. To this day I remember Zhenia with gratitude— she didn't leave me in misery and did a great good deed.

103

Translated by Cynthia Simmons

"SAVING, I AM SAVED"

Ol'ga Nikolaevna Grechina took pride in her Russian roots and her family's long history in St. Petersburg/Leningrad. Her mother's family came to the city at the end of the eighteenth century, and a number of her ancestors attained prominent positions in government and higher education. Her father, Nikolai Aleksandrovich Grechin, a doctor, was descended from Don Cossacks. Grechina followed in the footsteps of her maternal grandfather, Vladimir Ivanovich Lamanskii, who was a professor at St. Petersburg University, a renowned Slavist, and an acquaintance of Fyodor M. Dostoevsky. In 1941 Grechina was a second-year student in the Department of Russian Philology at the same university (Leningrad State University). Forced to withdraw due to the war, she took up work in manufacturing and as a caregiver in a children's foster home. In the course of the war, Grechina lost both of her brothers and her parents. In 1944 Grechina returned to the university, graduating in 1947. She entered graduate school, where she specialized in folklore and obtained a Candidate of Science degree (*kandidat nauk*). She worked as an associate professor (*dotsent*) at a number of institutions, including Leningrad State University and the Herzen Pedagogical Institute. In 1950 she married Vladimir Ivanovich Osorin. They had two daughters. Grechina retired in 1981 and afterward wrote her memoirs and conducted research on elements of folklore in the work of Alexander Pushkin. The excerpts from her memoir are followed by an interview recorded in June 1995.

From Ol'ga Grechina's memoir *Spasaius' spasaia* (Saving, I am saved), *Neva* 1 (1994): 211–82.

Foreword

Until 1978, everything that I want to tell people about today lived within me, physically torturing me—the memory of the stale odors of vacant frozen apartments, the taste of hot water with dried bread and boiled grass. The blockade and war would come in nightmares during illnesses, and I would suffer from insomnia when the moon was full (no doubt a reflex that was

N. Petrova. "In the tram" (*V tramvae*), 1943. This "slice of life" illustrates the demographics of the Siege—four women passengers and one young male. *The Russian National Museum*

awakened during the horrible bombings of September 1941—how we hated the moon then!).

In the years before I retired (1981), I worked with foreigners at the Herzen Institute in Leningrad. The foreign teachers of Russian took a lively interest in the blockade, and it was not simply a tourist's interest. They attempted to learn more about the nine hundred days in order to tell their students about it in class. Two or three times per year I would have to give a lecture on the blockade. In addition to my personal impressions, I had in my possession many books, newspaper clippings, and photographs, and my lecture brought many to tears. But I maintained the strict self-control of the "veteran reporter." I knew that if the wall within me that held the physical memory of the blockade were to collapse, I could not go on.

And then it happened, on the day of a joyous occasion in the family— when my first granddaughter was born. Suddenly, completely unexpectedly,

105

I dropped everything, and for two days and two nights I wrote the first part of my memoirs, calling it "The Fatal Winter."

It was 27 January 1978. It was horribly cold. The windows of our apartment look out over the Okhtinskoe Cemetery, where, 31 December 1941, we buried my mother. Someone was burning something at the gates of the cemetery, and suddenly there was a strong smell from the past. Those two days and two nights I did not eat and hardly slept, just wrote, cried, and wrote again, without stop. And when I finished, it was a year before I could bring myself to read it.

At that time I did not yet know that A. M. Adamovich and D. A. Granin had already begun their monumental work collecting material for their *Book of the Blockade.*

Finally I was able to break free from what had been buried so long in my memory, and life became easier. I also thought that the manuscript might help my descendants overcome difficult trials, if any should come their way after I was gone.

The second part of the book was created in a more reasoned and peaceful fashion. I gathered materials and wrote down my recollections of my colleagues at the children's foster home (*internat*), trying to preserve the unique "ethnography" of our everyday life at that time.

When everything was ready, my friends typed my work, and I gave it to my closest friends and acquaintances to read. Then people unknown to me read it and began to write to me . . . to thank me "for the truth."

So I do not know whether I have written well or poorly about the blockade, but I know that it is all the honest truth and that this is the blockade that I suffered, the one that is mine. . . .

∞

In one fell swoop, the announcement of war on 22 June put an end to our unfortunate youth, but we didn't immediately understand the full measure of suffering and responsibility that lay on our shoulders. . . .

Externally the city changed immediately. In the stores, people were feverishly buying up food, ration limits were instituted as early as 1 July.[17] There were lines at savings banks because withdrawals were limited to two hundred rubles per month. We didn't have any savings, so the lines at the bank genuinely surprised us.

At the Department of Philology, our idol Professor Gukovskii[18] spoke at a student rally and gave a rousing speech, calling us to enlist in the students' voluntary battalion. Many signed up right there. Everyone was agitated, and each thought about what he would do in these new circumstances. Everyone expected that Gukovskii himself would also enlist somewhere, since many teachers applied to be either translators or political workers. But Gukovskii began unexpectedly to appear in green house slippers and with a cane. Some said that he had acute rheumatism; others cautiously hinted that it was much more attractive to call others to action than to act oneself. . . . I really don't know whether he was sick then or not, but it was good that he was able nonetheless to write the book on Gogol. How much talent was crushed by that hellish war! His turn came a little later—in 1949 he was "repressed" as a "cosmopolitan" and died in prison.

৩

It was just at this time [August 1941] that I saw my school friend Dima M. for the last time. Everyone considered Dima the brightest boy in our class. Of average height, broad-shouldered, brown-eyed, with glasses, long hair that always fell in his eyes, he would brush it away with a customary wave of his hand. He was witty, loved to read, he knew a lot. Like me, he was a sophomore at LGU [Leningrad State University], except at the Biology Faculty. There was always a fun-loving group of people at his house— friends of his older brother Yura, a graduate student in archeology. . . .

Dima and I were friends from eighth grade on. We saw each other often, in the evenings we would walk our dogs together. . . . They didn't take Dimka into the army because of his poor eyesight. And then, in August 1941, Dimka and I said good-bye—on the following day his mother was to send Dimka with Yura, who had graduated from the university, to somewhere in Central Asia, where Yura was to work on an archeological expedition with Professor Ravdonikas.[19] I found out about their leaving and went over to their apartment. Muza Pavlovna was in a panic: "Today or tomorrow the Germans will enter Leningrad, and the pogroms will begin. I must save my sons at any price!" The boys were gloomy and silent, and this silence fell over us too. I couldn't understand how healthy and, in general, young, people could agree to be evacuated when everyone was trying to get to the front. Dimka said that he had an errand to do on Solianoi Lane, and I offered to walk with him. We left together, but my spirits were very low, and conversation was difficult. I didn't blame them for leaving, but I was

107

simply terribly surprised that they had agreed. And Muza Pavlovna's words made an unpleasant impression on me. These were the first words that I heard in Leningrad that expressed doubt in our victory. I waited while Dimka dashed down Solianoi; then we returned together and said good-bye at the door to his apartment. For some reason it suddenly occurred to me that we wouldn't see each other again, and I became terribly depressed.

A few days later in the evening Dimka's friend, Pasha Perelygin (my admirer since seventh grade), came to our house. He was upset and said: "Let's go to Dimka's grandmother's. She's asking for you." On the way Pasha told me that at the train station, seeing her sons off, Muza Pavlovna had cried so, and even fainted, that the guards on the train took pity on her and shoved her into the car with her sons. She left Leningrad without money or documents. When we arrived, the grandmother was in a desperate state: "What am I to do?! What am I to do?!"—she cried. It turns out that Muza Pavlovna, a lawyer by profession, handled guardianship for the insane. In her work, she dealt with these peoples' valuables, and while preparing her sons for evacuation, she pawned many of her wards' possessions. The grandmother showed us a pile of receipts and, crying, said that even if she were to sell "all this junk," she could never redeem the things that were pawned. In fact, the apartment looked awful—everything was turned upside down, and the poverty of this home had become even more noticeable. Pasha and I couldn't think of anything to do to console her, and we stood silently. . . .

In our hearts we blamed Muza Pavlovna, but her action was not a crime, just the outburst of blind and passionate motherly love. The old lady suggested we choose a book as a memento. I took the book *Marx and Engels on Art*, which Dimka had written his name in. I still have that book. We left, and as we were saying good-bye, the grandmother said: "There's nothing left for me to do but die, and as soon as possible!" We couldn't do anything to help her, or say anything to comfort her.

Muza Pavlovna took her sons safely to Central Asia, but in 1942, they were drafted into the army. They were together in a unit somewhere in the Crimea. Soon she received her last letter from them. Yurka wrote: "Mama! Tomorrow we are taking part in a decisive attack, after which we will be transferred to the jurisdiction of the People's Commissariat of Land (*Narkomzem*), or even better, to the People's Commissariat of Health (*Narkomzdrav*)."[20] Both of them died in that battle, and Muza Pavlovna went crazy. It became clear to us that her last action in Leningrad was already that of an abnormal person. The grandmother was one of the first victims of the siege. . . .

∞

It is very difficult for me to write these memoirs! I don't consider myself high-strung, or what is worse, weepy, but yesterday, having written about M., I just couldn't get to sleep, and the tears simply poured from my eyes. It turns out that everything is preserved in a person's memory, everything lies at the bottom of the soul, and just the surface is sprinkled with ashes, and it seems that everything is past and forgotten. And these memories, like a mine field—you just have to step on them, and you explode, and everything flies to hell—quiet, comfort, and your present happiness. Once again the reels of the movie of your life in 1941 begin to roll, and again you see the damp, dark apartment and the long lampless hallway . . . and the disheveled old grandmother again cries in hopeless despair, and again you don't know how to help her.

Can I describe everything as it really was?! Probably not. Because it was nonetheless someone else's grief. And how can I describe the guttering Christmas candle on the small marble table in front of which Mama died? Must I torture myself so? Isn't it almost like torture?! But perhaps it is the most valuable thing that I can leave people in memory of that time and of myself. After all, now, already, almost no one living in Leningrad after the war knows or wants to know about the siege. And how in the trams they insult the old women siege survivors of Leningrad! How vulgar of them to suggest that they sit at home and not take up seats in public transportation during work hours, and so on, and so forth. And when one of them tries to defend [the *blokadnitsy*], they all attack them: "We're tired of hearing about your siege. Everyone suffered during the war. In our village everyone starved too."

And the jokes about the dystrophics that everyone is telling now! . . . I can't listen to that! What kind of callous, indifferent people have made jokes out of tragedy!

No, still I must, I must write it all down!

∞

Interview, June 1995

Q: Is it true that Siege survivors felt that the defense of Leningrad was something exceptional?

Up to 1944 there was a feeling that Leningrad was exceptional. As Ol'ga Berggol'ts wrote: "We felt so exalted . . . that our grandchildren would have envied us."[21] It was a feeling that we could do whatever we set our minds to. Second, every person felt that she had some kind of internal reserve that she could mobilize in order to survive. For instance, once I fell down from hunger, twice I got caught in a shelling, but I knew that I would live, that I had to. Even when my ration coupons were stolen from me—at the very beginning of the month. Nevertheless, I bought grass, I picked nettles. They didn't give out replacement ration coupons. If they were stolen or lost, that was it. There was nowhere to go. That was in the beginning of May [1942]. It was already a little bit better. I walked to Rzhevka to the firing range. There were a lot of nettles there. They were still there, no one had touched them, because heavy artillery was continually being tested on the range. I would go there and pick nettles, and the soldiers would swear at me. But I would pick the nettles anyway. The soldiers themselves were starving.

My brother got surrounded near Kingissep. They managed to get out of there, they were all starving. He was killed near Shlissel'burg, on that postage stamp of land. It's horrible. And now they say that no one needed that little piece of land. There were horrible battles there; I don't know how many they buried. You can still find bones and weapons there. Some war buffs were digging up these bones and preserving them. And my brother died there too. No one knows where he's buried.

Q: And did the military leaders command respect, or did people talk about them like they do now?

No, no one had such discussions then, because there were always enough informers around. No one talked about the leaders, and in general, that theme was forbidden. Of course, the people didn't like Zhdanov, because he was a "fat cat," the only fat cat that we saw. Our lower-level leaders—Andreev, Popkov, Voznesenskii, whom Stalin had executed (he accused them of wanting to make Leningrad an autonomous city)—they were a little better. Andreev was a very good man.[22] They took care of the city. For instance, when it got very cold and there was no wood at all, we could buy a liter of boiling water for a kopeck. You see they placed these boilers in the cafeterias and on the streets, about every other block they set up warming stations, and there you could buy a liter of boiling water for a kopeck. But, of course, by the time you got it home (it was really freezing), it had cooled off. Many drank it on the spot. At these warming-up stations, there was an attendant, usually the yard woman of that building, and she sold the boiling water. She had to get hold of the wood herself. There were a lot of bombed-out buildings around, and you could drag out some boards. Well, true, a piece of wall could fall on your head. But they burned everything that was wood.

But I wanted to say that even though it was so deadly cold, and almost everyone's windows were broken, even then not one Leningrader cut down a living tree. No one ever did that. Because we loved our city, and we could not deprive it of its greenery. . . . They could tear down a fence, break up some kiosk, tear off an outer door. But they couldn't saw down a tree. They burned furniture, various rags, letters (it was painful to burn letters). They burned many books (also a pity).

Q: And your friends who had been evacuated, did you correspond with them?

Friends who had been evacuated didn't write me because their life was difficult too. They were almost as hungry as we were. For example, [the Germans] even bombed Saratov a couple times.[23] They didn't write about this, but they had air raids. All our boys died, except Yurii Lotman.[24] Yurii Lotman God saved. . . .

Q: And when did you get married?

In 1950. Our eligible young men had almost all been killed off. There were not many women in our generation who were able to find themselves a husband. But I was lucky. He was healthy and handsome. And during the war he was not at the front. He graduated from the Polytechnic Institute on 21 June, and his degree thesis was on vibration in airplane motors. And this was very needed. Therefore they sent him to the city of Perm, and he stayed there for the entire war. But it was very boring for him living there alone. His family died in the blockade—his father and mother. His sisters survived—there were three. To pass the time he went to the public library and read.

He started to read Hegel, then Marx, then Lenin, then Stalin, volume after volume. In 1948 he wanted to leave the factory, but they did not allow him to—the war industry was still at its peak. So he had no choice but to enroll in graduate school, the Philosophy Faculty, where he had never studied. And he had to pass eight exams in all the basic courses in the Philosophy Faculty. He got As on them all—they let him continue his studies. We met. I was in graduate school too. I was studying with Propp.[25]

Q: And when the "War on Cosmopolitanism" and the accompanying events took place, were you still in graduate school?

Yes, that was a repulsive period. And Propp was the only person who kept his dignity, didn't repent, didn't say he was guilty. But the graduate students and many undergraduates acted disgracefully. One Russian-language teacher said to Gukovskii: "Grigorii Aleksandrovich, we loved and respected you very much, but you gave us 'a stone instead of bread.'" It was so ridiculous, so vile! But Vladimir Yakovlevich Propp did not confess to anything. He was totally unlike everyone else. And incidentally, no one denounced him. Why? Because he was a totally different kind of person, outside of Soviet reality. He was busy with his science and was a totally amazing person, of unheard-of goodness, tremendously caring toward other people. I recall one incident from my own experience. There was an absolutely idiotic decree that female graduate students did not have the right to bear children. They had to write a dissertation. Abortions were illegal and women generally did not know how to obtain them. And a number of graduate students who were frightened by [the decree] arranged privately for a horrible operation in which iodine was poured into the uterus. After that they became infertile for life. But I very much wanted a child, and I had no intention of doing any such thing. And I immediately, instead of writing a dissertation, got pregnant. Now our rector then was the brother of the Minister of Finance Voznesenskii; he was Aleksandr. He was unusually concerned about the university and students. We called him "Papa Rector." . . . In general, he did a lot of good, but he was unusually vulgar. So he issued this decree that if an advisor allowed his female graduate student, instead of writing her dissertation, to have affairs or get pregnant, then a certain percentage of the professor's salary might be withheld. It was an absolutely absurd decree, and truth be told, he did not really enforce it, but he scared everyone half to death. Professor Berkov, for example, he was a stern and cold person,

112

he took it seriously and kept an eye on his female students.[26] And what did Propp do? Well, I had just come to him in 1950; we had just met and, can you believe it, in December I gave birth to a daughter. And I wrote him a letter: "Dear Vladimir Yakovlevich, I am sorry to have let you down. Perhaps you will experience some unpleasantness, but I must tell you that instead of a dissertation, I have produced a daughter, Mashen'ka." And he wrote to me: "Dear Olia, How nice that you have a daughter, Mashen'ka, and that into our world, not so very well equipped for the joys of life, she has arrived. And she will see that, nonetheless, it is good to live. Congratulations, and I wish you a little boy, Vanechka, too. Good for you!" With an exclamation mark. And he signed his name—Vladimir Yakovlevich Propp. Just like that. He wasn't afraid of anything, and he behaved as he pleased. By the way, he received a notice [at the beginning of the war], he was German of course, that he was to report to the police. He went to the rector, Voznesenskii, who took the notice from him and said: "Don't go anywhere. I'll take care of it." He went to the City Party Committee and managed to get a permit for the Propp family (his Russian wife and a son). And they left for Saratov. He was never exiled anywhere.

Q: Many say that the breakthrough in the blockade was a more joyous event for people than even the lifting of the blockade.

You know why? Because the breakthrough in the blockade opened a new artery, which provided the city with food, coal, oil, in general everything. Of course the breakthrough was a cause for great celebration. But when they lifted the blockade, 250,000 people perished. The majority of them were Leningraders and Siberians. They had sent hunters from Siberia, whom they had drafted into the army. They knew how to shoot, became snipers, and they sent them to attack. Since our [soldiers] were weakened from the blockade, they sent these Siberians. But the breakthrough was also an absolute nightmare. The first breakthrough came to nothing. My cousin was killed there. Almost all our women at the children's foster home where I was working became widows then.

Q: And what kind of work did you do at the foster home, where did the children come from?

It varied. In the first year of the blockade, the children came from orphanages. They were all orphans. But then they were evacuated over Lake

Ladoga. I started working there in the fall of 1942. The situation was already fairly decent. The children were no longer so emaciated, no one died of hunger.

We had one incident in 1943 when a child was found next to his dead mother. He was four years old. He was no longer able to cry, he was quietly squeaking. Neighbors, who were passing by on the stairs, heard a cat meowing. But since there were no cats left in the city—they had all been eaten—they remembered that they had not seen their neighbor for a long time, and they decided that something must be wrong. They broke down the door to the apartment and saw that the mother was dead. It was the winter of 1943, January, still before the breakthrough, but no one was dying any longer from hunger. She died of some illness. The boy was brought to the house-management office. At that time the caregiver with whom I worked as a team had come to get some information, and she saw the boy on a bench, his eyes shut, dying. And that little old woman carried him to us in her arms and put him in a bed next to the stove. . . . And our cook, a kind old woman, every two hours gave him some kind of liquid nourishment. . . . And we saved him.

Then suddenly in the summer of '43 an order arrives to check everyone's documents, who has parents and who not, and to evacuate those who have none. No one wanted to because the first evacuation had been to the front—they took them in the wrong direction, not suspecting that the area had already been captured. And they fell under bombardment earlier than in Leningrad. . . .

Well, when we found out that we had four children without parents, we decided not to give them up for evacuation. We took them ourselves. I took the boy. I was already twenty-two years old. I still had university ahead of me, and there was no money in sight. The boy's father was at the front. He had been seriously wounded and had been sent to Siberia to get his health back. He had sent one thousand rubles from there. But then that money was like water, like now. I paid for the boy for a year at the foster home, bought him shoes, and some other things. And [my co-workers] all fell on me: "Have you lost your mind! You have your whole life ahead of you. You will marry and have children of your own. What do you want with him!" But I said: "No, I'll take him." You know, I had to have him. Because that loneliness could have driven me mad. And even before the rector's order, I took Zhen'ka.

114

Later the situation became very difficult, when I entered the university, and there was nowhere for the boy to go. I could not take him home, because it was very cold at my place. So I asked to leave him at the foster home for a year and keep him out of school, to say that he was in poor health. . . . And he remained at the home, and I took him only for holidays. We slept together in the same bed, because it was very cold.

I started to write the father letters. And I somehow knew, felt, that he would return. Maybe fate spared him, because after Siberia he returned to the front. He transported shells; he could have been blown up at any moment. But at the end of the war, he returned to Leningrad. When he returned, I was already at the university, I was not at the foster home. He took his child, and they told him: "Ol'ga saved your child's life, you have to marry her." He was quite embarrassed by this. He was a good guy, simple, poorly educated, but kind. And he said: "You know, Ol'ga Nikolaevna, I thank you for taking my child. Maybe he would have died being evacuated. I'm a driver, a poor person, like you, but tell me what you need." And I asked him to bring some wood and also to set up a small stove for me instead of our big tiled stove. And he did all that for me.

Translated by Cynthia Simmons

Interview, July 1995

Natal'ia Borisovna Rogova, librarian and philologist, is a senior research assistant in the Manuscript Department of the Russian National Library.

It is the siege that connects me personally to the past. I work in the Manuscript Department, in which we preserve ancient manuscripts, letters on palm leaves, birch-bark documents, monastery manuscripts, very valuable [war] materials. It is the book of ancient relics. They are perceived on the level of art—somehow separate from me. And there is an element of the aesthetic in [the siege materials]. And suddenly I find in the department colleagues who experienced the siege and lived through that time. Like Ol'ga Borisovna Vrasskaia, Tat'iana Nikolaevna Kopreeva, Liudmila Alekseevna Mandrykina, who worked on the Akhmatova collection, [and] Konoplev, the musicologist.[27] In fact, there are many colleagues here who lived and worked, or began to work, here during the siege. And when I came here I met people who undertook to preserve the collections or to evacuate the collections to the rear. Ol'ga Borisovna accompanied the collections when they were evacuated. She told [us] a lot about how they prepared the archives for evacuation. Ol'ga Borisovna left with the archives, and Tat'iana Solomonovna Grigor'iants remained in the library.[28] She's in charge of the newspaper collections. At that time she was the head of the team that worked to protect and preserve the collections. She is an extremely organized person. She also directed work with the library patrons. Because during the war the library catalogues were evacuated, and many materials were lent out relying on people's memory. And she worked to keep the staff safe. And all that she did herself. It's no surprise that she is currently in charge of our work with the Veterans Union. And when I met people here whose lives were connected with the siege, it served as one more impetus for my "discovery" of the library. And I was somehow unwittingly drawn to prepare exhibits connected with the war. Elizaveta Fedorovna Fedoseeva and Petrova also worked on this topic, and they got me involved in collecting materials and setting up exhibits. And Valerii Nikolaevich Sazhin was also involved in this.[29] That is, everyone who was working on the collections made doubles of the cards for our card catalogue, and that was of interest to Adamovich. He was the one collecting memoirs from the library. And in *Book of the Blockade* there are extraordinary, vibrant, reminiscences from our colleagues, from Mandry-kina. They describe how beautiful and dead our city was. They went over Ostroumova-Lebedeva's materials. Ostroumova-Lebedeva's memoirs were accompanied not only by sketches but also by some relics that she had preserved. She had a piece of shrapnel in her walls, and she pulled out that shrapnel and we keep it stored here in the library. Well, this detail is very dear to me, because my mother kept, and our family still keeps, a piece of shrapnel from a bomb that hit our house and that lodged in the wall over our table in the dining room. And when I have to lead discussions about the siege (in the School of Choreography, in high schools—where I'm not the only one who leads discussions), I take this piece of shrapnel with me and set a candle in it and hold a moment of silence. And people sob.

I remember we had a meeting at which Ol'ga Borisovna Vrasskaia spoke about the preservation and evacuation of the collections during the war. Yurii Vasil'evich Yukhritin, who was an adolescent during the war, also spoke. His mother saved him, as he said, "through books." His mother would wrap him in blankets, set him on the stove, and leave him at home with books. And he read. And they asked me, as a colleague in the Manuscript Department, to speak as well. And I drew the audience's attention to the way that history and memory move through a people's age, from generation to generation. Ol'ga Borisovna worked during those years in the library, worked actively. Yurii Vasil'evich was that adolescent who was saved by the books of her, and then my, generation (which lived and grew up after the war). But I can speak as well, relying on what I know through them. On what reality do I rely? On a spiritual comprehension of the past. And that is a very important factor, which can lead to significant generalizations. I came to understand the significance of art, how people saved art (the treasures of the library and the Hermitage), then how they saved and defended the city; this includes medical services, the factories, and then, how they saved the children. And then the victory. This was also a tragic moment. For when those salutes of arms began, everyone was already so worn out that they took them to be a routine attack on the city.

117

People streamed endlessly to our exhibit, and we were continually extending its run. And I would end my tours by saying that we have shown you what is preserved here with us, but I am sure that in the recesses of your memory lie treasures of no lesser worth. And with this people would enter into a dialogue. We continually receive new materials. And we keep a record of incoming materials. Many contributions were made in connection with the thirty-five-year anniversary of our victory. At that time we received materials from the military newspapers, from ambulance physicians. Nothing was ever removed from these materials [for ideological reasons]. True, there really hadn't been any exhibitions for a long time, but now the need to have them is being felt more and more, because history is being written before our eyes, a true history. And we will search and search for memories.

⁊

So time goes by, and impressions surface. There are three generations. Ol'ga Borisovna Vrasskaia, who always spoke out, even when you couldn't really talk about it, would gather the young generation and talk about how they saved the collections, about the honor of the library. Then Maretina, who spoke just about the day-to-day aspect. Yukhritin, who talked about how he was saved, and myself. I remember how I felt uncomfortable in the company of O[l'ga] V[rasskaia], a veteran, but then I realized that time passes and it adds new perspectives. And time adds new meaning. I am like the daughter of those who survived the blockade.

Here it turned out that the views of those people who actively worked and lived in the blockade fell in line with my views. And those people who experienced the blockade as adolescents, and thus suffered, and they suffered so much then, here you have some kind of pattern. Those people who endured years of evildoing as children have an acute and not always just view of history. They were robbed of their health. Those people whose energy was directed at saving others, they survived more easily, they were spiritually stronger, like Vrasskaia. But those who were saved, for they were children, they were robbed of their health. The war revealed to them what children, perhaps, shouldn't see. And in this regard I find support in a story that Adamovich told me about how, while in a partisan detachment, he escaped from the Fascists. Still experiencing horror, he told how they hid under

118

bushes. They were separated from the road by only a sparse strip of grass. They were hidden from the Fascists, but he could see their boots going by on the road. And he talked about this. This naked vulnerability was so keenly sensed.

And something else. A child could not judge accurately how much attention was paid to him. When in fact people did a lot [for the children] when they themselves had absolutely nothing. But this resentment never passed. It was felt. Granin had a sense of the proportionality of the ordeals. But Adamovich was one exposed nerve. Because he had been a teenager. In the partisan detachment they cared for Adamovich like a child. But what could they give him, even when they gave him all that they could? And that's where all his acuteness comes from.

In that sense, I—I have nothing of that. I perceive everything in a mediated fashion. Through my parents. And it is the spiritual trial of those whom I love, who are the closest to me. It is their spiritual trial. Mama has talked a lot about it. Mama saved Papa during the blockade. Mama worked in a school, School #82. That school didn't stop working. She loved to talk about Tsamutali.[30] He is now a Professor of History. He was her student. And when I ended up here, he came by—for me this is a living impression of those years. And he was just a teenager [then].

Kruikov, Andrei Nikolaevich, he was also Mama's student during those years. He's a musicologist. That was a class for students from ten to fourteen years of age. The connection has been preserved. Tsamutali's mother taught literature, and my mother taught the lower grades in that school. My mother was a deputy, and Tsamutali's mother was a methodologist. For it was important then to devise lessons that stimulated the will to live. That also was a skill. After all, everyone's relatives were dying.

Translated by Cynthia Simmons

Interview, June 1995

Valentina Fedorovna Petrova, Research Assistant in the Manuscript Department of the Russian National Library, was raised in the best tradition of the Russian intelligentsia. Her mother, Elizaveta Mikhailovna (née Rodionova), knew several foreign languages and played the piano; her father was a civil engineer. At the beginning of the 1930s the Petrovs took up residence in an apartment on the Griboedov Canal. Their neighbors were the Osten-Sakens—of German aristocratic heritage. V. F. Petrova remembers the family well: the elder Osten-Saken, his arrest in 1934 and his return from exile; then the arrest of the entire family during World War II, and the return to Leningrad of the widowed Varvara Alekseevna (née Virileva) with her daughter Natasha.

Having lived more than sixty years in the same building, Petrova was rooted in the cultural and historical landscape of her neighborhood. She recalls the addresses of the schools she attended, she remembers the churches that continued to hold services during the war, she cites the addresses of the performers whom she visited while working at the Radio Committee [*radiokomitet*], she remembers the number of the grave at the Smolensk Cemetery where her elderly aunt was buried during the Siege.

Petrova's memoirs can provide readers with numerous details concerning the work of the Literature and Drama Department of Leningrad Radio during the war. Her memories of the Leningrad radio station during the blockade complement the story "In the House of Radio," written by another Petrova, the actress Mariia Grigor'evna Petrova, for the collection *Women of the City of Lenin*.[31] The terrible years of the Siege are for Valentina Petrova not only a time of loss, but a time when people knew how to be together, to take care of one another, to share to the bitter end.

As Petrova herself recounts, she had no intention of working in the Manuscript Department of the Russian National Library. In 1944 she began studying at the Herzen Pedagogical Institute. In 1945 she transferred to the university, and after hearing a lecture given to new students by Ol'ga Mikhailovna Freidenberg, chair of the Department of Classical Philology, she decided to major in Classics. Petrova studied at the university during the most unfortunate years for humanists, at the height of the infamous "*Zhdanovshchina*"—the battle against "cosmopolitanism" and "toadying to the West."[32] After graduating from the university, she was unable to find work in her profession, and she was pleased to be recommended to the public library as a librarian's assistant. In the Manuscript Department she met colleagues whose sole responsibility was the preservation of cultural memory. She herself prepared for publication the Siege diary of Liubov' Vasil'evna Shaporina, excerpts from which appear in this anthology. It has yet to be published in Russia.

Papa was a civil engineer in the army. . . . He directed the construction of defensive positions on the "Road of Life." And there his whole group was bombed. That was in the beginning of 1942. Papa sometimes would come from headquarters with dispatches. But once he didn't arrive. We went to headquarters. [They] said they didn't know anything. We went around trying to find out, and only sometime in May or June they told us that the whole group had been bombed. And nothing remained.

After Grandmother died, Mama didn't work. It was our custom that there had to be a housewife at home. Until 1936 there was Grandmother. After Grandmother's death, it was decided that Mama had to be the housewife. So everyone helped Mama out financially, and she ran the entire household. We lived as one family, and we turned our entire salary over to Mama to run the house. When the war began, my aunt and uncle were evacuated, another aunt was mobilized and lived in a barracks at her work, Papa was sent to work on the defensive positions, and we three remained: Mama, my cousin,[33] and I. My cousin had been studying at the university. But no classes were being held at the university, and they were sent to a military hospital that was set up at the Faculty of History. My cousin worked there as an orderly, and for that she got a worker's ration card, but Mama and I had dependents' cards. But then, when the hospital was evacuated (that hospital was considered to belong to the university), my cousin was drafted into the army. Mama and I were left to live on dependents' rations. But we were helped by the fact that just before the war began we had been getting ready to go to a dacha. Mama really loved the country and it was strange how she ended up in these villages. She was very sociable. At the market she would meet a landlady and her husband, and they would say to her: "Come to our place for the summer." And every summer we would wander like that. And so that summer before the war we rented a cottage in Rozhdestveno.[34] And on the day they announced the war, Mama, Papa, and I had gone to the store to buy groceries. We didn't know anything. . . . We bought canned

121

goods, macaroni, matches—for the first days. And Nanny and the dog were to remain here. And so that Nanny wouldn't have to go for groceries, we stocked up on grain, so that she could boil broth for the dog. We always had meat in the house. Therefore, when the war began, we had some food stored up. Our dog, a German shepherd, had to be put to sleep early on. We also had a little Spanish poodle. We kept him for a long time. Until the winter of '42. In our house, in general, children had no special privileges. Everything in the house was for everybody. Our nanny died 30 January 1942. On 31 January we buried her. We buried her, we didn't just throw her out. In exchange for bread, someone dug us a grave, and my sister and I took her on a sled to the Smolensk Cemetery. My cousin dug the grave herself, in exchange for bread and sugar, we found people to help us lower the body and fill the grave in. We set up a stick with a sign. It survived. After the war we found it. And my cousin and I look after the grave.

∽

From the winter of '42 people with foreign names began simply to disappear. Some were taken away, others were given a twenty-four-hour notice of eviction. At that time there were many older officers with German names living in our apartment house. True, they didn't arrest them, but they gave them twenty-four hours to leave. This became very common in the winter of 1942, they were sent over Lake Ladoga, well, maybe it had started even earlier, but in our house it began in the winter of 1941–1942. Someone would come from the police to deliver a summons to report to the police station. When they arrived at the police station, they were given an order to leave within twenty-four hours. That was it. And the next day they had to clear out. They went by convoy. And who was it they needed to move by convoy? They deported primarily women, no longer young, and children.

Q: Did anyone return?

To our apartment house, yes, some did return. The Osten-Sakens returned. And a military family returned too. He had been an officer in the Imperial Army, his name was Hahnenfeld, and there were the Germans Hautfobels; they returned. Men and women returned from among our close acquaintances. And I had a German teacher who lived in our apartment building; her husband was the famous tenor Karav'ia, a German. He was liquidated even before the war. And she, as the widow of someone who had been liquidated, plus the name. . . But I don't think she ever made it to the place she was to be sent to. They say she perished on the road. But some people did return nonetheless. And they've lived in the same building. We have been friends with these families to the very end of life. And it's interesting that they all had been Mama's friends, her friends from before the war, and they all died in the same years. In '71 and in '74, one then the other of her friends died. They all spoke Russian. They were Russified. They didn't even know German. Only the names remained, for which they suffered.

Q: **What about all these stories about rocket signalers and other signals—did you ever see any rocket signalers?**

We saw rockets. But rocket signalers I myself never saw. But they said they had caught rocket signalers. We saw rockets often enough, but what kind of rockets these were, God only knows. I saw a lot of German leaflets. But I didn't dare pick them up or keep them. And in school they forbade us, and Mama pleaded with me not to bring any home or take any from anyone.

∞

During the war I worked at the Radio Committee. . . . Before the war I was being prepared for the conservatory, and I studied with the concert master of the conservatory, Nikolai Ivanovich Isber. But he left and perished where he had been evacuated. When I finished school, one music school was still open, and Mama wanted me to study there until the conservatory returned [from evacuation], because during the war, our instruments went out of tune, and my skills disappeared. At that time one could find a job only through the Employment Bureau. And they were sending everyone to vocational schools. You couldn't even go to the university except by order of this bureau. Mama wanted me to get permission to study at the music school, but I didn't get it. But to our great surprise, they sent me to work at the Radio Committee. It was a military objective.[35] When I arrived there, they sent me to the Department of Literature and Drama. That was the summer of '43. My life was connected to this department for thirty years, maybe more. They treated me so well there. They liked me so much that when I went to study at the university, I still visited them; they called me and invited me to all sorts of parties—and that lasted as long as someone remained alive there who had been working there during the war. Being the youngest one there, I was like their daughter, like their sister. When I arrived there, the director of the Committee was Viktor Antonovich Khodorenko. The artistic director at the radio was Kalganov, the head of the department was Nison Aleksandrovich Khodza—a writer.[36] This department served during the blockade as the center for theater—Zonne, Gorin, Yarmagaev, Genkin, Nina Cherniavskaia.[37] Ol'ga Berggol'ts was a guest artist. These five people were the nucleus of the department and the "theater at the microphone," although "Theater at the Microphone" began officially when the Drama Theater (Bol'shoi Dramaticheskii Teatr) returned from evacuation. When I began to work there in '43, it didn't yet exist. Once this popular program appeared, large collectives took part in it. "Theater at the Microphone" put on "Dead Souls," "The Pickwick Papers." Those were the largest and most memorable broadcasts of '44, but the first year there were no big programs. There were readers, singers.

Mariia [Grigor'evna] Petrova read during the war. She worked in the children's section, and she performed on the radio literally up until the last days of her life. She read, and read, and read, and even the younger generations loved her. She had a particular kind of voice. Her voice was like a young boy's. Therefore she built a repertoire around very characteristic works. She read Kassil', Gaidar.[38]

Q: And did you become acquainted with Lidiia Yakovlevna Ginzburg at the Radio Committee?

No, at the university.

Q: Did foreign correspondents come to the Radio Committee during the war?

No, I don't recall that they did. I think we would have known.[39] But with the exception of Matvei Frolov, one of our most famous war correspondents, there were mainly writers there, who had been sent to the front: Dudin, Rozen, Aleksandr Germanovich; and among the women—Liudmila Popova, a poet. She had somehow been at the front.[40] And, well, Berggol'ts was there. She and Makogonenko were still working as a duo. Metter.[41] I somehow remember more actors. I remember those from the Bol'shoi Drama Theater: Granovskaia, Zhukova, Kibardina, Samoilov. Kibardina spent the entire war in Leningrad. I remember the day when the Drama Theater put on *Wolves and Sheep* (*Volki i ovtsy*).[42] We at the radio had gone to the performance. It's interesting that although we at the radio usually knew what was going to happen, this time no news had reached us. And

124

suddenly the performance was interrupted. Rudnik comes out on stage—at that time he was the artistic director of the theater—and announces that he just received word that there will be a military salute; therefore they were stopping the performance. And just as we were—the actors in make-up and the entire audience—we all went out to the embankment and kissed and hugged to celebrate the breakthrough of the siege. That evening I remember very well.

∞

I started out studying with Manuilov at the Herzen Institute.[45]... But I didn't like the conditions, I didn't like the big lecture halls, I didn't like the location itself. Therefore, as soon as the university arrived [from evacuation], I got my documents and set off for the university. It's true I lost a year.[44] Nothing transferred, and I entered as a freshman. I applied to the English Department (I had studied English in high school). One day before the beginning of classes there was a meeting of new students at which professors spoke, and there I heard the presentation of Ol'ga Mikhailovna Freidenberg, which decided my fate immediately and irrevocably. I took my papers from English and went to the Classics Department, and to this day I don't know whether I should regret it. On the one hand, thanks to that I ended up here [in the Manuscript Division]. If I had been in another department, I probably would have been able to find a job in my field.

∞

Q: And were your family believers, and did you go to church during the war?

Yes, yes. To the Nikol'skii. And the Nikol'skii Cathedral was open throughout the war.

∞

Our first Patriarch was Aleksei; later he was sent to Moscow. But I remember very well. He served in our church for the entire war, in the Nikol'skii Cathedral.

Q: Did you go to the same church as Shaporina?

No, Shaporina went to the Cathedral of the Transfiguration. She lived on Shpalernaia and went to Lord of the Transfiguration.

Q: And that one was also open during the war, and at the Smolensk Cemetery there was a chapel?

It was closed during some of the most difficult months, but basically it didn't close. . . . These were three churches in the city that were active.[45]

Q: But after the war there weren't many more?

You know, they've recently begun to restore churches. The church in Shuvalovo too. It was active even after the war. For Easter service we always went to Shuvalovo. It was impossible to get to [the Nikol'skii Cathedral]. People gathered there not only from all parts of the city, but from outside the city as well. People came prepared to spend the night, because there was no public transportation at night, and for the first years we went to Shuvalovo. Right in front of our house tram No. 21 went straight to Shu-valovo, and as an exception on Easter eve the authorities permitted No. 21 to run around the clock. So right from there, on No. 21, we were able to get back home. We went even during the war. I remember it very well, even though many years have passed.

Q: And are any of your classmates or friends still around?

No one's left. Strange as it may seem, they have all gone their separate ways, and we don't meet each other, although we were close friends. I don't know why. I don't see anyone, none of my old friends, from before the war, none of my new ones.

Translated by Cynthia Simmons

Oral history, recorded June 1994

Natal'ia Stroganova (née Evstigneeva), having learned of our intentions to publish an anthology of memoirs and reminiscences of the Siege, asked her friend Liubov' Beregovaia (whose *The Joyous and the Inimitable* appears in the section of documentary prose) to convey to us a tape that was made at an unofficial meeting of veterans of the war. At that meeting, Stroganova read from her memoir of the Siege. The following is excerpted from that reading.

I was in the besieged city for the entire nine hundred days. On 22 June 1941 I was with my mother and father in Leningrad. We hadn't gone to our dacha in Siverskaia, as we did every year, because Mama couldn't get ready in time. On that day we wanted to take a walk through Pavlovsk. Molotov had been speaking earlier that morning on the radio. I understood nothing and kept pestering my parents to take me for a walk. I was seven and a half.

Bombardments

The first bombardment occurred on 8 September, on my saint's day. The first days we hid in a bomb shelter. Many people took shelter there, many children, often carrying blankets and pillows. An older boy, Boria Riazanov, about twelve, from across the way, is drawing my portrait. I have a fire-fly badge on my hood.[46] Everyone wore these patches on hats or overcoats to avoid bumping into each other in the darkened city; it was dark everywhere. The portrait has survived. All the windows were covered up so as not to attract the enemy. The people on duty would constantly come into the apartment and say: "Your windows aren't properly covered." Strips of paper were crisscrossed over the windows. We believed this would protect the windows so the glass wouldn't shatter during the bombings. The glass did shatter. We would put plywood in its place. There is no electricity, heat. We have a *burzhuika*, in which we burn furniture.

New Year's Day

Mother managed to get a Christmas tree from an officer to whom she gave a bottle of vodka in exchange. We didn't have the strength to get our old ornaments down from the shelf. Mother bought new ornaments, which I make sure to put on my tree even now. She attached some thin church candles, gave me a gift of paints, and on the inside of the gift box she wrote: May your new year be as joyous as these paints.

We made special dishes to celebrate the New Year: pancakes from *duranda*, pancakes from coffee grounds (*gushchiaki*), and aspic from joiner's glue. Mama was afraid to give me too much aspic because of its poor quality. On my birthday a neighbor gave me a bowl of soup as a gift. On the following day another neighbor gave me a piece of bread and porridge.

One day my mother and I went to a bakery at the corner of Nevskii Avenue and Vosstanie Street, where the store "Nasledie" now stands. It was pitiful. My mother put me in the corner so that I wouldn't get in the way. She took her place in line. Next to me women were receiving their bread along with some scrap pieces (*doveski*).[47] Some woman thrust a scrap into my hand. I muttered something like: "What are you doing?" and gave the bread back.

Later, after the war, my father told me: "You are a heroine because you never once said you were hungry." Once, while sitting in a dark room, I recalled that before the war, stores displayed cakes decorated with colorful little mushrooms. I told this to my mother. She gave me several pieces of dry potato to suck on.

We slept fully clothed. One time I woke up in the middle of the night. I saw that the adults hadn't yet gone to bed. The radio was playing "The International."[48] I was taken by the music. Even now, I love to listen to the radio. I don't like television. They say that many siege survivors like the radio and are somehow indifferent to television. I remember one time Mariia Grigorievna Petrova was reading, I think it was, Turgenev's "The Watch" and several other short stories. It was then that I fell in love with the classics.

I was walking along the street with my father. He loved books very much. He approached a woman who was selling prerevolutionary children's books near, I believe it was, Kuznechnyi Market. He looked over the selection. "Why are you selling these; they seem to be very good?" Father asked. "My son is dead," she answered. "I'm sorry," my father said.

Papa and I were walking down Zhukovskii Street. It was spring. Two girls had lain down on a sled. The sleds were piled up with dead bodies. They were starting to drag the bodies out from the basements. Before there had been a laundry in the building where we had had our clothes washed. Now the laundry was filled with corpses. And other buildings too. In spring the MPVO began to remove them. So there it was, a big sled piled up with the dead, tied with ropes so the bodies wouldn't fall out. Heads, arms, legs were being dragged across the asphalt. Later Father told me that he felt I needed to see all this. Other times he felt sorry for not taking me away, for allowing me to stay and see.

Mother and I used to go to the hospital for our shifts. Mother took care of the wounded, as did I. I even read poetry to them. She wrote letters for the wounded to send home. One of them had no arm. He said to Mother: "Please dear, don't write home that I have no arm. Just write that I am only slightly wounded." In one of the wards the wounded set the table for me. They wanted to offer me food. But I immediately ran to my mother. For some reason my mother forbade me to take food from the wounded. The patients came to my mother to ask her permission to feed me. The hospital was located at 8 Vosstanie Street. It was constantly under bombardment. They said that the Fascists liked to bomb hospitals. There was a school in the same building. Before and after the war. I graduated from that school. Before the Revolution that building housed the Pavlovsk Institute for Gifted Ladies. Lidiia Alekseevna Charskaia, a writer of children's stories, studied there.[49] She was silenced after the Revolution, but the Soviet schoolgirls of that time remember. Now her name is rehabilitated. Her books are being published again, and there are even conferences dedicated to her.

In our old Petersburg apartment we were a family of nine. After the war only four of us were left. The first to die was mother's uncle, Vladimir Alekseevich Bystrov, a great athlete, an international soccer referee, a member of the All-Union League of Referees, a friend of Butusov, Dement'ev, and others.[50] He was my young great-uncle, almost my father's age. He adored me, and I him. They kept his death from me for a long time; they said that he had gone away. Then Aunt Tamara's husband died. His name was Pavel Ivanovich Davydov. He had been offered residence at the factory where he was employed. Before his death he kept hallucinating that all of the factory employees would receive a cup of hot cocoa. Pavel Ivanovich would walk around our large Petersburg apartment searching for as large a cup as he could find so he could take it to work with him.

Then Aunt Tamara, mother's sister, died. She died in the October 25th

Memorial Hospital. She had developed a very advanced case of tuberculo-sis. By coincidence she was diagnosed by another aunt on my father's side, a doctor who worked for her whole life, including the siege, in this one hos-pital. As a result of the test, she knew immediately that my aunt was going to die. My Aunt Tamara was the only one we managed to bury ourselves. Mother took her to the Volkovskoe Cemetery. Someone made a grave for her right then and there. The cross was made of metal pipes. Before she left, Mother tried to remember the exact location of the grave. When Mother was riding, or walking, back, there was an air-raid attack. At home my mother's stepmother worried that she would not make it back. But Mother did. Later my mother spent a long time searching for her sister's grave, but she never did find it. Maybe a bomb fell on it, or the cross fell off. Aunt Shura died, Aleksandra Nikolaevna Vorionova, Mother's stepmother's sister. She died having hallucinations brought on by hunger. She had lost her memory entirely and had visions of meat. And she screamed: "Wine, wine, meat!" We were not able to bury anyone ourselves, with the exception of Aunt Tamara. We don't know where any of them are buried.

After the war my aunt, a doctor, said to me: "Your family is like Tania Savicheva's, who kept a diary of the siege that ended with the words 'Every-one died, except Tania.'" In 1943, they arrested my grandfather, my mother's father, Nikolai Alekseevich Nikolaev. Under Article 58, paragraph 10, part 2, supposedly for anti-Soviet activity under extreme circumstances, in other words, during the war. They arrested people then too. Grandfather died. Where, how, we don't know. Now he has been rehabilitated posthumously. But that's another story.

Recently I transcribed all of the data regarding my relatives during the siege from our old book of house management. Fortunately, these books all survived. And so, once again, some data about my family:

1. Bystrov, Vladimir Alekseevich, my mother's uncle. Died 24 March 1942 at the age of forty-six.

2. Nikolaeva, Tamara, mother's sister. Died 12 August 1943 at the age of thirty-three.

3. Vorionova, Aleksandra Nikolaevna, sister of my mother's stepmother. Died 8 April 1942 at the age of seventy.

4. Davydov, Pavel Ivanovich, husband of Tamara, Mother's sister. Died 9 February 1942 at the age of fifty-one.

5. Nikolaev, Nikolai Alekseevich, Mother's father. Arrested by the NKVD. Died, as written in his document of rehabilitation, in transit to the site of detention and punishment.

Formerly a family of nine, four remained. My mother's stepmother, Margarita Nikolaevna Vorionova, died of paralysis in 1954, the year when the first rehabilitated people began to return home. She loved my grandfather very much, waited for him, placed his photographs all around her. No one in our family, not even in delirium, said that it would have been better if the Nazis had entered the city and fed us.

Forbidden

No one took food away from anyone else. Only once, Volodia Bystrov ate something that wasn't his. Mother yelled at him. She says she still feels ashamed about it.

Generally in the wintertime, corpses lay along the sidewalks wrapped in sheets, legs and necks bound by string. This is how their families buried them. Next to our entrance lay a woman who asked us to help her get up, so that she could make it to her building on Pushkinskaia Street. My mother didn't have the strength for this. For a long time afterward, that woman lay there dead.

During the siege my father taught me to read and write. The lamp would be lit, the wick dipped in oil, and the light even dimmer than the icon lamp—the only light in the apartment. They called these handmade little lamps "*fitiulkis*." I didn't understand something, and Father hit me. No one had ever struck me before, not even as a joke. Such were the old Petersburg traditions. But that time my father lost control. Later he told me that I said: "Daddy, it isn't my fault that I don't understand." He broke down and cried.

Our Janitors

Our janitors were Shura, Vania, and one more person. How hard they worked, how they cleared the snow! They kept watch at night, and we felt safe. All of the entrance gates were locked for the night, this was a prewar custom. The custom continued for some time after the war. The janitors knew their residents, and we knew our janitors. Our janitors never stole from apartments where people had died, were dying, or had been evacuated. I helped them clear the snow. After the war they continued working as janitors, and when they saw me they would shout: "Natasha, come help us clear the snow!"

Translated by Natalia Glazman and Cynthia Simmons

Interview, June 1995

Valentina Bushueva, eighteen at the beginning of the war, was orphaned first by
her mother's death, when she was three years and eight months old, and then by
the terror of the thirties—her father was purged and spent three years in Solovki.
Most of her life she lived with her aunt. An orphan and daughter of an "enemy
of the Soviet people," she was forced to demonstrate her loyalty to the state. At
the age of sixteen, during the war with Finland, she was drafted as a forced la-
borer together with thousands of other Komsomol members. She worked in a
canteen for officers (*komandiry*), sleeping on the average only five hours a day.
After the end of the Finnish war (March 1940), Bushueva returned to her aunt's
apartment on Decembrists Street and found a job. But with the outbreak of war
with Germany, Bushueva was once again drafted to labor for the defense of
Leningrad. She was sent to build fortifications near the town of Luga. From
March 1942 to December 1943 she worked, again as a conscript, in the fuel and
energy system. After the war, she was assigned to work in a freight office. As she
mentions during the interview, she was one of the first women sent to truck-
driving school, got a driver's license, and worked as a truck driver for four years.
She had to quit this (usually) man's job in 1948, due to liver disease. For the next
thirty years, Bushueva worked at the Baltic Plant as a dispatcher. She is married, has a son and two grandchildren. Like all survivors of the Siege, she has a
medal "For the Defense of Leningrad." Bushueva regularly attends meetings
and functions of the Society of Veterans (*Soiuz veteranov*).

This interview with Valentina Bushueva occurred spontaneously, at a meeting with Antonina Maslovskaia (whose "Blockade Lullaby" appears in the section
"Documentary Prose"), which accounts in part for her manner of speaking.

I worked in a stationery store as an apprentice to the salesman. After that I
found a job at the Industrial Factory in the Petrograd district where I worked
on the looms. We made lace for, I guess, textiles. While I was working there,
the war began, and we, the young, were mobilized immediately. First to the
Luga line.[51] There we constructed antitank barricades—with crowbars,

133

shovels, pickaxes, working twelve hours a day. The regimen was very harsh and demanding—fifty minutes work, ten minutes break. Then the next shift followed, and so it went. Then the Germans began dropping bombs on us, and we left that place ahead of schedule. So we returned home. Then very shortly afterward I was sent to dig trenches in Kuzmolovo, not far from here. Then the fall, the first fall, and that winter of 1941–1942, that most horrible, most terrible time, I was in Levashevo, in Aspen Grove. We dug trenches there.

I lived on the site because we were labor conscripts (*trudarmiia*), not a real army.

Q: Was it better than being in the city at the time?

Yes, of course . . . as a worker I received 250 grams of bread a day. Also they gave us, what should I call it, some kind of slop. At first they made regular soups for us, you know, pea or lentil. Later it was—I don't know what. Well, in short, those three days when there was no bread at all, that's where I was.[52] And during those three days they gave us, I remember, something blanched. I can't remember what it was . . . maybe *shroty*. But for three days they fed us this whitish water; there wasn't even any salt in it.

When we finished digging the trenches, they allowed us to return home. Now, what does it mean—they allowed us to return home? They just said: "Go home." How? There was no transportation of any kind, no buses, the trains were not running. So we simply walked along the tracks. . . . But, you understand that first we had to reach the Finland Station, and from there I still had to walk—it's a long walk—to Decembrists Street . . . about twenty-five kilometers. The first night home, I screamed the entire night from pain. Then, since I was home, I had to report to work. Now, from where I lived to where I worked it was fourteen tram stops. I covered that distance on foot. I would arrive at the factory, others would too . . . no electricity. So they would gather us girls and say: "Here, take this sled." The sled wasn't little, a rather large sled, and there were all kinds of pails on it. "Go and fetch water." And we used to go to the Neva for water, dragging this sled. We would fetch water. Then we would bring it to the plant.

Q: For what purpose?

I don't know. The production lines weren't working, it's true. I guess they needed it for something. We were instructed to do this, so we obeyed. Sometimes they would order: "Go cut firewood." We would cut firewood. And I continued walking there every day for as long as I physically was able to.

Q: Could you stay at the plant overnight?
No, we had to return home. Home.

At home, first of all, we had to buy our bread, at that time it was 250 grams, on our ration cards. There was no grain of any kind any longer, there was nothing. Only this bread. I used to eat all of it right on the spot. I wanted to eat. I simply couldn't wait. Well, then, we also had a *burzhuika*. It had to be heated. There were two rooms, a large one and a small, dark one leading into the large room. In the large room, the windows were blown out. There were several windows; the glass in all of them was shattered and replaced with plywood. We had nothing to feed the stove with. No firewood, nothing. . . . Firewood could be obtained only by bartering bread. Firewood could not be bought with money. You'd have a children's sled, and you'd pull the sled with a bundle of firewood on it. And this small bundle of firewood cost two hundred grams of bread. We would buy this wood, chip the small logs, and with those chips we would heat the stove. We also had to barter bread for kerosene for our wick. Only for bread. Now, what else? To get water we had to walk to the Priazhka [River]. One day, I remember, I felt worn out, and my aunt was in a bad way, but I went out because someone had to bring water. To walk as far as the Priazhka was unthinkable. And that day there was a big snowfall and I collected snow. When I walked outside, the synagogue was burning. It had been burning for several days already, well, you know, sort of smoldering. Old Jews used to go there to warm up near the fire. It was already 1942, after the New Year. So, I collected snow, and my aunt decided to make soup out of bread crumbs. And, you know, it turned into such a tragedy for us, it was such a pity. Because when this snow melted and my aunt cooked this soup, it turned out to be absolutely inedible. Because of the smoke. That smoke in the air . . . I don't have words to describe it, this acrid smoke. . . . Well, the cold, it was dreadful. We went to bed in our coats, wrapped in kerchiefs, and whatever we had. But, what else could you do when you would wake up and see the water in a glass frozen!

I continued reporting to work for as long as I could; then I gave up. March and April, I stayed in bed. I could no longer walk, so I stayed in bed, and was really prepared . . . Nothing mattered any longer, you see, I was re-

135

ally prepared to die. My belly was swollen from dystrophy. And yet, if you can imagine, before quitting going to work, I went to the outpatient clinic. Because discipline had to be maintained. How could I be truant! And there I was—lining up in the street, in a winter coat, and all the rest. And still wearing my coat and everything else, same as I was outside, I walked into the doctor's office. She's sitting there, with her coat on, and with her gloves on, only the ends of the gloves are cut off. She sits there writing. Then she glances at me as if wishing to examine me. Only there wasn't much point in examining or looking—everything was obvious. She wrote: "Dystrophy of such and such degree," I don't remember now which stage of dystrophy it was, and then she issued a sick-leave certificate for me. And so for two months I stayed in bed, and then I received a paper from my work stating I was laid off due to the length of my illness. It meant . . . well, it meant that starting from the first of the next month I was qualified for the ration card of a dependent, which meant I would receive only 125 grams of bread.[53] . . . Then, suddenly, out of the blue, really, four or five days later, I received a summons to report to the October District Council on an assigned day, at an assigned hour and to bring my personal possessions with me. And you know what? Whether it was our upbringing, or the feeling of, shall we say, duty, or perhaps patriotism, I don't really know, but I got up and went.

I went and they sent me to the peat bogs.[54] This was in May. And this moment marked the beginning of my participation in providing the city of Leningrad with fuel. Until the end of the war, I worked in the system of fuel and energy.

They looked at me, saw I was tall and, at first glance, healthy, and said: "This one—to the quarry." Before there were prisoners doing that job. They died, probably, did not survive the work. There were no more new prisoners. However, new girls did arrive. So it was ordered: "Bushueva—assign her to the quarry." Now, what did this mean?

It meant a deep pit and two very powerful fire-pumps on its edge. There was an engine and a pipe, and this pipe carried liquid for many kilometers. At the bottom of the pit there were squares called cards. When the engine started working, it produced peat liquid, which was pumped into pipes and carried to those squares. As for me, I stood there alone in that pit, you understand, and with a stick I drove away pieces of floating wood, icicles, and this in the month of May, and I am standing there up to my waist in that liquid. I have canvas trousers on, a canvas jacket with a hood, a canvas cape on top, and also boots reaching up to my thighs.

They had to pull me out of there. Just imagine, twelve hours in a pit. When they brought us some gruel, they had to pull me out. But then we were given five hundred grams of bread there.

Q: That wasn't enough?

Of course, it wasn't. By that time we were worn out. It took some time for them to pull me out of there, then it took me time to reach our barracks —we lived in a tall barracks. There I got undressed—every piece of clothing on me damp, wet, the shirt—brown from the water. But most of the time there wasn't any place at the stove to hang my things to dry—the space near the stoves would be taken. And then I developed boils on both legs. It was scurvy; it meant I was totally debilitated. So again I stopped going to work. I just couldn't anymore. Then they selected the weakest among us. I still remember—nineteen women. Only I no longer cared. I did not care where I'd be taken, what would happen to me. Just think, I had really given my all there. There had been no holes or corners to retire from sight. Everyone could see me. Besides, you know, there was this awareness that others depended on you.

Anyway, they took us to Ladoga—not to any hospital, no. That wasn't their concern. We were taken to Ladoga. They took us . . . I will read it to you. I have the citation. "This is issued to Comrade Anastaseva, née Bushueva, to confirm that she was indeed mobilized in accordance with the instruction of the Military Council of the Leningrad Front on 21 February 1942 . . . and she was sent as a labor conscript in a separate women's coal workers-battalion to Lake Ladoga in order to perform work aimed at supplying the city of Leningrad with coal fuel, and she stayed there from 6 June 1943 to 9 December 1943."

Thus I worked on both shores of Lake Ladoga. I'll tell you what happened on this shore. A barge would approach carrying *topliak*. *Topliak* is a very heavy wood, so heavy in fact that it's impossible to lift it.[55] . . . Now, there are freight cars standing on the pier, and these logs have to be loaded into the cars right away. You lift the log on your shoulders and carry it along the ladder to the cars. And don't even dream of looking around! The commander of our group would be watching, and you'd hear her right away:

137

"Bushueva, what's going on? Come on! Faster, faster!" We worked that way for twelve hours at a stretch. Fifty minutes work, ten minutes rest. One month—day shift; the next—night shift. We lived in a dugout; inside there were communal bunk beds that slept sixty people one right next to the other. That was our life, day in, day out. One month day shift; the next, night shift. No holidays, no days off, nothing of the sort, no let up.

Bombardments were constant. German planes were always overhead. There was a lighthouse in Osinovets where one could run for shelter, but I almost never did, except once when there was a particularly fierce bombardment. . . . Several piers stood there side by side. At one of them ammunition, boxes with ammunition, were being unloaded. And we were unloading a barge with *topliak*. And an awful air raid started. I still cannot bear the memory of it. When a plane dives. . . . Even in movies I cannot watch this. A plane dives, but it is always diving at me. It happened to me. It was flying straight at me, and our barge was right there. This plane dropped a bomb, but it just grazed the barge. But first a bomb hit a motor-launch, and a bollard flew at us. . . . A bollard you know is a thick post on a wharf you secure ropes too. So pieces of this bollard and logs were flying at us. There were usually many boats there, reconnaissance boats, motor-launches, many of them, and as soon as there was an air-raid alert, they would quickly go out into the lake. This boat for some reason stayed behind. And a log, a two-meter log, broke through the deck and hit a sergeant in the belly. He lived for forty minutes after that, died when they were carrying him on the stretcher. So this bomb hit the stern of our barge as we, there were the two of us, were already sitting down below. We somehow had seen no point in coming up because it was complicated, it involved climbing the scaffolding. And then the boat started sinking. We got frightened and rushed up. I don't know even now how I did it, but I simply leaped onto the pier. And we ran to the lighthouse. When the air raid was over, we still had forty minutes to go on our shift. The commander of our battalion, Mankevich, came and ordered: "Back to work!" We were in such a state. That bombardment was, you know, like a cloud of mosquitoes. But what could we do? We went back to work.

Well, that was on this shore. On the other shore . . . this is where Spit Kobona is, the village of Lednevo. . . . There we . . . What did we do there? We unloaded coal from railway cars into a barge. . . . And again there was a horrible air raid. It was summer. And, you know, there was nowhere to run for shelter. We ran past the pier. Where to hide? Where? There were no bushes, nothing. We crawled under a railway car. But listen what happened! Three girls hid inside a car carrying coal. They took a direct hit and were burned alive. Some colonel was walking by on the road, and he was killed too. And there we sat under a railway car. It was so terrifying . . . I can't tell you.

To make a long story short . . . we were there when the blockade was broken. On 7 February the first train got through to Leningrad.[56] And shortly after, I was summoned to the commander of the battalion, Colonel Bagrov: "Bushueva, you will accompany a train with coal to the city." Thirty cars—coal cars and tenders. . . . I went to Voibokalo. A train with thirty cars of coal was formed, and I accompanied this train. What can I tell you about this? It was the beginning of March. It took us four full days to reach Leningrad, whereas usually it takes several hours. The first night I spent in Voibokalo—the train did not get permission to depart. Then we stayed in the village of Shum. The Germans were four kilometers away. The train would move a little and then stop. There Germans kept bombing the railway. They would let an empty train go by, but if it were a hospital train, or a train with food or fuel, they tried to stop them.

That was the first and second nights. The third night . . . The third night I spent in Peter's Fortress,[57] but in the switchwoman's or someone's hut at the railway station. And one night I spent in a railway car. It was terribly cold, you can imagine, at night, in a car. At the beginning of March. In the morning our train's team said to me: "You go and see a military commandant (RTO) and ask him to let us pass." So I went. I arrived. I found him in a dugout, he was a colonel, and there was another officer with him. I handed my papers to him and explained that I was from a coal battalion accompanying a train with coal. He looked at the papers. And suddenly a terrible air raid began. We walked outside and he said: "We'll attend to this matter later." And the two of them, imagine, went to the shelter, and did not even invite me along. I remained sitting at the door of their dugout and sat there through the entire air raid. . . . This rail line . . . Our authorities called it the "Road of Life" (*Doroga zhizni*) after the blockade was broken. But the Germans called it the "Road of Death."[58] They fired on, I don't know, every centimeter of the tracks. In a documentary they showed how our soldiers repaired this railway. Do you know how they worked? Lying down, without raising their heads, just their hands were moving while they repaired tracks bombed by the Germans.

Well, on the way to Leningrad, people asked me to take along whatever they had for their relatives and friends in the city. I arrived. I also brought my aunt, who had become dystrophic, some bread, two packs of tea, some canned food. And several days later, on the 17th of March, I went back. And when we reached Ladoga, that is, Osinovets, I had to find a way to get to the other side. Several vehicles had already fallen through the ice. The ice was weak, and I was in a car. Then they said we should go through Morozovka. There was a ferry there. And when we arrived there, there was such a line, a tremendous line. And they were letting only specialized vehicles through. Well, we waited and waited. And everyone, the drivers, and military personnel, everyone had left every crumb of bread in the city, with their relatives. And we sat waiting and waiting, wondering what would happen. Luckily, it turned out that our driver had some alcohol on him. And that's how we got out of that situation. They let us through.

Translated by Alla Zeide

SILHOUETTES OF TIME

Avgusta Mikhailovna Saraeva-Bondar' was an art historian and, from 1950, a research assistant at the Leningrad State Museum of History. She kept her double name in memory of her parents; her father, Mikhail Saraev, a worker and participant in the revolutionary movement from 1895 on, and her mother, Zinaida Bondar', a country school teacher who in 1917 became the head of a regional department of education. In her book *Silhouettes of Time*, Saraeva-Bondar' dedicates a chapter, "The Great Resistance," to her memories of the Siege. In the other chapters, she recalls writers, artists, and actors whom she knew, and with whom she worked while organizing exhibitions at the Museum. Central to the narrative are her recollections of her husband, the art photographer Vladimir Vladimirovich Strekalov-Obolenskii.

In the 1930s and until 1941, Saraeva-Bondar' and her parents lived in the Leningrad suburb of Pushkin. In July 1941 the daughter traveled to the city of Ivanovo to visit her father, who was working there at the time. Saraeva-Bondar's mother had allowed her to make the trip, not understanding the seriousness of the situation so soon after the outbreak of war. When Saraeva-Bondar' finally reached Ivanovo, she fell sick, and only with great difficulty did her mother manage to travel there and find her child. The entire family returned home in August 1941, but the German army reached Pushkin in September. Their home was destroyed, and they fled on foot to Leningrad. There they found lodging in a small room near the Kazan' Cathedral.

From A. M. Saraeva-Bondar', *Siluèty vremeni* (Silhouettes of time). St. Petersburg: Istoricheskaia illiustratsiia, 1993, 56–61.

Before every New Year's celebration a bazaar is held in the garden of the former Palace of Pioneers.[59] The merchants' stalls are decorated with garlands of electric lights, tree ornaments sparkle gold and silver, and there is music playing. A heart could hardly resist this festive peal. And happy little children hurry here with their mothers and fathers, grandmothers and grandfathers. Those who have no one with whom they can decorate a tree or share a New Year's dinner also come. On this night they will be all alone

141

with their bittersweet thoughts. Their dear ones, their unborn grandsons and granddaughters are there—in the Piskarevskoe Cemetery, there—on those unnamed heights, there—in the mass graves of the soldiers of the Fatherland.[60] I can pick out these Leningraders in any crowd, I recognize them with my heart, I see on their faces that special stamp.

As you rush to the New Year's bazaar in search of quiet pleasure, turning from Nevskii Avenue onto Ostrovskii Square, pause a moment at the Rossi Pavilion.[61] Here you will see one of the first wounds of Leningrad.

. . . It happened at the end of September 1941. The Fascists had been bombing the city fiercely every day. Finally we got a gloomy, overcast day, with low clouds and a lazy drizzle. Not flying weather, it would seem . . . but at 4:00, as if on schedule, the air-raid alarm sounded.

My mother and I were returning from the city's Council of Education, located on Proletcult Street (now Malaia Sadovaia), where they had given Mother work orders for School #239 in the October District. Several of my mother's friends—teachers—were leaving [the building] with us. They walked along, overwhelmed by sadness at the thought of their abandoned homes, schools, and students. We heard the alarm when we reached the Eliseev store. All the trams, trolleys, and buses on Nevskii Avenue immediately came to a standstill. The officer on duty made us run across Nevskii and take cover quickly in the trenches in the Catherine Garden.[62] Shelters like these had been dug in all the city's public gardens. We had barely reached the railing when we heard overhead the slow whining of an enemy bomber. Shoving each other, we plunged into the darkness of the trench. We groped our way to some seats (they had also been dug into the earth and were covered with boards) and we started a roll call: had everyone made it?

"Be quiet!" A woman's voice was suddenly heard from deep inside. "My kids have fallen asleep."

"Oh! So we're not alone here," I thought, and for some reason felt more at ease. Suddenly a deafening blow rocked the shelter. The floor was giving way beneath our feet, some kind of sand was falling on us from the ceiling and walls, and generally it seemed as though the earth was closing in around us. People were screaming in strange voices; we were all deafened. I clung in terror to my mother. Everyone froze, afraid to budge. A few minutes later someone [from outside] raised the bulkhead to the entrance, now all covered with dirt, and asked: "Well, is everyone alive? All right! Come on out, and go straight to the bomb shelter at the Theater. We are still under at-

142

tack." "Consider yourselves born under a lucky star," the policeman continued. "That bomb probably weighed a ton and blew up right beside you."

And "right beside" was exactly the place near the Rossi Pavilion where
the garden railing begins and where they now hang announcements for the
New Year's bazaars.

Coming out from under ground, we saw the mangled trees in the garden,
blown-out windows in the Pavilion, and the fountain, shooting straight into
the sky (no doubt the pipes and plumbing had been damaged); ambulances
carried off the injured. We saw everything, but we heard hardly anything:
we were still in shock.

At the bomb shelter of the Pushkin Theater we were greeted without
enthusiasm. True, they offered "guest" seats and tincture of valerian. I was
surprised by the atmosphere in the bomb shelter—there were some women
in kerchiefs and aprons, stern, unapproachable. Some people's sleeping areas
were separated by screens. It was very warm and clean there.[63]

The next day we went to the spot where the high-explosive bomb had
landed. Before us gaped a huge crater full of metal pipes that had been
blown to bits. Mama hugged me to her and said:

"Remember this, Asen'ka! For time will pass, everything will start to
grow back, to scar over, and only silent witnesses will remember this bomb
—the handsome ancient Russian warriors, and some of us."[64]

I often pass by them [the bas-reliefs] and say: "Hello there! Do you remember the war?" They are silent. People say: "Silence is a perfect herald."
It means they remember!

. . . I remember how one of the children in our class (I went to School
#218 on Sof'ia Perovskaia Street,[65] where the acquaintances lived who gave
us shelter after we fled from Pushkin) suggested that we go after school to
look at an apartment building that had been bombed during the night on
Kirpichnyi Lane. We set out on Gogol Street, talking on the way about bombs
and shells, their relative strength, and about a quick breakthrough in the
siege. We had already begun to feel hungry, but hunger, with its horrible
power, had not yet touched our psyche, and we were for the time being, and
in general, ordinary prewar school children. Along the way the conversation even turned to our favorite films. And there we were at the building, or
more precisely, what remained of the building. Its facade, from the top to
the bottom floor, was torn away. We stood facing the strange warped segments of the apartments that had survived, with the remnants of some

143

things, clothing, hanging from the beams. Below there was a mountain of debris; it smelled as though something was burning; it seemed as though the smoke from the bomb had still not dissipated. We froze; we were terrified. The spectacle reeked of death and destruction—it could happen to each of our homes. The children looked at me in silence, for in my class I was considered a veteran, having already smelled some gunpowder. Suddenly from the ruins I heard a human voice.

"Hey! There's someone in there. Maybe they need help."

We rushed to the guard standing at the other end of the building, who was not letting anyone come near.

"Now go home, kids. There's no one left alive, and the voice you're hearing is from the radio. There's a loudspeaker hanging over there. Do you see it?"

And then we saw it. In the debris of the fourth floor, a radio speaker [reproduktor] dangled back and forth from which we now heard the peaceful ticking of a metronome.

The blockade metronome, which after the war went on exhibit in museum expositions, was then the pulse of life in the besieged city. When its resonant knock was interrupted (A. A. Akhmatova called the ominous sound the "voice of calamity"), everyone knew—an air raid was near! The siren would howl in alarm and terror, on the street and in homes. Its sound would penetrate inside, carrying with it a horrible feeling of helplessness, dependence on the luck of the draw; perhaps of approaching death. This soul-rending howl was followed by an announcement, delivered by an agitated male voice:

"This is the local air-defense headquarters. Air raid! Air raid! Air raid!"

And again the siren. I remember each note of its melody even now. And I can reproduce it in that siege tonality. Once, after the war had already ended, I imitated the siren, in jest, in the building where some acquaintances of ours lived. We barely managed to revive the lady of the house, and because of my foolish joke, we severed for a long time our relations with these dear people, who had lived through the siege.

The fall months of 1941 were divided into two distinct periods of time: during the air raids and after them. And a good portion of this time was spent in bomb shelters. The cozy, well–cared for basements, to some degree reinforced with partitions, became for Leningraders not only a place to hide, but a place to live. Many elderly inhabitants gathered their necessities and migrated there on the days of particularly fierce bomb attacks. Our beautiful Leningrad buildings, which seemed so mighty, so solid, were destroyed by a direct hit, like a house of cards. And people who had sought refuge in the basements ended up being buried alive. These people, who went gray instantaneously, who had grown old, and were psychologically traumatized, were dug up and brought back to life. But the feeling of what they had experienced never left them. The pandemonium of the siege hell was fixed in their memory in the same way that the outlines of the inhabitants of Hiroshima, incinerated in the atomic explosion, were imprinted into the asphalt and onto the walls of houses. The deafening strike, the entire building quakes, the cracking of something falling apart overhead, darkness. . . . And in the silence blanketed with terror, a thick dust permeates your mouth, your nose, making it hard to breathe.

I survived a direct hit in the courtyard bomb shelter of building No. 1/3 on Sof'ia Perovskaia Street. We were saved because the left side of the bomb shelter caved in, and my mother and I were on the right side.

How many bomb shelters there were in the life of Leningraders, and in mine! Under Kazan' Cathedral, under building No. 32 on Nevskii (next to the Èngel'gardt house), in building No. 9 on the Griboedov Canal (which had an annex for writers), [another one] underneath the Aleksandrinskii Theater. The bomb shelter between the Theater of Musical Comedy and the Philharmonic, another one beneath the famous building No. 18 [on Nevskii], steeped in the memory of the last days of Pushkin, and still others.[66] These shelters are best remembered by their inhabitants, native Leningraders, who had assimilated the history of the city, its culture, its traditions. Unable to be unethical, dishonest, insolent, and cruel, not wanting to become shameless procurers of additional means of sustenance by looting abandoned apartments, they were the first to take leave of life. With them something very important disappeared, something unique. . . . That genuine high culture [*intelligentnost'*] that corresponded not only to the spiritual life of our city, but to its external appearance as well—the architecture, avenues, embankments, gardens.

∞

And this happened at the beginning of October—an encounter with the enemy inside the city, in Leningrad itself!

About 8:00 in the evening my mother and I were leaving my uncle's

145

place (my mother's brother), who lived on the embankment of the Fontanka, in building No. 80. I intentionally note the address, because buildings No. 74–76 housed (as they still do) the State Bank, and across the way there was the Volodarskii printing plant, where the courageous *Leningrad Truth* was printed along with all food-ration cards. On their maps the enemy had designated this area "Objective T-1" and fired on it from the ground and from the air with particular ferocity.[67]

We had to get to Sof'ia Perovskaia Street. Air-raid alarms were sounding at brief intervals one after the other. During each interval we had to cover a certain distance. We managed on our first attempt to reach the Chernyshev Bridge. An air-raid alarm forced us to take cover immediately in the entryway of the neighboring building. The entire sky moaned in response to the attacking aircraft. The anti-aircraft guns, roaring, struck at the enemy, the intersecting beams of the searchlights furrowed the dark sky, flames began to dance—fires had broken out. We left the doorway and, pressed against the walls of the building, tried to determine what was burning where. Suddenly we heard the sound of a window vent (*fortochka*) quickly being opened, and I instinctively turned my head [in that direction]. In the glow from the fires I saw some gadget, which first cracked, and then with a hissing sound took off into the sky, shining bright-green. What could it be? A rocket?

"It's a spy's signal," it dawned on me, and I screamed: "The enemy! The enemy! Comrades, the enemy's here!" I ran to the side of the bank, where soldiers were always patrolling. Several men came running.

"What are you yelling about? Where's the enemy?"

"Quick, come quickly," I hurried them, "and I'll show the window where they launched the rocket."

The air raid continued. We remained on the street; the men quickly entered the building. After just several minutes they led out two suspects with hands tied.

"The bastards, the rocket launchers are still warm, you scum!" they swore at them. "And good for you, little girl! Only next time, be more careful. These beasts are armed. They could easily have shot you . . ."

They left, and only then did I begin to feel terrified. My teeth were chattering—I had actually come face-to-face with the enemy. . . .

Translated by Cynthia Simmons

Interview, July 1996

K. M. Matus was an oboist with the orchestra of the Leningrad Philharmonic, having been hired even before the orchestra returned from evacuation in Novosibirsk. In 1942, as a student of the Conservatory, Matus played in the orchestra of Leningrad Radio. Kseniia Makianovna is one of the few musicians still alive who took part in the famous concert on Leningrad Radio when K. I. Èliasberg conducted Shostakovich's Seventh (Leningrad) Symphony. Not long ago Matus contributed her diaries and memoirs to the museum. "The Muses Did Not Keep Silent" (*A muzy ne molchali*) documents the history of music and theater in Leningrad during the war. As Kseniia Makianovna describes herself, she has always been an "activist"—she took part in philanthropic concerts organized by the Conservatory or Philharmonic, performed in musical ensembles before workers and soldiers at the front, and helped in the restoration of buildings that had been destroyed. A member of the Veterans Association, she takes pride in the medals and certificates that she has been awarded and is eager to give interviews to Russian and foreign journalists. At eighty-plus years of age, she is cheerful, relishes her cigarettes, takes an avid interest in world affairs, and rejoices at the accomplishments of her daughter and granddaughter.

I

The more time goes by, the harder it is to talk about it. I feel as though I've lived three lives. The first life was before the war. The second was the horrible years of war. The third is now. There's a lot to say. They sent us to dig antitank trenches. But it made no sense, because our soldiers were running our way, black and burned, and yelling: "What are you digging for? The Germans are at our heels."

At the end of February [1942], they continually announced on the radio: "We ask that all musicians remaining in Leningrad report to the Radio Committee (*radiokomitet*) for registration. The Symphony Orchestra is going to start performing again." When I took up my instrument, I saw

147

that it had turned green. The valves were green; the pads were coming off. It was impossible to play it. I took it to be repaired to someone who lived far away, and the trams weren't running. I arrived and opened the door. There he sat wrapped in a rug, dressed warmly. He recognized me. I told him: "I'm going to work. I have to get this instrument fixed." He said: "All right, let's take a look. Do you need it right away?" And in the corner he had an armchair and lying on it were various pelts—like muffs or collars. I was embarrassed to look at them for too long. And when he agreed to fix my instrument and I asked "What do I owe you?" he replied: "Bring me a little cat! I have eaten five little cats already." I said: "Oh, there are no cats, or birds, or dogs left in the city. They've all been eaten. I can only pay with money." But he repaired my instrument anyway.

And here I was on my way to the House of Radio. When I arrived at the House of Radio, I was horrified, because I had known all the musicians before the war. And here they were, some sooty, collars turned up, in their winter coats; on the collars of some there were even lice crawling. Well, I tried to wash and keep myself clean, but, who knows, maybe they were on me too, and I didn't see them. And this was our first meeting. The first rehearsal was on the fifth of April. Èliasberg conducted.[68] Even though he was also dystrophic, he would ride from apartment to apartment, because he knew that people had taken to their beds. And he would say: "Come to work and there will be food. We have to get to work." And that's how he got the people together. Later they arranged for us to be fed. We ate in the Bol'shoi Drama Theater. For dinner they gave us an appetizer—a small handful of salad, a first course, a second course, and some bread. By that time my mother had become very ill; she was already bedridden. And I knew that I must eat only a little there and carry the rest home to her in small dishes or jars. The portions were very small.

The first rehearsal was the fifth of April. We had no strength at all, and the rehearsals were very short—forty minutes. But the first concert was in the Pushkin Theater. So we arrive at the Pushkin Theater. And the theater is cold. It's 8° [C]. At that first concert we played the Glazunov overture; then we played the waltz-chardash, then something from "The Nutcracker," then someone sang a piece from "The Maid from Orleans" [*Orleanskaia Deva*], and Kastorskii sang Susanin.[69] And when we had finished the last piece, the audience began to applaud, and I'll tell you, in the concert hall there were only the ghosts of listeners, and on the stage, the ghosts of performers. Because the men who played the brass instruments couldn't hold them in their hands—they were beginning to freeze. So they cut out the fingers of their gloves, and played that way. They themselves were dressed in tailcoats over quilted jackets. That's how our men looked. Karl Il'ich [Èliasberg] came out all starched, in tails. But when he started to conduct, his hands shook. And I had this feeling that he was a bird that had been shot, and any moment he would plummet. But at the concert his hands shook for just a while and then stopped. He began to conduct.

When we had finished a piece, everyone started to applaud. But there was no sound, because everyone was wearing mittens. And if you looked at the crowd, you couldn't tell who was a man, and who a woman. The women were all wrapped up, and the men were also covered in scarves and shawls. Some were wearing women's fur coats. But after we played the first concert, we were all so inspired, because we knew that we had done our job, and that our work would continue.

And right after this concert the Committee on the Arts, along with Karl Il'ich, began to talk about how we must do the Seventh Symphony. We knew that Shostakovich had written the first two parts in Leningrad in September. When he spoke on the radio, he said: "If I finish composing this symphony, it will be called the Leningrad Symphony."[70] But he was evacuated. And since then it had been performed in New York, in England, in Moscow, in Tashkent. It had been performed practically everywhere. So Leningrad definitely had to perform it—after all it was the *Leningrad* Symphony.[71] Well this, of course, took a great deal of work. There was no score; there were no people to play it. While they tried to get hold of a score, there was a search for musicians. This was already the summer of 1942. They would find out which units the musicians were in and would send out a dispatch that so-and-so was needed to perform the Leningrad Symphony. But when they came to Leningrad, they came on foot—there was no public transportation—and they were given a pass. The patrol would say: "Your documents!" And the pass said: "Permission to enter Leningrad to perform the Seventh Symphony with Èliasberg." The fact is, musicians from the front had started to work with us even before the Symphony. But the Symphony also needed a wind ensemble. Well, we did have a military orchestra [in the city], so they were able to negotiate. And when the rehearsals began, they came marching in. The military orchestra was called "The Crew."[72] We didn't know any of them.

149

We began to prepare the Leningrad Symphony. We needed the score, and we needed to write out the parts. Everyone worked as hard as possible copying these notes. And finally the rehearsals began. Naturally everyone's spirits had been raised. Would we be able to do this or not? Of course, without Karl Il'ich there undoubtedly would have been no symphony. He stood on the podium and conducted the orchestra. And there sat the first trumpeter—he had a solo. But the trumpet was lying on his knees.

—Karl Il'ich: "Why aren't you playing?"

—Karl Il'ich, I don't have the strength.

—What do you mean you don't have the strength. And do you think we have the strength? Let's get to work!

That's how demanding he was of everyone. But of course the rehearsals were not long—we rested more than we played. But to make up for this, he worked with each group separately: with the violins (the concertmasters helped with them too). But with the wind instruments, flutes, oboes, and percussion instruments, he worked on each musician's part separately. And finally the day arrived when the posters were hung on Nevskii Avenue. We were told to wear something dark. This was the 9th of September. In general that summer had been cold, but women wore dresses to the concert nonetheless. Because there was no public transportation, women walked to the concert wearing their fine dresses. But the dresses looked as though they were hanging on hangers—everyone had lost so much weight. And when I was approaching the Philharmonic I saw military vehicles in front, and climbing out of them soldiers in boots and sheepskin jackets, carrying machine guns. They were always everywhere in the streets, and here they were at the concert. It began early, at 7:00. We were anxious when we came out on stage—could we hold out and play before an audience? Govorov was in the hall, a general in the army, and his retinue.[73] . . . There is no recording. A tape was made, and a film too, but it has all been lost somewhere, and whatever recordings we have were taped at a later date. When we entered the hall and went out on stage, a floodlight shone from the balcony onto the stage to make it a little warmer. But of course when we began to play, they turned it off. Karl Il'ich came out and everyone stood up and applauded. He had us stand up, and this all went on for a long time. And the symphony itself takes fifty minutes without a break. There's no time to catch your breath. But we played it, thank God! But listen, there had been other concerts at the Philharmonic before this one. And as soon as we would start to play—u-u-u-u—the air-raid signal sounded. And the conductor would put down his baton, and everyone would go to the bomb shelter. And sometimes concerts would end that way. But this time there were no sirens, no air-raid alarm. True, we heard people saying: "Here they come, they're flying overhead." And we thought: "Now it will begin!" But there was no alarm. So we finished the symphony, and they applauded for a long time. Of course we were all inspired, because we knew we had done something great. In fact, the concert was broadcast all over the world. And we proved that even in such hunger and cold, in such living conditions, Leningrad could still perform this symphony.

After the concert was over, Govorov approached Karl Il'ich. He congratulated him. Karl Il'ich thanked him for coming. "And you have not only that to be thankful for," Govorov said.

—What do you mean, not only that?

—You see, the concert was a success. There were planes flying overhead, but still the concert was a success. I gave an order to all of our units to bomb the German batteries so that no plane from their side could take to the air, so that no one would be able to fly over and bomb the Philharmonic. And the concert took place.

And several years later, after the war was over, the Board of Directors sent for Karl Il'ich and said: "Karl Il'ich, some Germans are here and they want to meet you." "Me!" he said. "They tried to kill us! So many people died, so many horrible things." He was half German, half Jewish. But they said to him: "Karl Il'ich, it's an order." So someone was told to accompany him, and he went to the Astoria.[74] He sat down and was then approached by some men from a nearby table.

—Karl Il'ich, hello. We are very glad to meet you and we want to express our gratitude.

—For what?

—For the symphony. We were sitting not far from you, in the trenches. We were bombing you, and the planes were flying—our airfield was there. After all, we had orders to destroy Leningrad. But we sat in a trench and listened to your symphony. And we burst into tears and realized: "Whom are we bombing? We will never be able to take Leningrad because the people here are selfless."

Certainly, that's a touching fact. But that's how the symphony was completed. Later there were other performances. In the House of the Navy and elsewhere. But later, when the Seventh Symphony was performed, Karl Il'ich always conducted.

II

All right, I'll tell you my story. V. was my gallant, from before the war. We used to rehearse together at the Conservatory. I played the oboe; he—the flute. He often came to our home, and my mother treated him well. It was that kind of romance.

And then the war began and he was drafted. One day, it was in August, he called me on the phone: "Kena, I'm on my way to the Finland Station. I've been called up." I went to the Finland Station. The train was already there to take them all to Vsevolozhskaia.[75] I knew they were sent there for three days. That is, for three days they were trained how to use a rifle and then they were sent straight to the front. Cannon fodder. My God, even now it hurts to remember.

An article appeared in the newspaper that said that fifth-year students who were also recipients of the Stalin stipend were temporarily deferred from the draft. But V. had already gone. And yet he was a fifth-year student, receiving the Stalin stipend. I cut out this article and rushed to the conservatory to get him a letter of reference; from there to the Military Registration and Enlistment Office (*voenkomat*), where I was told to go to some City Military Office. And for three days I rushed from one office to another, all of them located in different parts of the city—you know how it is here. And finally I managed to get an exemption for him and a pass for myself to go to the front. And I went.

I took off my gold watch, my ring, and I gave these and my ration cards to my sister.[76] You know, in case.... "I am going." I told her. "Don't say anything to Mother." So I set out. Of course a good part of the way I had to go by foot. Anyway, I found the headquarters and entered. "How do you do," I said politely, and started to explain myself. "And here I have a document...." The officer stared at me in a strange way, looked at the paper; then again at me. "You know," he said, "they should build you a golden statue. I have never seen anything like this. What an effort it must have been for you to get this paper!" "Yes," I said, "So?" And then he asked: "And who are you?" "His wife," I answered right away. What else could I say? Who was I? His girlfriend? Big deal. I wasn't his sister, or his relative. To make it short, the officer told me to go to some road nearby and to wait for their return ("They will be returning shortly from their training exercises"). "Tell him," he said, "not to leave the lines or he will be punished. But tell his sergeant to send him to headquarters."

When I saw them, my heart sank. It was his third day there. His feet were wrapped in rags. He had some old boots on with holes in them. They all wore some kind of worn-out field jackets. And all of them were blue with cold. Their hands were blue from the cold! Well, cattle to the slaughterhouse, that's how they looked. He caught sight of me, and tears came to his eyes. "It's all right," I said to him. "Take it easy."

When they got back, I walked up to the officer in charge. He sent V. back to headquarters. And he asked me whether I had brought civilian clothes for V. I hadn't. "That's bad. Now tomorrow he'll have to return to bring back his uniform." "All right," I said. "He will."

We walked all the way back from Rzhevka.[77] But we made it. Now we had been going out for a long time, holding hands, kissing, hugging. And V. was a big guy, and I knew it wasn't easy for him. So one day he says to me: "You know, I can't take this any longer. Why don't you want to marry me?" "I don't want to get married," I told him. "I want to have my own career. I want to stand on my own two feet. I don't want to get married." But I could see how it was torturing him, so I said to myself: "To hell with it. I'll just give in!" So I went and told him. He nearly went berserk, he was so surprised. And after that ours was a warm and friendly relationship. So when we got back to Leningrad, I went to his place. Besides, it was too far for me to walk home. And again he cried: "How did you pull this off? You're so smart!"

In the morning I told him to take his uniform to the Military Office. When he got there, they looked at his letter of deferral and ordered him to return to the front. "A newspaper article?" they said. "What do you mean, a newspaper article? Everyone should be at the front. Forget about returning your uniform. And you can go back where you came from." And he went back. And I started rushing from office to office again. . . . It took me some time, but I finally succeeded in getting another deferral. This time I packed his clothes, and when I arrived, the same officer was in charge. He asked me: "Where do you get your stamina? Where do you get so much energy?" And I said: "What do you mean? For someone you love. . . ." So I got him out a second time.

153

Next we had to decide what to do—we knew he would be called up again soon. A friend of mine conducted a band in the Gorky House of Culture. I told V. we should go see the conductor. I pleaded with Vasen'ka [the conductor] to help us. "I can't," he said. "I don't have any openings." I knew he didn't. But I continued pleading: "Find any kind of job for him, even a street sweeper." And he took him. After a while the band broke up. Then I told V. to join a military orchestra.

Once he joined this military orchestra, he started visiting like he used to. Mama would be making *duranda* pancakes, but there wouldn't be a bit of firewood at home. He would come and sit down:

"Come on, give me a kiss."

"A kiss, are you kidding? I'd like to eat something, and you've got kisses on your mind. Look, Mother's making *duranda* pancakes, and there isn't any wood!"

And I think to myself: "If I were in his shoes and heard those words, I would jump up from the chair, and even if it were only a plank from a fence, I'd bring it. . . ."

But things went on as before. Then the October celebrations came. Our conservatory group was sent to Avtovo, a place very close to the front line. We arrived to give a concert, and he [V.] came with us. I had told him: "Let's both go. They'll feed us." After the concert we went outside. We were warned to be quiet—whisper, no smoking. But then we saw some distance away what looked like lights burning. It turned out it was the Germans smoking. They weren't afraid of us at all. It was we who were afraid of them.

Afterwards we were invited to have supper. The tables were set nicely —meat cutlets, pasties, bread, vodka. There was no great selection, but . . . I, fool that I am, began filling his plate with this and that. And he began eating right away. Across from me a commissar was sitting—there were still commissars at that time.[78] He gave me a strange look, then stood up and gave a short toast: "Dear friends, thank you very much for coming. You made my boys' day. They have at least had some chance to relax for a while." Yes, I forgot, I was the only woman among them. The rest were men, that is, boys. . . . He finished his toast. Everyone had already started eating, but my glass was empty, and my plate was empty. He gave me a look and said: "Well, well! There is only one woman here with you, and you aren't taking care of her? How can that be?"

I must admit I have a terrible disposition. He said this and it was as if something in me broke—suddenly my love was gone. To begin with, I my-self felt ashamed. And second, [I realized] his shameless selfishness. He was hungry, all right! How about me? Wasn't I hungry?

After that they filled my plate with everything, and I ate. Then they put us up. Well, he tried to get close to me, and I just kept my distance. "What's with you," he asked. I didn't say anything. "I'm not in the mood." In the morning we had to go back to the city, and he was the first to leave.

"Kiss me!"

"Go ahead, kiss me."

"I don't understand a thing."

"You don't have to understand anything. I'll figure it out myself."

So this was a real turning point for me. Afterward, there was no feeling left. For a while he kept coming, got down on his knees, kissed my feet.

"Please forgive me, forgive me. We used to be so close. We were as good as married. You might end up alone . . ."

"Don't worry about it," I said to him. "I don't need anything anymore, not kisses, not tenderness. Because the most important thing is missing. How could I unite my life with yours!" And how could I? With such a person! And that was the end of our relationship.

Translated by Cynthia Simmons (I) and Alla Zeide (II)

Excerpt from THE DEFENSE OF LENINGRAD

Yuliia Aronovna Mendeleva received her medical training in Germany and began work as a physician before the Revolution. Her membership in the Communist Party dates from 1905. Mendeleva became director of the Leningrad Pediatric Institute in 1928; she was a good administrator and succeeded in attracting the best specialists as teachers and clinicians. As a long-time member of the party, she commanded authority in the administrative and governmental apparatus and made good use of her official connections. When the evacuation of children began in June 1941, Mendeleva decided that the Institute should not leave Leningrad: "since a population of children will to some degree remain in the city." Thanks to her standing in the party, she was able to provide staff, students, and patients with the kind of supplemental sustenance that she describes in her article. She did not fear foreign contacts, and more than once the Pediatric Institute received relief packages of medicine and food from abroad. During the war, the Pediatric Institute saved the lives of thousands of children in Leningrad.

Mendeleva's accomplishments as an administrator and party functionary were used against her during the Leningrad Affair. She was arrested in 1949, charged with anti-Soviet activities and Zionist affiliation. She was sentenced to ten years of hard labor in the gulag. Mendeleva served her sentence in the camp for women invalids on the river Abez' (northern Komi Autonomous Republic). She was rehabilitated in 1954 and set free "for the absence of corpus delicti."

The following excerpts from Mendeleva's memoir were published in *Oborona Leningrada (1941–1944): Vospominaniia i dnevniki uchastnikov* (The Defense of Leningrad [1941–1944]: Memoirs and diaries of participants). Leningrad: Nauka, 1968.

By the time the war began, we already had a large collective of professors, teachers, and scientific staff. The clinic at the Institute was fully operative, with 1,200 beds. There were a number of scientific-support and management operations. Our dairy (*molochnaia stantsia*) served not only the Institute, but the children's institutions of the Vyborg district as well.

156

∞

In response to the demands of wartime, we had on call: 85 hematologists, 367 nurses, 25 surgical nurses, 1,800 nurses of the Russian Red Cross (ROKK), and 275 orderlies.

In 1943 we trained five hundred wartime nurses, twenty-five completed our courses for health and hygiene instructors, and seventy-five our program for dietitians. We organized monthly courses for the advanced professional training of 1,570 Leningrad doctors. In addition we trained: thirty cooks for infant-care centers, thirty-five chefs for soup kitchens, thirty-five elementary-school doctors, thirty directors of kindergartens and orphanages.

The Institute was engaged in training doctors for the army and for the rear. During the siege, of the 947 doctors that were trained, 360 worked in the public health-care system, and the rest for the Red Army.

Personnel received special training so that during air raids they could move the children to bomb shelters in the minimal amount of time necessary. We were able to get this time down to two to three minutes.

∞

There was one very serious episode during the siege, when, as a result of damage to the water-supply system, the city had no water. No matter what, we had to save the food-processing operation, the autoclaves, and the laundry. In the bitter cold of winter, all personnel, from the director and professors on down to the rest of the staff, formed a bucket brigade each night, bringing several thousand buckets from the cistern to the boiler-house, and in that way they saved the Institute's central heating. We had filled tanks in the courtyard with water—that assured us heat. There was coal, but it was very difficult to get hold of it. Initially our heating system was fueled by heating oil, but later it was necessary to convert to coal and firewood. In order to ensure heat for the Institute, the staff took to dismantling wooden houses.

A great deal of attention was given to the Institute's gardens and orchards.[79] The entire collective was totally dedicated to this work, which greatly contributed to the discovery of ways to increase the food supply. In order to build trenches in Rzhevka, it was necessary to dig up several fields of raspberry bushes; workers from the Institute's gardens carefully transported the raspberry bushes to other places. Because these measures were taken, the Institute had an adequate reserve of vegetables, various fruit preserves, vitamin-rich juices, and the like.

The enemy wanted to starve us to death. Severe cold and an insufficient amount of fuel made it worse for Leningraders. Pipes froze, as did our staff in their unheated apartments. The absence of electric lighting, the absence of kerosene forced the scientific staff to work in their coats and to carry on their research (*nauchnaia produktsiia*) by the light of old-fashioned oil lamps. And under just such conditions master's theses were written, and doctoral dissertations.

In order to save the lives of the workers, it was first necessary to bring them closer to the Institute. It was beyond the strength of most of the workers to live far from the Institute, walk many kilometers in the -40° [C.] cold (in the winter of 1941–1942), through snowdrifts, and all this under threat of bombs and artillery fire. What is more, most of them lived at home without light, heat, or water. We had to crowd together those who already lived at the Institute to make room temporarily for those whose health was most weak and for workers who were the most essential. . . .

Establishing at the Institute a cafeteria for supplemental feedings for those who were starving, establishing a hospital ward for those who were dystrophic and could no longer work—all these measures made it possible to save the lives of the people on our staff.

The later evacuation of many professors and of other medical institutions (in particular the Military-Medical Academy) whose professors worked in our Institute as well put us in an extremely difficult position. In our institute alone, we lost in the course of the evacuation all the M.D.s on the teaching staff, a professor of diseases of the ear, a professor of diseases of the eye, etc. Many of them returned before the siege was over. Those professors who remained had to take on the extra burden. For example, one of them had to supervise the work of three departments of closely related disciplines. We had to find new department heads. As a matter of fact, we were able to attract Professor of Anatomy Shilova, who stayed on with us at the Institute.

Even though we had a reduced teaching staff, we were able to work it so that throughout the war we still maintained the full five-year program. Teachers and students worked with unusual fervor; they dedicated all their strength not to fall behind the prewar curriculum. Students and teachers alike participated actively in the resistance, in the defense of the city against a horrible enemy. For many of the Institute's workers, neither cold nor hunger nor artillery shells nor bombs could force them to abandon the institute they cherished. . . .

We were most occupied by the question of how to feed the infants. Under the supervision of our Institute a council on children's nutrition was created. I was its chairperson. And despite great difficulties, the department of nutrition, the dairy, and the food-processing operation worked without interruption. As a result we succeeded in working out a system that would accommodate the changing availability of ingredients and would allow us to switch from one formula to another without compromising the overall caloric content and nutritional value of the mixture. During the siege, the dairy and food-processing center served 7,000–8,000 children daily, providing up to 13,000 servings a day. The scale of our work at the center, in comparison with what it was before the war, increased twelve to sixteen times, and despite this fact, all the children we served were fed adequately and on time.

I was particularly concerned with the issue of physical development in newborns. I have been conducting research in this area since 1938. We study their weight, length, the circumference of their heads, the circumference of their chests. In 1942 we experienced a catastrophic drop in all these indicators; there occurred an amazingly sharp drop in the weight of infants born in Leningrad—more than six hundred grams [one and one-half pounds], and the length of newborns dropped two centimeters from the prewar average.

I succeeded in familiarizing Comrades [Aleksei] Kosygin and [Anastas] Mikoyan with the information I had gathered on the physical development of Leningrad infants when I was in Moscow, attending a scientific conference of the Soviet People's Commissariat of Health (NKZ) on the topic of dystrophy. Comrade Mikoyan familiarized himself thoroughly with the data and diagrams I had presented and at the first opportunity posed the question: "What measures do we need to take?" To this I answered that children are not capable of normal development if they do not have natural whole milk. Anastas Ivanovich immediately asked, "Would one thousand cows be enough for you?" I felt feverish from worry when I realized that there might not be enough feed in Leningrad for these cows. I called Comrade Popkov on his direct line and I received a confirmation from him the following day. In this way Leningrad received during the siege one thousand cows from Vologda and Yaroslavl'. Our Institute was allotted fifteen cows.

Throughout the siege less than 1 percent of the children who were admitted into the hospital were of normal weight; and it was not unusual to treat children who weighed one-third the normal weight. Of course, one thousand cows played no small role in improving the health of infants.

In light of the research that showed that the physical development of newborns in 1942–1943 was unsatisfactory, I sent a memo to Comrade Mikoyan in April 1944 on the absolute necessity of increasing the ration for pregnant women. And, indeed, after the decree of the Presidium of the Supreme Soviet of 8 June 1944, the physical development of newborns dramatically improved, and in the first half of 1945, the weight of newborns, as well as the length, reached the prewar average.

∞

In 1942, many babies were stillborn, and among the live births, many were premature and weak . . .

The Institute was first hit in November 1941, when a high-explosive incendiary bomb exploded nearby and collapsed a four-story building in which our hospital was located. The entire support structure of this building was destroyed, so we had to transfer the hospital to another location. . . . On 4 January 1942, the Institute was the target of intense artillery fire. Twelve shells fell on the grounds of the Institute. As a result almost all the buildings lost the glass in their windows, and in some, the walls were damaged. The quick actions taken to shield patients and staff accounted for the fact that during this artillery attack, and those that followed, there was not one casualty on the territory of the Institute.

The next intensive artillery attack on the Institute occurred in May 1942, when we were hit by ten shells, one of which fell on the clinic for nursing babies. The shell tore through the roof and exploded on the second floor, destroying several storage rooms. There were no casualties. The attack began during the night; it was long and unrelenting. . . .

On that memorable night at the Institute, a woman in the obstetrics clinic gave birth to a boy. She was in no condition to be taken to the bomb shelter, so her bed had been moved to a wall without a window. The midwife and the doctor calmly performed the delivery. . . . The mother would not give in to fear and was even in a good mood. She was elated at the arrival in the world of her new son and decided to call him Viktor (the victor). The next morning when I walked down the hall with Vera Inber, who had come to the Institute, almost everything had been cleaned up—the glass as well as the broken plaster. The staff demonstrated discipline, recognition of their responsibility, and their love for their work. As a result of this heavy attack, we lost most of the window casings, several roofs were ripped off, the tops of the poplars in the park were cut off by the shells, and metal sheets from the torn roofs hung from the trees like leaves. But once again, there were no casualties.

Often shells fell at tram stops, and this sometimes resulted in a large number of casualties. In August 1943, a shell actually fell right on a tram car, near the Institute. Among the passengers in the tram was one of our young, talented graduate students, who perished along with the other sixty. There were many wounded. At the height of the attack, workers from the Institute themselves carried the wounded on stretchers into our surgical clinic. We intended to bandage them and transfer them to the hospital for adults. However, I figured that this could have an adverse effect on several of the injured; in light of which, in the children's surgical clinic we set up a section for adults.

In August 1943 the attacks became considerably more frequent. Although they did not cause a great deal of damage, it was necessary to be on constant alert.

On 12 October 1943, a shell once again fell on a tram that was passing under Litovskii Bridge. In the midst of the attack, putting their lives in danger, workers of the Institute (the Civil Air Defense [MPVO] and others) rushed to the site of the catastrophe to administer aid to the wounded. . . .

A large number of people were wounded on 14 and 16 October 1943, from shells that exploded not far from the Institute, on Karl Marx Avenue.

∞

During the war the Institute experienced an extreme shortage of medical personnel. Many positions went unfilled—for 35 percent of the doctors, 60 percent of the nurses, and 65 percent of the child-care workers. Only in 1943 did our situation begin to change for the better.

The dairy, headed by Dr. S. I. Poliakova, received the highest honors among the managerial organizations. During the most difficult days of the siege, in the absence of cow's milk, the dairy prepared formulas from dry and condensed milk, from soy and other products (eighteen substitutes in all). The dairy organized a distribution center for mother's milk, which was so essential for nourishing premature and sick babies. During the war and the Siege, the dairy distributed 697,000 liters of formula and 4,871,320 servings of mixtures for baby formula. . . .

The numbers of births in clinics:

1941, 3rd quarter—654; 4th quarter—418
1942, 1st quarter—250; 2nd quarter—176; 3rd quarter—65; 4th—20
1943, 1st quarter—88; 2nd quarter—235; 3rd quarter—118; 4th—280
1944, 1st quarter—338. . . .

Translated by Cynthia Simmons

"The Saltykov-Shchedrin National Public Library
(of the Order of the Red Banner of Labor)"

Lilia Solomonovna Frankfurt entered Leningrad University, the Faculty of Social Sciences (FON), in 1924. There she became an ardent student of the history
of the Revolution and the sociology of the literary process. She was a member
of the Komsomol and lectured workers on the foundations of communism. She
joined the Party in 1928. After graduating from the university, she worked in the
publishing house "History of Manufacturing Plants and Factories" (ZIF). In
early 1937, the press was closed, accused of promoting an "anti-party line," and
Frankfurt was expelled from the Party.[80] That same year Frankfurt's husband,
expecting to be arrested, committed suicide. However, toward the end of 1937,
Frankfurt succeeded in having her case reviewed by the Party and was subsequently hired to work in the Public Library. In 1941 she was appointed Expert
Advisor to the Director. During the Siege, Frankfurt and her colleagues continued to serve patrons. They compiled a catalogue of wartime publications, and
they saved approximately 60,000 rare books and more than 100,000 (artistic)
prints. As the Director of the Public Library Rakov wrote in 1948, she "remained
on the job throughout the war, doing a great deal to ensure that the library did
not cease functioning for even one day. She engaged in all the library's activities,
both great and small, and rendered considerable assistance to the new [post-
war] directorate as one of its oldest and most esteemed workers." In October
1950, Frankfurt was expelled from the Party for hiring personnel who were ide-
ologically suspect and for political errors in her published work. On 9 January
1951 she was arrested on articles 58-10 and 58-11 [anti-Soviet activity]. Frankfurt
served her sentence in the same camp as Yuliia A. Mendeleva, and, like Mendeleva, was completely rehabilitated in 1954.

Lilia Frankfurt's memoir "The Saltykov-Shchedrin National Public Library (of the Order of
the Red Banner of Labor)" was published in *Bibliotekar'* 2–3 (1946); 32–39.

Tremendous trials and tribulations befell Leningrad during the Great Patriotic War. Along with the entire population of the heroic city, these trials
were borne as well by the staff (*kollektiv*) of Saltykov-Shchedrin Public
Library.

In the very first days of the war, the library was faced with new, extremely complex and difficult problems. It was necessary to put all work quickly on war footing and to ensure the preservation of the holdings. The war resulted in many new responsibilities in the area of acquisitions. We ceased receiving a requisite copy of all new publications. The besieged city was deprived of current books from the Soviet press. As a result we had to prepare a full accounting of all lacunae, in order to replenish [our holdings] at the first opportunity. For this we kept a special card catalogue in which all entries were checked against the *Chronicle of Books* (*Knizhnaia letopis'*). In this way we could identify gaps in our acquisitions and keep track of publications that had come out in other cities in the Soviet Union and that we were missing. In addition we compiled a full list of all publications in Leningrad during the war and transmitted this to the All-Union Book Chamber (*Vsesoiuznaia Knizhnaia Palata*), which was deprived of the opportunity to receive and register what was published in Leningrad (*leningradskaia pechatnaia produktsiia*).

In order to serve library patrons without interruption while under siege it was necessary to reorganize the work of all departments: acquisitions, cataloguing, preservation, inventory, and the reading rooms. The volume of work at the library was significantly curtailed at the beginning of the war, especially in 1942, and began to grow according to basic indicators only in 1943, and significantly increased toward the end of the war. . . .

The work in acquisitions was distinguished also by the significant growth in purchases of second-hand books and rare editions. During the siege, the booksellers at the market were overwhelmed with a huge quantity of books, and the library staff felt obligated to acquire and add to the library's holdings everything that was significant and valuable. All in all, in the course of the siege the library bought 58,892 books, 112,640 prints, and 48,411 rubles worth of manuscripts.

Among these acquisitions, the following were of particular interest: very valuable items related to Pushkin from the library of the famous Pushkinist N. O. Lerner;[81] the collection "Cities of the World," comprising more than eighty thousand postcards; the library of Alikhanian, with rare books and reference materials on the East; the archive of the writer D. V. Larionov, who took part in the Battle of Tsushima;[82] the archives of the journal *Russkoe bogatstvo* (Russian treasure)[83] and of L. B. Deich; the manuscripts of V. Ya. Briusov, and much more. In 1943 we were even so fortunate as to acquire seven incunabula.

As a result of bomb and artillery attacks and fires, many libraries of private individuals and institutions were left totally unguarded, in ruins or open to the sky, and they were destroyed by fire, water, or inclement weather. The library staff took it upon themselves to gather and preserve this wealth of books. This work demanded incredible strength. The books had to be picked out of destroyed buildings, lowered through the window frames, extracted from under piles of bricks, and carried on one's back (only much later was the library supplied a car for this).

A large quantity of books, packed in boxes, was transferred to the basements or to the lower floors, including the entire reference library of more than fifty thousand volumes.

Under wartime and siege conditions, it was necessary to reorganize totally our way of serving our patrons. In the very first days of the war, instead of eight reading rooms, we created one—at first it was located in the exhibit hall, and later in the manuscript division. If an air-raid warning was sounded, patrons would take their books to the bomb shelter, where they would continue to work.

From 1 May 1942 to 1 November 1944, the reading room occupied one of the rooms of the administrative offices of the library, which was heated by a wood-burning stove. The relocation of the reading room required a great deal of strength. It involved the transfer of thousands of books then being used by individual patrons and the entire system of reference materials.

[On] 26 January 1942, the library lost electricity. The heating and plumbing system had stopped working even before that. Cold and dark reigned in the stacks, the reading rooms, and everywhere else on the premises. Now the patrons had to settle down to work in the only place where life still glimmered—in the director's office. The stove was lit there, and a kerosene lantern, a "bat."[84] During the winter of 1941–1942, all operations involving patrons were conducted by the light of lanterns, and when the kerosene ran out, we had to search for books on the shelves with a burning piece of wood in our hands.

And nevertheless the library never ceased functioning even for a day. Just as before, books were requested and bibliographical inquiries were received. The profile of our patrons did change—students and researchers were replaced by commanders of the Red Army, doctors, military specialists, political agitators, lecturers, and political workers. There were changes in the traditional methods of serving our patrons—requests for books and bibliographies were processed more quickly. Everything possible was done so that the resources of the library could assist in routing the enemy. A book turned out to be a weapon.

During the war, the library served more than forty-one thousand patrons, discharging to them approximately 1,500,000 books, journals, and newspapers. There were requests for engineering books, medical articles, historical literature, political brochures, periodicals, and works of fiction. From the various requests for bibliographical searches, it is apparent what literary sources were needed in a besieged city. We cite here a sample of the literature searches that were processed by the library:

The study of just and unjust wars;

The Leningrad Komsomol in the Patriotic War;

Leningrad scientists in the Patriotic War;

Bogdan Khmel'nitskii;[85]

The history of the Kronstadt Fortress;

The images of Suvorov, Kutuzov, and Aleksandr Nevskii in works of fiction;

Illustrated materials on Suvorov's crossing of the Alps;

Heroes of the Patriotic War of 1812;

Brusilov's breakthrough;[86]

The representation of Germans in nineteenth-century classical literature;

The honor of the officer and military education in works of fiction;

Standards and behavioral norms of officers in the old army;

Party work in the army (an historical purview);

Textbooks on tactics;

Anti-aircraft cannons;

The love of a Russian soldier for his regiment;

Fire fighting abroad;

The hydrology of Lake Ladoga;

The processing of soy;

Edible wild plants;

Scurvy and vitamin deficiency;

Sanitation in a besieged city;

The establishment and functioning of hospital bomb shelters;

Shrapnel wounds;

The treatment and cure of dystrophy;

Famine edema;

Cold sterilization of surgical instruments;

Secondary shock;

Plaster casts in the treatment of wounds;

Wounds and trauma to the hand;

Traumatic fistula of the urinary tract;

Russian and foreign literature on the restoration of architectural ensembles and monuments.

All holdings of the library, the entire reference department that it had taken decades to establish, all the staff's efforts were directed toward satisfying the patrons' requests, the retrieval of a book, reference materials, or a map to serve in our defense.

∞

Work continued uninterrupted on the general systematic catalogue. During the course of the war nine manuals and eight catalogues were compiled, among these a catalogue on the history of philosophy, the history of the Middle Ages, the history of Great Britain, the history of agriculture in the USSR, biology, zoology, plant husbandry, mining. Work continued on the new arrangement of the stacks, which had been introduced in the library for new acquisitions beginning in 1940.

Groups worked on planned bibliographies: "The Bibliography of Russian Bibliography," "The Bibliography of Russian Periodical Publications." Old card catalogues were filled and new ones established: military-technical, military-surgical, and others. Large projects were begun—"The Bibliography of Slavic Studies" and "The Library Bibliographical Encyclopedia." A special group of colleagues was commissioned to gather publications on Leningrad and to compile a bibliography: "Leningrad in the Great Patriotic War"; 62,736 items were gathered—various books, brochures, magazines, newspapers and other, miscellaneous, materials. Of particular interest among these are the partisan newspapers of the Leningrad district, a set of newspapers "Building the Barricades" (*Na oboronnoi stroike*) and "In Defense of Leningrad," posters and leaflets, a collection of photographs, application forms for food-ration cards (including the 125-gram "starvation" bread-ration card), publications of the Leningrad Front and the Red-Banner Baltic Fleet. The materials of this collection, along with the bibliographic card catalogues, numbering around ninety thousand entries, represents, of course, the sole source of its kind for anyone working on the history of the defense of Leningrad in the Great Patriotic War.

Work continued on the preparation for publication of a scientific catalogue of Voltaire's library and a catalogue of incunabula.[87]

∞

During the war a great deal of energy was expended defending the library against enemy air raids and artillery attacks. On the very first day of the war we began to prepare the buildings of the library for enemy attack. First of all the attics were spread with sand, and all wooden ceilings were painted with superphosphate. All these tasks were accomplished through the efforts of the library staff alone.

In the cellars of the library buildings gas and bomb shelters were built. In the first days of the war, a special unit of the MPVO was set up, composed solely of the staff of the library. All 102 members of this unit stayed in barracks, continually kept watch, and vigilantly and selflessly protected the library.

The library, located in the center of the city on one of its main thoroughfares, was continually the target of bombardments from the air and artillery attacks. With the exception of two shells, one of which fell in the area of interlibrary loan, but fortunately did not explode, the library received no direct hits. Nevertheless the library suffered considerably from shrapnel from bombs and shells, from shock waves, from the lack of heating, plumbing, etc. Total physical damage done to the library is estimated at 77,147,941 rubles.

The library collective, reduced by July 1942 to 158 persons, demonstrated in their work the epitome of discipline and dedication. Among the staff members there were many casualties, those who perished at the front and those who could not endure the hardships of the siege. Elder and eminent librarians died—V. È. Bank, M. È. Orlovskaia, I. I. Slonimskii, N. D. Ignat'ev, M. D. Kransfel'd—as did the young graduate students Tseitlin and Andreeva and such excellent workers as Ya. Ya. Zakorina, Bisnek, and others. The library suffered a terrible loss with the death of the director of the manuscript department, the great Russian scholar I. A. Bychkov.[88] During the war he proved himself to be a faithful son of his people and an ardent patriot. He refused to abandon his native city and worked up until the last days of his life. In 1943 the scientific and library community of the country observed the eighty-five-year anniversary of his birth. The government awarded him the Order of the Red Banner of Labor.

Those who remained worked on production, defended the library, kept the night watch, stockpiled and transported wood, fueled the stoves, tidied the grounds, transferred books, repaired the roof, volunteered at hospitals, cleaned up the courtyards, removed snow from the streets, gave lectures and speeches, defended dissertations, worked to raise their ideological and political consciousness and their professional qualifications.

For good reason the medal "For the Defense of Leningrad" shines on the chests of 153 members of the library staff, and it is not by chance that among the best soldiers of the MPVO, the Order of the Red Banner of Labor was given to a colleague in the library, Zina Ivanova. Within the library collective, well-deserved respect is enjoyed by such comrades as V. N. Struleva, O. P. Zakhar'ina, M. V. Kal'fa, E. M. Soloveichik, V. V. Bessonova, E. M. Egorova, P. F. Gorbatenko, and many other colleagues, who took upon their shoulders all the hardships of work during the siege.

[On] 1 November 1944, with great ceremony, the general reading room was [re]opened at its former location. On this day the library received congratulations from various organizations and patrons.

At present the Saltykov-Shchedrin National Public Library, according to basic indicators of production, has made great progress in comparison with the difficult time during the war and the siege. However, the library collective must still do more in order for the work of the library to reach its prewar level.

Translated by Cynthia Simmons

Interview, July 1995

Ol'ga Il'inichna Markhaeva is a historian and senior research assistant at the now reopened National Museum of the Defense of Leningrad. She began the interview by recalling the tragic fate of the first museum, closed in connection with the Leningrad Affair.[89] A series of trials that occurred from 1949 to 1953, the Leningrad Affair claimed as its victims "thousands of party, soviet, agricultural, trade-union, Komsomol, and military workers, scientists, representatives of the creative intelligentsia, members of their families, relatives, and other citizens."[90] Among them was Lev L'vovich Rakov.

Rakov organized the exhibition "The Soviet Nation's Great Patriotic War against the German Invaders," which opened in Leningrad in the spring of 1942 in a building on the corner of First Red Army Street and Izmailov Prospect. Displayed at the exhibition were examples of confiscated ("trophy") weapons, shrapnel from ammunition shells, and tokens of daily life in the besieged city. This exhibit, together with items from the anniversary exhibit "25 Years of the Red Army" (at the Leningrad House of the Red Army, February-April 1943), formed the basis of another exhibition, "The Heroic Defense of Leningrad," in the area of Leningrad known as Salt Town. This locale was the site of the first Museum of the Defense of Leningrad.

In 1946 those who had founded the museum were indicted by investigators from the Central Committee VKP(b) (All Union Communist Party of the Bolsheviks), who claimed that they had "created a myth about Leningrad's peculiar fate during the Siege, had diminished Stalin's role, and, under the pretext of exhibiting trophy armaments, had amassed ammunition for a terrorist act and an attempt of the life of the leader."[91] Some of the museum's collections were destroyed; those that survived were distributed among the other city libraries. Rehabilitation of victims of the Leningrad Affair began at the end of 1954. Relevant documents were reassessed in March 1988.

170   Our museum was "repressed" and closed as a result of the Leningrad Affair and then, in 1985, a campaign got under way; that is, Leningraders did not forget our museum. That museum was huge, thirty-seven rooms, and it

took up this entire block.[92] The museum extended beyond its walls. Nazi "trophy" military hardware, which was brought here, stood along Market [*Rynochnaia*] Street. There were German tanks that were called "Ferdinands," "Tigers," and "Panthers," and guns. Therefore, there was a great deal that was tied to this museum and the siege. And when the days of perestroika arrived, a thaw, a campaign began, under the influence of this democratic wave: "Give back our Museum of the Defense of Leningrad." And many well-known public figures in Leningrad supported this campaign. And indeed, the Museum was reopened in 1989. When the museum was closed, it took them a long time to close it—it is impossible to close such a huge museum all at once. At first it was closed for "reconstruction," then for "major repairs," then for an "exhibition change," and thus they began to close it in '49, but closed it once and for all only in '53.[93] Our museum's collections were transferred to various museums in the city, and some of the exhibits have been preserved, but not here. They're in other museums, I think even in Moscow. And some of the exhibits were simply destroyed. People witnessed the burning, in the inner courtyard of our museum, of documents that were considered "useless." All the ordinance was blown up on the firing range or turned in to be melted down, because one count of indictment in the Leningrad Affair was that Leningrad was collecting a "military arsenal," and that it was being collected at the Museum of the Defense of Leningrad. It's an absurd indictment, but in those days you could claim anything—that someone was an agent of the English or American intelligence agencies, for example. And people believed, or pretended to believe, because of fear. People were afraid.

And so when the museum reopened (in a certain sense, we are the successors of that museum, by virtue of our name), that which the old museum possessed no longer belonged to us. In this sense, we are a new museum. They didn't return the old archives to us, but we are trying to get them. But I don't know if we'll be able to or not, because museum holdings are very expensive to purchase.

They've begun to reconsider many pages of the war. For example, not long ago I read an article about whether it was necessary to bomb Dresden. And now they're saying that it wasn't necessary, and even Churchill expressed his regret that it was bombed.[94] Now that is all in the past. But every time humanity faces new problems—moral, philosophical, ethical problems—then, I think, we can look to our past. Of course, at that time of hatred, the question never occurred to anyone—is it necessary to destroy Dresden or not. We are the ones who can look back now, through the eyes of a person of the late twentieth century. And that, I think, is good, very good.

To return to our museum, in 1989, when our museum opened, we announced on the radio that we were accepting items for exhibition. And Leningraders started to bring us things that they had from the siege. The chronological framework of our museum is very broad: 1933–1953.[95] And naturally, as time has gone by, it has become impossible to restore the old museum. Time passed and the character of the exhibitions has changed. In the former museum, there were overhead exhibit mountings, from which "trophy" airplanes hung. There were tanks and cannons. We had a tram that had been hit by a shell, it had been by the Eliseev store, and they brought it here too.[96]

Now the character of the exposition has changed. We have a very good manuscript division. When you read what was written at that time, you begin to feel that these were people of a different culture. Indeed, much time has passed, and radio and television have fundamentally changed people. But then people had great trust in paper, and it was common to keep a diary. Of course, Tania Savicheva's diary is unique.[97] It was found after the war by Rakov (he was the first director of our museum). It is now exhibited in the Museum of the City's History, but it was our exhibit. That little girl, in third or fourth grade, was left alone, utterly alone. And she wrote: "Today uncle died. Today Aunt Leka. Today Mama died." You can't bear to read it. This famous diary was even at the Nuremberg Trials as proof of Fascist crimes. But we have a collection of diaries that is comparable to that of Tania Savicheva. We have quite a lot of diaries. Students wrote diaries. Very ordinary people. And it is very strange, that during a siege people would write. . . . Thanks to these sources, our exhibits have taken on different characteristics. . . . Right now I am keeping a diary, it is a diary of perestroika. But in fifty years this diary will acquire a different meaning. And that's exactly what happened here. Many things that no one attributed any significance to in those days now have acquired great value. Especially manuscripts. For instance, a young girl writes: "Mama dear, why have you left me?" No one knew that there would be a siege. No one thought that there would be a war. And if a war did occur, then it would be short. And if

172

there were a war, then it wouldn't be on the territory of the Soviet Union, but beyond its borders. And therefore people were absolutely unprepared for war, because our communist propaganda, although it was primitive, was still effective. It worked. Mass propaganda always reaches the people quickly and spreads quickly among them. And people were so patriotic.

∽

While Ol'ga Markhaeva was being interviewed, a staff assistant entered her office and led in Ol'ga Anatol'evna Trapitsina-Matveenko, a former chemist, whom she had called without our knowledge and urged to come right away to the Museum. Ol'ga Anatol'evna was only one of the Siege survivors this staff assistant was eager to have us talk to. This was not an uncommon occurrence— that knowledge of our project solicited an immediate response and unsolicited interviews. Our talk with Ol'ga Anatol'evna is, then, an impromptu interview within an interview.

Although Ol'ga Anatol'evna spoke generally with reserve, two memories brought her immediately to tears. More than fifty years later, it was still agonizing for her to recall how her grandmother's corpse, which the family had dragged downstairs with great difficulty and had hoped to bury the following day, was cannibalized in the courtyard overnight. And that her beloved father accused her of "stealing" their bread and hit her when she returned with the family ration that was missing a small piece of crust.

When the fire broke out in our building, I was sleeping. My sister Zhenia was by the wall, and I was by the stove. Suddenly they started pounding on our door. It was about 6:00 in the morning. And Papa said: "Who's knocking like that, like there's a fire?" And that's what it was. Who was knocking, I don't know. We got up, Zhenia and I. Papa no longer could walk. And you know why they didn't take him into the army? He was sent to Novgorod. He worked there as a public prosecutor. And we lived there too. But when the "terror," as it's called, began in '36, Papa was expelled from the party. And his friend who worked there as a party secretary, he was simply shot, and his wife was exiled.

I don't remember anymore what Papa dragged downstairs. It was the third floor, and I was going upstairs, and my legs were like rags. It was dark, and I was going upstairs, recalling where everything was. And I grabbed something and carried it downstairs, and all I was thinking was: "Don't forget your sister's blue skirt and blouse." Her boyfriend had given it to her. And what else? Silver, glass-holders (*podstakanniki*)—I didn't think about

173

them. And just then one of our political activists came in with some man and said: "Here are the trunks. Save them." And Grandmother had told us earlier: "Now if we're bombed, put all the silver and clothes into that sack there. And there I stood, but there was no way I could lift that sack. That man took a trunk in one hand and the sack in another and left, and I followed. And when we had come down, he said: "I'm tired." And I said: "OK, when you've rested, put the trunk by that man over there" (it was Papa). When I got to Papa, I turned around—the trunk was still there, but the man and our sack were gone.

I remember the siege all the time. After I had retired, I worked as a cleaning woman in a bookstore, and the director and I had a good relationship. Well, I'm conscientious and neat. And so I read in the TV guide that *Book of the Blockade* had come out. The next day I said: "Sergei Timofeevich, do we have *Book of the Blockade*?" And he said: "You've got to be kidding, Ol'ga Anatol'evna, it's gone" (that is, sold out). But he knew I was a siege survivor [*blokadnitsa*], so he called one director, then a second, then a third, and in that way managed to get me that book. It was a gift from him. It cost three rubles. As soon as I read it, I took it to my sister. I was shaken by the diary of Yura Riabinkin. And the next day my sister said: "The book upsets me very much. I can't think about it. I'm not going to read anymore."

I often go to our old house. I look at the windows. But my sister says: "Whatever happened—there was good and bad—you can't return to the past." Well, that's a controversial question. Many treat the siege survivors badly. Is it some kind of envy?

Translated by Cynthia Simmons

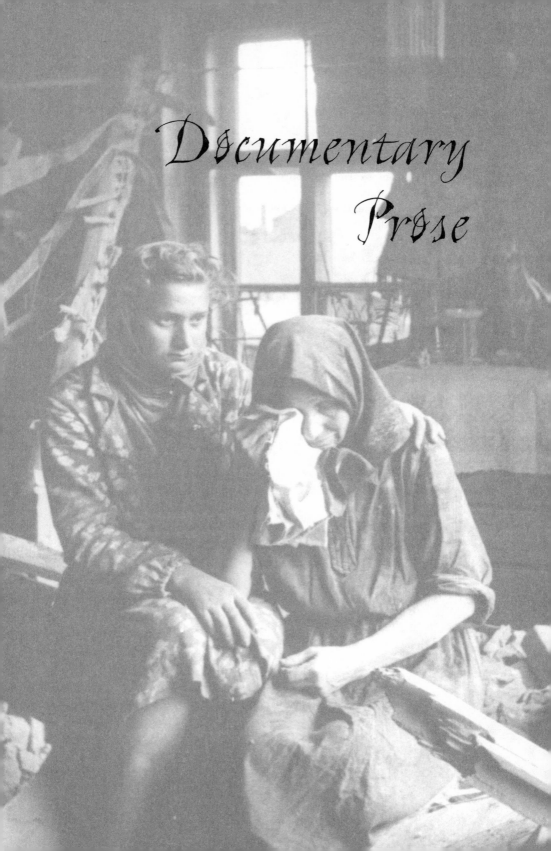

Documentary
Prose

Some women conveyed or recalled their experience of the Siege in artistic forms and autobiographical fictions. We gathered the works of documentary prose that follow from a variety of sources. When available, we have provided background information about the author. For other works that we selected from the literature of the Siege, we know nothing more about the author than what she has suggested therein.

GRAVE MONTHS FOR THE BLOCKADED CITY
(excerpts)

Elena Oskarovna Martilla, theater artist, set designer, and instructor of painting at the studios of the Pedagogical Institute and the City Palaces of Culture,
became fascinated by art while still a child. In 1934, her drawings received
awards at the All-Russian Competition in children's drawings, and she was accepted into the school for gifted youth at the Academy of Art. Unfortunately, fate
had something else in store for her.

The war began six days after Elena Martilla came of age. As did many girls
her age in Leningrad, she enlisted in a civil-defense unit; later, along with her
former classmates, she went to work as a nurse's aid in the Krupskaia Hospital
on Vasil'evskii Island. In 1941 a shell hit the house in which her family lived, and
Martilla, along with her mother, Evdokiia Vasil'evna Mishina, their neighbor Zinaida Yafarova and her two children, moved to a small ten-meter room on
Vasil'evskii Island. Martilla's father was then living in the barracks at work, but
sometimes he visited his family and brought a little food from his military ration. As Martilla recalls: "You might say I grew up and became responsible for
others. Due to shellshock, Mama turned into a helpless child—she couldn't
dress herself, feared everything, spoke in a whisper. Then I had a revelation. I
informed Mother that for the time being I would become the mother, and she
my daughter. I would run things. From her look of gratitude, I understood that
she not only agreed, but was even glad."[1] Martilla served as the "elder," even
among her former classmates and their families. In November 1941 she entered
the only remaining art school in the city, on Tavricheskaia Street, No. 35.[2] The
director of the institute, Jan Konstantinovich Shablovskii, whom Martilla always
recalled with warmth, managed to have the students assigned to the cafeteria of
the Tavricheskii Palace and later was able to organize a cafeteria for the students right in the institute. Martilla remembers that her teacher told them more
than once: "Look around! Look around! You must tell people about this!" From the
fall of 1941 to April 1942, Martilla painted numerous portraits (among them, the
portraits of the painting instructors Ekaterina Ognevaia and Ja. K. Shablovskii)
and produced a series of sketches of besieged Leningrad. On 12 April 1942,
Martilla and the Yafarov family left the city on the "Road of Life," by way of the

177

Kobon station to Riazan', and then on to Moldavia, the native territory of Zina Yaforova.

Martilla's drawings were preserved, and in 1991 they were shown at an exhibit in Berlin entitled "What We Endured" (*O perezhitom*). As she recalls: "The very first question was how do I feel about Germans. I answered: 'There are Fascists, and there are people who aren't Fascists. For Fascists of any nationality I have negative feelings. Toward people of all nationalities I feel positively.' I remember an old man. He came up to me and with sadness in his voice told me that his father had died at the Leningrad front. I answered, with emotion, 'My deepest sympathies.'"[3]

The excerpts that follow are preserved in the Museum of the Defense of Leningrad. They demonstrate how Martilla in her later life used her own diary, written when she was eighteen, to recall and slightly refashion the formative events of the Siege. An excerpt of Martilla's documentarty prose is presented here, and is followed by the diary entries which informed it.

Winter 1942

Leningrad is under siege. January, February, and March are the most deadly months. Death has reaped an immense harvest on Leningrad's frozen streets, singed by severe frost.

Silence. Not a sight to be seen, not a rustle to be heard, not the sound of cars, nor steps.

A magnificent tragic silence. (Such as I have never experienced, as if you have been lowered deep into a well, the shaft filled up with earth and everyone has gone far away for a long time. Terribly quiet.) And like a single distant and weak but living pulsation: tic!. . . tic!. . . tic!. ., like the pulse of a fatally ill patient in the silence of a ward, the radio reverberates in the hearts of those awaiting a miracle—recovery—no, death. Hopes. Valia Ermolaeva is dead. The neighbors in apartment 74 are dead. Fima Efimova's son and many more are dead. Especially men and boys.

A shell fell on our apartment house, Number 19, on the Eighteenth Line of Vasil'evskii Island. The windows and doors gape, fragments have wounded all the furniture. We remained intact by chance. We all moved over to the apartment of friends in the same building. We all huddled as closely as possible. Seven of us lived together and from then on endured the rest together. We were based in the kitchen, since there were no windows there—it was warmer and there was less danger that fragments would fly in. But there was no protection from a direct hit. No sooner had we settled in than a bomb hit and destroyed everything. I was on my way home and near the house heard one person tell another: "A bomb has hit the seventh floor of Number 19." I could not walk up the stairs, I crawled on all fours and howled in horror that all those dearest to me had perished; we lived on the seventh floor. From above two neighbors descended and seeing me waved their arms and said, "They're alive, alive, alive!" I sat down on the stairs and started crying bitterly, from joy. My legs couldn't move.

Then we had to drag ourselves to some other friends (now our hapless relatives). It was forty below. Ten days later the same misfortune befell us there. In January, having gathered the residents who had lost their apartments, we went to my father who was put up in a barracks at his place of work on Volkhov Lane. In a ten-meter room all the victims and vagabonds found shelter—at times there were nine of us. But we had it good there, it was warm. Then many began to stay the night at their workplace or with someone who lived closer to work. Ol'ga Unuchek, Zina Yafarova, Nikolai Lepintsev. . . . In February I sometimes walked through the whole city to the Leningrad School of the Arts. Walking was the only means of travel. The weak and corpses were transported on children's sleds.

I walked along alleyways as far as the university, then descended onto the ice by the Strelka at Vasil'evskii Island; from there on the ice to the Field of Mars, across the field to Swan Bridge, farther along Pestel Street across Liteinyi Avenue and along Peter Lavrov Street to the Tauride Garden, and from there along the gratings to Tauride Street and an even longer gate . . . to Number 35. The School of the Arts. Along the way I met more dead than living—ten dead for every five alive. Some had been felled by hunger; others by shrapnel from shells and bombs. . . . At one point in February I understood that I wouldn't make it until morning; were I to lie down, I would no longer be able to get up (I had already been having fainting spells two to four times a day). I didn't dare lie down and that was that. And how bitter I became: I'm a young woman and I'm forced to be snuffed out in my bed as if my life were worth nothing . . . Bah! Says who? That Fascist Hitler! And not in battle, but in my bed. . . . I'll die, but at least it will be like an artist with a brush in my hands—that's how I calmed myself down and felt stronger, because I was no longer sniveling. I took out a piece of paper, some blue paint and a brush and looking at myself in a little mirror, I decided to paint what I saw. The wick glimmered weakly, but I was carried away and didn't want to think of death, I was my own model, and I kept painting. Maybe in the future people will understand that Leningraders didn't give up so easily. As I wielded my brush, the night passed. Suddenly raising my eyes, I saw a weak light through the cracks of the curtain in the window—morning. The morning of a day I had not expected to see. I was victorious. I had overcome death and had not succumbed to Hitler's order —to exterminate all Leningraders.[4]

This morning I saw through death and realized that I will not die. I will live—this I felt with every cell of my dystrophic organism and it infused me with strength. Now I had caught my second wind, no, my tenth.

I even became happy and . . . calm.

From Elena Martilla's Diary 1941–1942

FEBRUARY

Received coupons for February, can I make it to March? Can I really submit to these wretches? Lie down and die? It's painful to sit, difficult to walk. But I walk with a cane. I saw Beyer at the Young Viewers Theater, he's in a bad way. People call me grandma.

FEBRUARY 1942

Last night I drew myself in a mirror—to keep me from lying down, because then I wouldn't get up. . . . Now I'm afraid of nothing and no one's afraid.

I often have fainting spells, but it's nothing, it's from hunger.

Olga's husband, Pavel, has returned—it's a miracle! They've reconciled.

Aunt Dora has some kind of visions, as if someone were strangling her. I bring her bread and boiled water. Sometimes I buy firewood at the market.

FEBRUARY

In school it was bad. No classes, we simply warmed ourselves in the office. They gave us a soufflé of who knows what, you could chew it but you couldn't get it down. Hardly made it home. All the way I set up points for me to rest, but it's impossible to sit down. I got my bread on the corner of Kirochnaia and Chernyshevsky Streets, and put little pieces in my cheek and wouldn't swallow them until a certain corner, bridge, street.

FEBRUARY

Papa got hold of a briquette of dried peas—paradise! The soup is very filling. That is all we would need for everything to be all right. How can Papa bear to share it with us?

MARCH 1942

Zina's petitioning for evacuation with the kindergarten children and is trying to persuade us to do the same. I don't want to, the city and I are together forever.

MARCH

I was at school, and very few kids came for their ration tickets, maybe they'll come tomorrow. And on the way there, I saw more dead than living.

When I was walking home, I met Zoia and Raia. Zoia's face is so made up, it's terrible. (It's dark at home and there's no place for her to wash.) Jan K[onstantinovich Shablovskii] advises me to evacuate.

MARCH

When I eat *olifa* I faint less.[5] Mother's like an eighty-year-old woman. In line someone called me "grandmother." I'm walking with a cane.

MARCH

Someone came to our family from the front and gave Papa a briquette of wheat and one of dried peas. And also two little fish—*voblia*. For the third time Mama has boiled the bones in a little piece of cheese cloth for soup and the smell is everywhere. We still have it better than others since in the apartment the oven is lit and we're allowed to cook. In our room it's usually warm since we heat the stove (with shelves, school desks, etc., that I broke up in school). At times I can exchange cigarettes for little bundles of firewood (Papa doesn't smoke and sometimes a pack is given out for ration coupons).

APRIL

In school there was a proclamation about the city clean-up of filth and debris. Raia, some other girls, and I were in neighboring courtyards and cut ice and dragged it out on plywood. . . . We got very little done. The little ax which I now wear all the time on my belt helped me, actually it's on a rope which I use to belt my [sheepskin] jacket. [. . .]

181

6 APRIL

Zina took some children for the evacuation; they're staying with us.

I was at Koze's, you can't imagine a more terrible picture: Roza Markovna sat at the table in a cold dark room and, with her arms and clenched fists on the table, she howled! Like an animal—people don't shout that way. She howled!

Marik and Izia, both dead, are lying right there, so long and skinny (they're fifteen), but there's no Koze . . . what happened to her, it's terrible to say . . . arrested for nonappearance at the Tenants Cooperative Association's clean-up post. I want to howl, how can R. M. survive such a thing? How can I help?

8 APRIL

I was at the TCA [Tenants Cooperative Association] on the Eighteenth Line and got an evacuation form. It was approved at the Regional Executive Committee, but I don't believe I'll be leaving. How can I leave my hometown? It can live without me, but I can't live without it . . . .

And what about Mama? The children—they'll perish.

10 APRIL 1942

I was at school. Jan K. ordered me to go. He says that despite his efforts, the Leningrad School of the Arts can't be evacuated, the city won't get to us. He gave me a form.

Translated by Arlene Forman

"To the People"

Lidiia Razumovskaia was born into a happy and nurturing family. Her mother was dedicated to the three children: in addition to Razumovskaia, her older sister, Mirra Samsonovna, who became a teacher of literature, and her brother, Lev Samsonovich. She recalled that her mother would say: "I have three five-year plans," because the children were each born five years apart. Her father, Samson L'vovich Razumovskii, was an engineer and designed the renovated sewer system in Leningrad.

Razumovskaia was a good student and studied in the Russian Department at the university for three years. Her professors included Gukovskii, Propp, Riftin, and Piksanov. During the Finnish War, she worked as a volunteer at the Otto Clinic. Then World War II broke out. Razumovskaia remembers that after hearing Molotov's speech on 22 June 1941, she rushed to the university. There she and her friends were enlisted to deliver draft notices: "The rest of the day and all night we entered the apartments of strangers and called them to war. Many had gone to volunteer before we arrived. Some came along with us. In every home there were tears." The following day they entered the university auditorium—her professor of Western European literature was there, and they took their exam. "After the exam, we went to a wedding party. Yes, Ira and Sergei had come to the exam straight from the Registry Office. The next day Sergei was leaving for the front. Later I read a lot about such weddings, they were shown in films, but just then I was shocked. My girlfriend's eyes were filled with such despair, the young husband spasmodically clutched her hand. It was such a mournful wedding."[6]

During the war Razumovskaia worked in a military hospital in Leningrad and then in a field hospital in Eastern Prussia, on the border with Poland. In the difficult years after the war, she worked in a publishing house and continued to study for her undergraduate degree at night. She completed her degree in 1948, but the birth of her son kept her from entering graduate school. Later she applied to a literary institute and submitted a paper she had written on Tvardovskii. When she went for the entrance exam, a professor accused her of "advertising Cosmopolitans"—the names of Danin and Andrei Redzhiev appeared in her bibliography, and they had only recently been denounced. Thus ended her hopes for graduate school. She went on to teach at the elementary level.

Razumovskaia wrote her memoir forty years after the war. At the fifty-year reunion of the class of 1938 (the year Razumovskaia entered the university), she read some entries to her former classmates, and someone recommended she show the memoir to Dina Isaevna Dikman at the publishing house Sovetskii pisatel'. As with her attempts to earn an advanced degree, her attempts to publish always came up against some obstacle. At Sovetskii pisatel', for example, one of the three readers delivered a negative report. That reviewer stated: "All of this is just about herself, there is no background."

Razumovskaia was married in 1948. She celebrated her golden anniversary in Israel. That is where her daughter lives with her husband and two daughters. Her son lives in St. Petersburg with his wife and Razumovskaia's two grandsons.

Razumovskaia's fictionalized memoir, "To the People," is held in the Museum of the Defense of Leningrad.

At the end of January 1942 a boy named Alesha appeared at our hospital— "son of the regiment" we called him.

We found him early in the morning by the entrance. When the hospital attendants went to work they discovered the child, stiff from cold. They thought he was dead, but he was still breathing. They easily picked him up and carried him in their arms.

"He weighed almost nothing—a real dystrophy patient," said Marusia through tears; she was the first to notice the boy. We brought him to our ward, warmed him, put him on an IV. He lay there very skinny, not merely pale but completely bluish white, and indifferent to everything. Slowly and carefully we started to feed him. At first he didn't even react at all to food. He lay turned to the wall and was quiet. Then, after he pulled himself together a little, he told us that his mama and papa were at the front and his grandmother had died. He said this and for the first time started to cry. Through tears and sniffling we listened, how before she died, his grandmother ordered him to go to the people.

"And so I went."

"But how did you find out that our hospital was here?" we asked in amazement.

184

"I don't know. I just walked and walked. In the morning I left my house on the Second Line and kept walking. I don't remember how far, and on the corner of Nevskii and Sadovaia, I fell. Some old man with a cane picked me up, stood me on my feet, and asked, 'Can you walk?' I said, 'It seems I can, I just need to hold on to something.' 'Well, hold on to the walls as you walk. There's a hospital near here, in the courtyard.'"

Alesha was quiet for a while. It was clear he was remembering his difficult journey. Then, as if summing up what had been said, he said, "That's how I got here."

"Alesha, what about the neighbors in your building? Why didn't you turn to them? Why, you must have known people in your building, didn't you?"

"There was no one left. Some of them were evacuated, and those who stayed all died," Alesha said somberly. We were all quiet for a while.

Soon Alesha Korolkov became everyone's favorite. We all tried to fatten him up, be nice to him, do something pleasant for him.

Little pieces of bread, little packs of sugar cubes, a few raisins—that's what we each could spare from our own meager rations. And we brought these priceless gifts with pleasure, although we ourselves were just barely staying on our feet from hunger. Kira pampered Alesha more than anyone else. Always sad, she smiled when she saw the little boy, and somehow he too singled her out from the rest of us immediately, and reached out to her with his child's heart.

When Alesha called her Mama-Kira for the first time, we couldn't help smiling. It seemed funny and strange to us. Kira wasn't even twenty, and it turned out Alesha was already nine. Then we got used to it and when the little boy would ask, "Where's Mama-Kira?" we would readily tell him what she was doing at the moment.

One evening at the dormitory Kira said that she wanted to take Alesha home with her.

"What do you mean, home with you?" Galia asked in amazement. "I don't quite understand you."

"What's not to understand? I'm taking him home as my son and we will live together."

"He has parents."

"Well, if his parents return, what's the problem? Of course he will go back to them. But if not? Sasha and I will raise him."

I raised my eyebrows in surprise. What was she talking about? What was with her? Sasha was not alive! Hadn't we received his death certificate not long ago?

"Why are you looking at me like that?" Kira said with irritation. "Can you really believe every little piece of paper? Sashka is alive—alive! My heart feels that he is alive."

"And what if Sasha doesn't want Alesha to live with you?" asked Galia.

Kira's eyes became completely round.

"How could he not want it?" She asked incredulously.

"Well, just like that. Doesn't love him, doesn't want him."

"That couldn't be, that could never be. You don't know Sasha."

Kira was so convinced that it was pointless to argue with her. She was always a maximalist, our Kira. If she loved, it was for life. If she was your friend, she would sacrifice everything for you. If she worked, she would sweat her guts out, without a rest.

"Kira, why aren't you getting some sleep? Your shift ended two hours ago already."

"Oh, girls, Petrov asked me to write a letter for him."

"Kira! Why are you so pale? Are you sick?"

"Oh, girls, I couldn't leave the ward, and I missed dinner again." And this during the siege! And always, without fail. True, we all were like that, but Kira had this special strength.

When Alesha was discharged from the hospital, Kira organized a tea party to celebrate. Each one of us received a big mug of boiling hot water and a tiny piece of bread sprinkled with granulated sugar—the so-called "blockade pastries."

Now Alesha was constantly with us. At night he would sleep on my bed, as Kira and I worked shifts. During the day he would help the nurses—distributing thermometers, going with us to the pharmacy for medicine, and chatting with the sick and wounded. The patients loved him and treated him just like we did. The presents he received covered the bedside table. Sometimes I would find some pink soapdish or little handmade knife under the pillow.

"Alesha! Where did this come from?"

"Oh, Uncle Petia gave it to me."

All of us at the hospital were like his uncles and aunts. Dressed in his little white doctor's robe, which we had combined our efforts to tailor for him, he looked so cute that you couldn't look at him without smiling. Alesha was included on the hospital roster and went with us to the cafeteria. It took great effort on our part to talk him into taking off the robe, even only for

186

the dinner break. That's how our little favorite lived with us, our "son of the regiment."

Alesha didn't mention his parents often. But sometimes at night he would cry, and it was clear that he was dreaming about his mama.

Once a week one of us would set out for the Second Line of Vasil'evskii Island, where Alesha had lived. The walk there was long, hard, and cold, but we would go without complaint. We all took turns—no one forced us to drag ourselves around the ice-cold city from Sadovaia to the Second Line after our daily duties. We needed to do it for Alesha. But there was still no sign of any letters. Then the house disappeared—it was destroyed by a bomb, and our trips ended.

Toward summer Alesha got healthier and put on some more weight. His little face became rounder. He no longer resembled a little old man, but simply a very thin and pale boy. We gave him coniferous pine extract to drink—the whole city drank it to prevent scurvy. All day long he would crunch cabbage and carrots from our supplementary vegetable garden. We ordered an army uniform for Alesha at the workshop. So then he wore a soldier's shirt and boots. On his head he wore an officer's service cap. True, it constantly fell down over his eyes because the right size could not be found, but Alesha was happy.

As before, he wouldn't part with Kira.

"Mama-Kira," he would say, "when Mama and Papa return we will all live together—me, you, Mama, Papa, and Uncle Sasha."

Alesha did not know that his mama and papa were not going to return —they both had died at the front.

Rushing ahead, I will tell you that Kira and Sasha adopted and raised Alesha. Now they fuss over grandchildren—Alesha's children. They all live together as a big, happy family.

Alesha's grandmother was right when she sent her grandson to THE PEOPLE.

Translated by Katherine Hardin Currie

COLD SUN: STORIES

Cold Sun: Stories **was published at the author's expense. The following synopsis appears on the copyright page:**

> The trilogy *Cold Sun* brings together stories that document the tragic valor of Leningraders in the cruel days of the Blockade, difficult wanderings in evacuation, and the uneasy return home.
>
> Through the psychology and perspective of a child and [her] simple, clear language, the reader discovers the complexity of human relations in the inhumane conditions of a war for survival. Everything in the narrative is true—everything was experienced by the author herself. The book can also be considered as documentation of the inordinate trials that befell children, people's courage and readiness for self-sacrifice in the name of victory, truth, and goodness.

Excerpts are taken from the title story, "Cold Sun." It is narrated by a young girl, Stasia Yasnitskaia, with interpolated radio announcements.

Kholodnoe solntse: Povesti (Cold Sun: Stories). St. Petersburg: LIO Redaktor, 1992.

Radio: "A regulation from the Department of Trade of the Leningrad City Executive Committee (*Lengorispolkom*). The Department of the Executive Committee of the Leningrad City Soviet announces from 12 September 1941 a reduction in the bread ration: blue-collar workers and technicians—500 gr. per day, white-collar workers and children under 12—300 gr. per day, dependents—250 gr. of bread per day."[7]

—Lenechka, it's you!—Grandma's voice is heard from the hallway.

—Yes, just imagine, in person, dear Anna Aleksandrovna! They let me out of the barracks for a cultural excursion to the Philharmonic.

—You're going to the Philharmonic!?

—Yes, to a concert of Lev Oborin.[8]

—That's wonderful!

—And where's my beloved wife?

—She'll be right back. She went to the store to buy food for the next ten days. We've somehow run low . . . we've eaten all our reserves. And what reserves did we have!? We haven't had any for ages.

—What do you mean we haven't?! What about the expedition for potatoes?

—We ate them all. There aren't any.

—How can't there be any potatoes? What did you do with them all?

—Well, after all, there was quite a horde living with us—they cleaned out everything right down to the rusks, and then since we had nothing left, they went back home. It turned out that it wasn't so relaxing here, it's dangerous . . . Right!

—Well . . .

—Papa shrugged his shoulders and he and Grandma looked at each other and laughed.

—And how are you doing, sweetheart?—Papa asked while he stroked Stasia's cheek and looked into her eyes.

—I'm doing fine.

—What's keeping you busy?

—Sand bags, a bomb shelter.

—Oh, so much to do. And here's one more thing,—and Papa pulls out a book on which is written: Mark Twain, *The Prince and the Pauper*.

—Oh, Daddy, thank you!—Stasia kisses him.

—And what else did Mark Twain write. Do you know?

—About Tom Sawyer, right?

—That's right, good for you! And how's the piano here getting along without me?

—Not well. It misses you.

—Really?—Papa sits down and pensively runs his fingers over the keys, as if caressing them.

Stasia took a place nearby on a little bench. Her chin propped on her fist, she was completely carried away by the amazing sounds flying out from under her papa's big, kind hands. But then the sounds became disturbing, appealing somewhere, demanding something, and even frightening. Stasia shrank back and became all tense. . . . But then exultant, victorious chords   189
were struck, and they straightened her up and let her breathe freely.

—That, Yason'ka, is the German composer Beethoven.

—A Fascist?!—Stasia exclaimed, horrified.

—No, Yason'ka, not all Germans are Fascists. Here, listen!—He started to play and to sing: "*Po raznym stranam ya khodil . . .*"[9]

—"*I moi suro-ok so mnoi.*"—Stasia took up the tune.

—"*Podaite groshik, ya-a odin . . .*"

—"*I moi suro-ok so mnoi,*"—they sang together.

—Who wrote that?

—Beethoven?

—That's right. And then there's Bach . . . do you remember?—Papa played the familiar chords of a fugue.—They're all Germans, great Germans! And then there's Ernst Thälmann; do you remember, I told you about him?[10]

—Uh-huh,—Stasia nodded.

—And Ernst Busch! Do you remember, he sang in Spain! "Arise, the Party is in danger!" Papa sang "The March of the Swamp Soldiers."[11] Remember, Yason'ka, there are no bad nations. There aren't! Remember! But in each nation there are good people and bad people.

—And are there bad Russians?—Stasia asked in surprise.

—Of course there are. And what's so special about us that we would have only good people?

∞

The following scene takes place on the national holiday commemorating the October Revolution.

Already yesterday Mama and Papa decided to visit Grandma Vera and Aunt Zosia. Mama put on a black dress with intricate, cream-colored lace, Stasia a dark-blue dress with a white braided collar, Papa a white shirt and a new tie. All dressed-up for the holiday, they left home and took a tram from the Palace Bridge for the Petrograd side.

—Lenik, dear brother!

—Zokha, sweet sister!

—My dear boy! Oh! *Dobrze*! ([It's] good [to see you]—Polish)

—Happy Holiday, Mama dear!

—Stasia, Nina! How nice you've come!

They hugged for a long time, for a long time looked at each other. Once Stasia and Varia linked arms, they would not let each other go.

—I've already grown some fringe,—Varia stroked her head,—but you haven't.

—No. Just right here a little bit,—she pulled at a little forelock.

Four months had already passed since they had had their heads shaved like little boys before the evacuation had begun, and the hair just would not grow back.

—And do you remember how we hid the roll under the burdock?

—Uh-huh. Wouldn't it be nice to have it now?

—And do you remember the porridge they gave us at the station, all covered in butter?

—And do you remember the wild strawberries? To have them now! And Uncle Lenechka just couldn't make us eat them . . .

—And where's Polia?

—She's in Perm with the ballet school.

—And do they bomb you a lot here?

—A lot. And they fire at us too.

—Us, too. . . . But do you know the song "The Blue Shawl"?[12]

—No-o.

—On the twenty-second of June, exactly at four o'clock, they bombed Kiev, they announced that the war had begun.[13]

—*Proszę, pane* (Please, ladies [*panie*—Polish])! Let's celebrate our holiday,—Grandma Vera called out.

—Vera Adamovna, here, we've brought our share: bread, sea biscuits, saccharine for the tea.

—*Dziękuję*, (Thank you—Polish), Ninochka, thank you. Sit down, *Proszę*.

Into the bowls Grandma Vera poured real soup, prepared from canned fish and rice.

—Well, you've made a dinner fit for a king, exclaimed Mama, and Grandma Vera blushed with delight.

Everyone ate without hurry, savoring it, for if you eat in a hurry, you won't really feel it.

—Let's have a drink of my homemade bilberry liqueur, saved especially for this day—Grandma poured everyone half a liqueur glass.—I think that under these circumstances, we can pour the children some. What do you think?

—Of course you should pour them some; it's nutritious.

191

—My dear ones,—Papa stood up, and everyone else along with him,— we have only one toast: to victory!

Stasia and Varia followed everyone and took a sip from the tiny liqueur glasses—it was tasty, like jam, only it had a bite.

—And do you know that there was a parade today in Moscow?—Aunt Zosia asked.—They reported it on the radio.

—That was probably after we had left. So today in Moscow there was still a parade! Yes, that was a great political statement!

—The Germans must be furious!

Grandma Vera remained standing, looked around the room, and said quietly:

—Children, let's drink the last sip for Narten'ka . . . . He's somewhere out there . . .

—Yes!—Papa went up to Grandma and hugged her—To Nartik! I believe, I believe, Mama, that it's a mistake. When this mess is all over . . . when the war ends . . . everything . . . everything will get straightened out! Only now . . . now . . . now is not the time for that.[14]

—Yes, Lenik, yes . . . —Grandma whispered and wiped her eyes.

Papa blinked back tears, Aunt Zosia quickly went into the other room, Mama blew her nose in her handkerchief.

—Here, I have a present for you,—Aunt Zosia said, returning, and holding out a small iron stove.

—Good Lord, Zokha, how did you get your hands on a *burzhuika*? We've been killing ourselves—we haven't gotten one.

—They make them at our factory.

—Thank you so much, Zosen'ka! It's the best gift possible!

—And how is it here—have they been pounding away at you?

—Well, you probably saw on your way here—the second building over is destroyed, and on the corner of Vvedenskaia . . .[15] A lot, an awful lot . . . And how about your place?

—Well, yesterday a delayed-action bomb fell on our building. Today they dug it out, disarmed it, and there was a message [in it] in Russian: "We do what we can to help!"

—That's interesting. Who was it?

—Friends . . . We have friends everywhere! Not all Germans are Fascists . . . Don't forget, there were, and are, Thälmann, Busch, Marx, Goethe, Beethoven . . . We have to remember that!

—You're right, Lenia! Right!

Translated by Cynthia Simmons

"Sweet Earth"

"Sweet Earth" is held in the Museum of the Defense of Leningrad.

At the start of the war the mother would come home from work later and later to feed her little girl and then immediately would go to bed. The little girl was alone all day, locked inside with no one to talk to, save her doll Katia, and she could only watch passers-by from the window. The window was almost even with the roadway; across the fence was the garden of the Karl Marx Hospital. The German air-raid attack began late at night while the tired city slept. The little girl did not wake her mother; she listened to what was happening outside. But the explosions came nearer and nearer, something beyond the wall began to rumble, then thundered loudly, and outside the window it became very bright. That night the city was bombarded by incendiaries. But the little girl didn't know that, she was only six years old. Outside her window the whole street shone with a crimson light. The girl began to shake her mother by the shoulder, "Mama, Mama, look how beautiful it is!" Her mother awoke, scooped her daughter together with her bedding up into her arms and ran outdoors.

Outside a fire raged. By the building's blind wall, wooden sheds were burning. The garage by the Samson Bridge was on fire. The Vyborg side was aflame. The whole city was ablaze. Across the entire city the sky had turned pink. Suddenly something in the shed exploded and burning boards flew out in all directions. One of them struck the little girl a glancing blow, leaving a deep cut on her forehead and her right cheek. In a nearby hospital she was given stitches and some good-natured teasing: "Don't cry, it will all be gone by your wedding day."

The sheds had almost burnt down, and mother and daughter returned to their basement apartment on Orenburg Street. Once again, the little girl was alone each and every day; only in the evenings did her mother come from work. New food appeared for the little girl—sweet earth. It was ashes

193

and dirt from the fire at the Badaev Warehouses. Mother brought the sweet earth home up until the freezing temperatures set in. At first she did so by instinct; then later by plan: the city's starvation from the blockade had begun.

"I will make it through the winter." Fewer and fewer things remained in the room. The round stove in the corner devoured much wooden furniture, so from a cauldron and a bucket the mother fashioned a makeshift heater in which, on tiptoe, the girl could boil water and heat the room. Each time on her way home the mother would peer into her window with fear. . . . Her daughter was alive. Her little girl!

The girl would hear her mother's footsteps from afar and would crawl to the window. How much joy there was in these mother and daughter reunions, for war and hunger were all around. They were two old women, grown wise through their experience of war. The mother wore a quilted jacket, quilted pants, and a gray kerchief. Her wrinkled face resembled a skull with living eyes. The daughter, in a hood, warm coat, and felt boots, had bleeding gums, a wrinkled face, and everything else that goes along with dystrophy and scurvy. Yet despite everything, they were two individuals.

"It's all right, dear, we'll make it through the winter," the mother would say every time. "We'll make it through," the daughter would echo and they would tell each other about the events that had occurred in the day or two since they had last seen each other. For the most part, it was the mother who spoke, while scrounging about for kindling for the stove; the little girl would suck on the last centimeter-sized cube of bread as if it were candy. She would listen and wait for the water to boil and for her mama to give her bread. Maybe mama would give her soy cereal or soy milk for dessert. The mother would report that a high-explosive bomb had hit a building on Astrakhan Street, but did not go off. Inside was a note: "We do what we can to help you."[16] About the ice road and the increase that would come in the bread ration—all this the little girl learned about from her mother. There was no radio at home. The neighbors upstairs had one, but the little girl could not make everything out. The girl would tell her mother how many times they had been bombed, how many big dolls lay covered up by the hospital fence, what the rare passer-by would say outside the window, but she never complained about the cold or her hunger. Toward the end of the winter only the tall iron bed and the heater remained. The little girl was no longer able to stand up and spent all her time in bed, playing in the corner with her doll Katia. More and more often the sun would shine outside her

194

window; the fence and the earth thawed and blades of grass began to appear. "We've made it through the winter," Mother said. She got out her last prewar dress and took it to the bazaar. She returned with a piece of *duranda*, purposefully mixed it up with water and some grass and made patties which she cooked in a dry frying pan. "Oh, how delicious," the girl murmured. "We've made it through the winter," she repeated, echoing her mother. In their district, at Poklonnyi Mountain, overnight kindergartens were set up, providing high-calorie diets. The mother now knew that her little girl would recover.

First grade in Leningrad in 1943. The bombing raids were replaced by shell fire. The mother and her little girl now lived in another building, in a large room with a balcony and green grass in the courtyard. The girl had started first grade. School would take place in a bomb shelter more often than in a classroom. Of course, you had to run to school under the fire of artillery shells. That fall was sunny and clear. During one of the air-raid warnings, two first-grade girls ran out of the bomb shelter. They ran into the school courtyard to find out what was in the car that had just arrived. A teacher ran out after them to drive them back into the bomb shelter. At that moment a shell hit the school courtyard. The girls, the teacher, and the driver were all buried in closed coffins. On the walls of School No. 5 pieces of the shell fragments still remain.

Arithmetic came easily to the little girl—she had learned to count during that very hungry winter. She was smallest in the class. Not all of her teachers were pleased by her independence of thought and behavior. The girl was hardly talkative, but she could recall and recite verse well.

The Germans had a bombing routine: early in the morning they would sleep. The mother would leave for work at 5:00 A.M., and the girl would leave for school with her. The little girl did not fear the darkness; she knew that the door to the school bomb shelter in the courtyard was always open. Until the school bell rang she would sleep in the quietest place, in the natural-science classroom in a glass-front cabinet filled with stuffed animals. There it was warm and quiet.

The school observed a strict routine. All tardy pupils were called into the principal's office, and the girls would return to class in tears. So the little girl became clever. She joined her classmates long before the first bell, so no one ever found out about her secret. There was only one time that she did not come to school. This was after the second fire. Her mother was working

195

the night shift from Saturday to Sunday and, as always, the girl was locked in the room. Already at work the mother heard that a fire had broken out on Lesnoi Avenue, on the third floor. Running toward her building, she saw that burnt rags were hanging outside a third-floor window (the window of the room where the girl had been left faced the courtyard), and smoke was coming out of the small window vent, although nothing was destroyed. A twelve-room apartment had been divided into three apartments by partitions. The apartment with windows facing the street had gone up in flames, but all the partitions were intact. The firemen were told that a little girl was locked in one of the apartments. The whole room was filled with smoke and only with difficulty did they find the little girl. With a blanket thrown over her head, she was standing by the balcony door. She had pulled out the quilting that had caulked up the door and was breathing in the air from the street. She suffered a very mild case of smoke inhalation. At the neighbors' the mother found the little girl quite well, but the doctor had given her a release from school for one day. After that, her mother left the little girl with keys to the room and the apartment.

Bombing raids grew less frequent. Suddenly one day cannons began to roar so closely that the mother and daughter ran to the bomb shelter, but no one was there. Everyone was standing on the street looking at the illuminated sky. It was fireworks saluting the lifting of the blockade.

Translated by Arlene Forman

"Blockade Lullaby"

From *Blokadnaia tetrad'* (Blockade Notebook). Leningrad, 1990.

—Sleep, dear son, while there's no bombing . . .
—And Mama, will you cook me some barley?
—Now sleep, my dear son, I'll cook it . . .
—But Mama, where is that barley I didn't eat, before the war?
—The little birds ate it all. Now sleep, my dear . . .
—And where are the little birds now?
—They've flown away to safety . . .
—Let's fly away too . . .
—When we get a letter from Papa, we'll fly away too.
—And does Papa like barley?
—He does. Go to sleep, my dear . . .
—Cook us a lot of barley.
—I will, sweetheart . . .
—Mama, do you like barley too?
—Go to sleep, my dear . . .
—Then cook lots and lots of barley.
—I certainly will . . .
—And Mama, will the war end soon?
—It will end, it will end . . .

Translated by Cynthia Simmons

"Vitamins, or Ode to Grass"

Along with Miliutina's memoir *Evacuation*, in the previous section, this work of poetic prose appears in *By and about Vera Miliutina.*

How agonizing the desire to eat was in the winter of 1941–1942. . . . And as if that was not enough, long distances had to be covered on foot, and because of this life became even harder. In the city's empty streets there sometimes appeared trucks carrying the military. They were coming from the countryside and had pine and spruce branches with them. I would usually pull some tobacco out of my quilted jacket—if the truck stopped, I would offer it to the men in military overcoats: "Comrades! Have you got any twigs? Here is some tobacco for you!" The sailors of the Palace Embankment turned out to be particularly generous. They once tossed me a heap of aromatic pine branches. I gnawed on them all the way home. I totally devoured their tender bark and needles. They were extracting vitamins from the pine needles, and this infusion, I had heard, worked miracles on the starving wounded in the hospitals. But at home we had neither the strength nor the time to cut needles and put them into boiling water. And those twigs and branches had such a wonderful smell of the forest!

Yes, in the spring of 1942, grass was as much our salvation as were glue and leather straps. Those also had to be prepared and then cooked, which required time and . . . fuel. But grass, it was growing everywhere—in the streets, in empty lots. It even poked through cracks in the asphalt.

Questions such as these were asked: "Say, how do you know which grass is edible, and that some grass is not poisonous?" I used to answer: "Well, just eat what you used to nibble in childhood, one blade after another, the taste of which you remember. Just rely on your instinct." The person asking assumed I was reluctant to reveal my secret to him—he had not nibbled any shoots in childhood and so timidly continued to question: "People say you should eat plantain and goose-foot . . ." But I had never eaten either.

V. Miliutina. "The Hanging Garden in the Hermitage (A kitchen garden on the roof)" (*Visiachii sad v Èrmitazhe* [*Ogorod na kryshe*]). The Hermitage's "Hanging Garden," intended as a replica of The Hanging Gardens of Babylon (one of the Seven Wonders of the World), was transformed during the Siege into a common kitchen garden. *The State Hermitage Museum*

As soon as the sun warmed up our devastated and starving Leningrad, green sprouts immediately started forcing their way through all the cracks. There were no more dogs in the city—all of them had been eaten. Children, looking more like old men, were not running around trampling down the grass, and besides, there were so few of them left in the city. The grass kept growing. Grass-plots were dug up; seeds, obtained somehow, were sown. However, real gardens appeared in the city center—the Summer Garden, the Field of Mars—only the following summer, in 1943. They did not last long. Those on the outskirts of the city turned out to be more viable. Years after the war was over, Leningraders could not deny themselves the pleasure of traveling to these plots with spades and planting potatoes there.

But in the spring of 1942, the hunger was unbearable. The sun was shining; yet you were so cold that you could not even think of removing

199

your quilted jacket. . . . Rations were slightly increased, but you never felt full—emaciation had reached inconceivable proportions. Scurvy, vitamin deficiency, boils, pellagra, even blindness—all of these besieged us. The yearning for food was immense; especially for greens!

In the morning, before setting out with two pails to fetch water from neighboring buildings, I could go with scissors and a basket to empty and deserted lots—abandoned trenches or rubble from buildings destroyed by bombs. Or I could simply walk to some quiet street (although by that time all the streets were quiet). In all those places it was easy to cut heaps of new spring chamomile—its fluffy and aromatic little leaves went so well with the tender feather grass, which usually grows in the shade, close to houses. In the past it was used as food for canaries. I made a delicious salad out of it to supplement the morning portion of our bread ration, which we received at five-thirty in the morning in a former bakery lit by two dim kerosene lamps. A portion of this grass and the remnants of the bread ration would be left for an evening meal.

And then there were the sticky little linden leaves of spring! You could eat them, or you could make soup out of them. And the sour leaves of barberries! And shepherd's purse! It says in science books that the latter helps to fight vitamin deficiency and scurvy. But there was not time for studying science books, whereas the feeling of hunger was always present. And my basket was filling up with all kinds of grasses.

How grateful I am to it, my dear, green, fresh, dewy grass! In the years since then, much has gradually disappeared from memory, but the memory of those bright spring mornings will never fade.

—c. 1965, Moscow

Translated by Alla Zeide

THE JOYOUS, THE INIMITABLE . . .

Schastlivoe, nepovtorimoe . . . (The Joyous, the Inimitable). St. Petersburg: Papirus, 1997, excerpts.

"In Urshak"

I'm eight years old. I go to school.

They proudly call us "Leningraders" and [then] add the long, ugly word —evacuees. As for what happened before we arrived in Urshak, I try not to think about it. When they talk about Leningrad, I remember the window in our room, and in the window, like in a picture, roofs. In the narrow aperture there's a sidewalk and people crawling below. The roofs smelled of heated paint, sun, and a calm life. In Urshak the house drew back its walls for me. I don't remember a room in the barracks, where we—the evacuees —lived, but the street.

Our barracks divided the street, like a partition, long and low. In front of the barracks, on both sides of the dusty colorless street, stood two rows of wooden houses. The houses were crowded with women and children. Many children. Along the houses there was a lot of greenery, either large bushes or small trees. That's what they call a street.

The customary silence is broken now and then by a squeaking—someone is getting water from the well. Across the street, old roosters are roaming, and emaciated chickens walk mincingly.

Behind the barracks—a wasteland, an immense world. A river flows there, and there is a forest. Beyond the forest the sun goes down, crimson and so huge that the black forest is silhouetted in it, as in a round fiery frame.

Everything beyond the barracks is different and unknown. Fairy tales live there: Alenushka and Ivanushka walk about, and in the warm swamps the Frog Princess hides.

On the street in front of the barracks life goes on as normal. A little building is stuck to the hill—the mess hall. Every aspect of life in Urshak is saturated with the smells of this mess hall. The smells waft far and wide all over the *sovkhoz* [state farm]. Overcooked cabbage, that looks like the head of a mop, smells like something moldy.

That's what the whole evacuation smells like.

Every day the food is the same—buckwheat with horse meat and cabbage soup. The tough meat hardly reminds me of horses, which I love and stroke behind their warm, firm lips, breathing steam. Horses are one thing, and horse meat is another, it's . . . just a word.

The only reminder of life before the war was a nickel-plated teapot—they carried cabbage soup in it—and the rough feel of a clean, new oil-cloth—they covered the tables with that kind in the kindergarten.

Zabirov

In my eight-year-old world there were important discoveries—the world is huge and limitless, it is not limited by buildings, huge ones, that reach the sky. It is like the field, the forest, the river, that begin beyond the empty plot of land and the garbage pit. And another discovery: the most important profession in the world (after a teacher) is a postman.

In every house, everyone knows him, waits for him, and fears him. The postman can bring a letter from the front and make everyone happy. But the postman can also bring a thin envelope with a sheet folded in two, on which everything is typed, but the name is written in by hand.

In the house where they receive such envelopes, life changes: the children play less, they talk more quietly, and the women put on black scarves and grow even paler. The grown-ups with pity call the children orphans and try to stroke their heads.

This frightening paper doesn't always deliver the truth. The grown-ups talk about this with hope and describe various incidents. I know about one myself.

It was the winter of 1942. In the first house from the school there lived a big family. The small dried-up woman from that house would meet the postman on the road. She often received triangular letters. But we hadn't received any triangular letters from Papa for a long time. Mama was always rereading yellow and gray pages, but they had arrived a long time ago. The grown-ups talked to each other about the hold-ups in the delivery of letters, about how letters can get lost. That's what Auntie Anisa Zabirova must have thought when the postman hurried past her house.

But a letter arrived. In a thin envelope. A death notice. A quick, fussy woman became slow and forgetful. She didn't cry, didn't complain, just looked somewhere off into the distance and probably saw something that wasn't visible to others. The grown-ups went to help the Zabirovs. A young nice-looking girl helped too, Zoia, the sister of our teacher. She was in the tenth grade and seemed to me to be grown up. She was tall, slender, with black hair and blue eyes, and always calm.

We weren't surprised when, during our lesson, Zoia opened the door to our classroom. But when she shouted, "Zabirov is coming!" we made a racket. Zabirov had earned the title of "hero," and after the hospital, he was sent home for a stay with his family. He dispatched a telegram that he was coming.

Lessons were postponed. Everyone got ready for the welcome. On the white snow by the Zabirovs' house stood everyone who lived in the *sovkhoz*. Tapping one foot against the other, stamping their feet, clapping, the women stood, and the kids scurried about. The women were dressed up, and suddenly it turned out that they were young, rosy-cheeked, and knew how to smile. And someone started singing. Only Zabirova herself stood off to the side, frightened, and her eyes were huge and sad. Everyone pestered her and spoke very loudly. Why isn't it like this every day?

When the car carrying Zabirov (he was called a hero) drove up, it was strange—everyone got quiet. A man in uniform got out; he was limping. He made straight for Auntie Anisa, but for some reason stopped, then quickly blinking back tears, moving slowly and uncomfortably, waved his hand. Everyone tried not to look at Auntie Anisa, now come to life and sobbing like a child, who in a moment was at her husband's side. Everyone quietly dispersed so that they could get together in the evening to give him a hero's welcome in the club.

And all the while I thought and wondered—the hero is short and on his sheepskin coat, there isn't any medal . . .

Back in Leningrad, in '46, I learned that Zabirov had been killed in the fall of '44. Again a death notice arrived. This time it was the real thing.

Leningrad

The beginning of June, 1944.

We've been riding in a freight train for eternity. Then—Moscow and more people than I have ever seen in my life. In Moscow we switch trains, and after sleeping through the night, we approach Leningrad.

So this is it—Leningrad . . . a gray, gray station—Moscow Station. A gray sky. A gray sun. Quiet. Mama says, "This is Nevskii Avenue." What kind of avenue—one sailor and a woman with a little bag . . .

The wheels of the wheelbarrow make a thumping sound. The sailor helps us carry our things. I look beneath my feet—huge stone slabs with cracks, and in the cracks, grass. This is a sidewalk. And here's our building. The walls are made of small, smooth yellow bricks, like elephant bone. The [tile] facade. The courtyard is narrow and dark, like a gorge.

Women with cloth bags come out of the black emptiness of the main entrance and ask which apartment we are going to, look at us indifferently, and leave. We go up the stairs. The last flight—narrow, narrow. Oh, how high! My heart is pounding. The key jingles in the keyhole. A dark corridor. A small door. A door into a room. Ours. Mama can't get the key into the lock. Now she'll open it, and how the sun will burst upon us! Right into our eyes!

The door scrapes . . . So why did I used to think that our place was so huge? That in our room the sun was more brilliant than anywhere else in the world? Something gray clouds my eyes. Or is it a gloomy day? The chairs are pulled out from the table in disarray. Things are spread over the table, and for some reason, two wrinkled, dried-out old spirals of lemon rind.

Mama stands, her arms hanging at her sides, and looks in front of her, and I rush to my familiar blouse that is lying on the table. "Don't touch," Mama says wearily, "Dust."

I don't listen, pull on my favorite children's blouse, and look in the mirror. That's right, dust. I write with my finger in the dust on the mirror, "Hurrah!" And I see that the blouse is not pretty at all, but old and small. In Urshak I thought that in Leningrad everything was good. And now I want to go to Urshak, where there's green grass, sun, everyone speaks loudly and knows each other.

Mama sat down on a chair in the middle of the room and folded her hands on her knees. "Soon it's time for bed," Mama says. How can I sleep if it's still light? Outside the window it isn't even dusk, but just a little faded, as if the weather is a little unsettled—a soft and tender light, how strange, sad but joyful too. I don't feel like sleeping at all, but sit at the window and watch, watch, discovering the secret . . . We sit on the divan. I look at the wallpaper. I squint and see various patterns. Suddenly Mama glances back toward the wall. I look over there. What is it? So small, so gray, so many of them, and all in one pile, as if someone had thrown a rag, and it's moving. Mice! I jump up on the couch in fright. In various directions, like arrows, from the middle mice rushed to the walls. And so small, I had never seen any like them, the size of a thimble!

That's how we began to live—alone and not alone. The mice weren't afraid of us, and when we would stop walking and talking, they would gather in the center of the room. I had begun to look them over and wasn't afraid— little beady eyes on a velvety coat.

But there weren't any cats. They said that there hadn't been any since the blockade. But at the Kuznechnyi Market one time they were selling a cat. I saw it myself and asked Mama to buy it. But a cat cost a lot.

Death Notice

Now the war was over. After the intoxicating joy of fathers returning from the front, families returned to their day-to-day lives. Those whose husbands had not returned repeated each day the legends of a miraculous return from prison, from some camps, even after completing a special mission.

We had a hope that was not imaginary: a return address—"Special Ski Battalion." Mama was writing wherever possible; the first days after she had sent off letters, we would run to the mailbox several times a day. Then it would begin to seem to me that they had by chance printed too many of the forms "Not included in the lists of killed, injured, or missing in action." Nevertheless, we persistently and confidently awaited a miracle.

On the streets I would peer at every tall man and sometimes for a long while would follow those who seemed familiar on the basis of particular characteristics I had chosen—a nice wide smile, broad shoulders, and tightly curled hair, but they never paid any attention to me.

As for stories with another outcome—fathers who were alive but did not return to their families—I simply didn't listen. Nothing like that could ever happen with my father.

I would imagine how it would all be. He'll ring. I'll go to open and will ask, "Who is it?" I'll recognize his voice, will throw myself on his neck, and then, taking him by the hand, we'll go into the room. I would even talk to myself, telling him about school. Whenever anyone would ring [the bell in] the apartment, I would be the first to run to the door.

Then the slender envelope arrived with the death notice—Died from wounds 13 May 1942. That precise indication of time prosaically canceled any belief in a miracle.

They set up a pension for me from my father—a young, cheerful, smiling man in an unbuttoned white shirt. That's how he looked in a photograph; that's how he remained for my whole life in my memory.

True, there remained one small bright light—the story of Zabirov. But fairy tales don't repeat themselves twice. And that fairy tale also had a sad ending.

I don't know where my father's grave is. Every summer at the Pioneer Camp I would take flowers to place at the foot of the small tower with a star —the grave of an unknown soldier. Every 13 May I go to the Piskarevskoe Cemetery. First I put one flower on the slabs where the name "Boris" is written, then on the slabs that show my father's year of birth. There are never enough flowers . . .

The First German

I often thought about what I would do to Hitler if he had been caught. Gouge out his eyes, like they do to bandits and cyclopses in fairy tales? Brand him with the Fascist sign, like the Germans did to our partisans with a star?

I saw my first live German when I was twelve years old. I didn't see him in the movie theater, or in a picture, or in a photograph in the paper. [I saw him] on International Avenue, far away, at its very end, almost outside the city, where there were gardens, and Leningraders would plant potatoes and were building new blocks of apartment buildings. At the building site Germans were working. It was early spring. There was a nasty cold wind blowing. It blew fiercely, but no buildings up to the sky could stop it, because there were no buildings.

We kids run to have a look at the Fritzes. My heart is pounding and ready to burst, and my head swarms with cartoons, sketches, evil faces, like on a poster. We all run and run past people bent over shovels, pounding crowbars into the hard, frozen earth. We stop, tired. So where are the Fritzes? There aren't any. There are people working, men. Then looking closely we see that on their uniforms there is no shoulder strap, they only have service caps. They aren't ours.

Closest to me stands a tall, emaciated man. A pale and gaunt face with colorless, bulging eyes and whitish eyelashes, without eyebrows, and all somehow grayish white. His neck is wrapped with a woman's scarf, and his legs are emaciated, emaciated and long. Sensing my gaze, the man stops working, leans on the crowbar, and looks down, at me. His nose is red, and at the very end hangs a drop, just about to fall off. His lips, thin and moist, have turned blue. He whispers something—or did I imagine it?

Why look at him? Why feel sorry for a Fritz? I should take a rock and throw it right on target. He looks at me and smiles with his blue, drooling lips, and the drop still doesn't fall and keeps on hanging from the end of his nose. They did tell us that Hitler forced the soldiers to go to war, and they didn't want to. If it had been Hitler I would have hurt him, but I can't do it to this one. He probably didn't want to go to war . . . And there is that drop on his nose.

With head lowered, I walk away from the man. He's a German. The first live German that I have seen. I don't want to think about him. It seems that the Fascists that the children play at being are not like these, but like the ones in the cartoons. I was sorry for the German prisoner of war. I didn't go to look at the Germans anymore. I didn't feel like it.

Translated by Cynthia Simmons

THE COMPREHENSIVE RESPONSIBILITIES OF THE WOMEN OF LENINGRAD, both public and private, affected the traditional understanding of war and siege as much as it affected their own identity as women. In this collection of narratives, the *blokadnitsy* recount their experiences in the traditional male spheres of government administration, industry, and defense. In the domestic women's domain, in which they continued to function, they chronicle their superhuman efforts to nurture both body and soul and, when that failed, to take leave of their loved ones with the greatest possible dignity and respect. The broad scope of the documents included here conveys the impression that women struggled, and generally coped, in all spheres of human endeavor and that women in an essentially women's world succeeded in preserving the structures of Soviet-Russian society. The reader's sense of the heroic woman's contribution to the Siege effort has been corroborated in Soviet and Russian history, even if the full account remains to be written.

However, in gathering these stories of valiant resilience, we could not help but sense a persistent, if underlying, motif—these women, though victorious, suffered tremendous losses. Their greatest tragedies—after the death of their beloved children, husbands, brothers, parents, and friends—are revealed when we identify those aspects of a woman's natural peacetime existence that remain in this collection *unchronicled*. They all have to do with life lived without men. None of our informants ever mentions a marriage; only one, Kseniia Matus, recalls an affair of the heart (and even that is poisoned by war); and the only woman to discuss the birth of a new life, Dr. Yuliia Mendeleva, the director of a pediatric institute, reports on the birth rate that waned with each passing month of the war (sixty-five births in Leningrad in July-August-September 1942; twenty births in October-November-December 1942).

The "small stories" that these women contribute to the history of the Siege of Leningrad add dimension to the chronicle of the nation's shared tragedies. Their greatest revelation, however, may be of their excruciatingly personal sacrifice of love, marriage, and childbirth. This suggests not only a fleshing-out of the history of the Siege and war, but other histories as well. These would be all the histories affected by the material and emotional repercussions, during and after the war, in a city of millions in which the heads of household were women, where women could hardly expect to marry and have children, and where the predominant discourse and other forms of interaction, on nearly all levels of daily life, were primarily female.

In addition to augmenting the sources already available on the defense of Leningrad (construction of the Luga line of defense, service in the civil defense forces), the continuing functioning of government institutions, or the preservation of cultural monuments, these documents raise issues that have received little or no attention in the official history of the war or Siege. Soviet ideology underlay the writing of official Soviet history, yet these documents generally reveal a perspective that is not strictly or predominantly Soviet. It is as if the cataclysmic destruction of the nation led to a similar fragmentation of self and a reassessment of identities and loyalties. With the single exception, perhaps, of the teacher Mariia Kropacheva, none of the Siege survivors indicated by what she said or wrote that she defined herself *first* as a Soviet citizen or as a member of the Communist Party. Instead, we find in the personal narratives the particular viewpoints of a woman, a Jew, an ethnic German, an artist, a Russian woman of a particular cultural background. Paradoxically, in a country founded on the principles of communist internationalism, our informants continually highlighted individual differences. Equally paradoxically, most of these besieged citizens discovered in this catastrophe that they belonged, indeed, to the "world of nations." Ostroumova-Lebedeva ponders the emotions of *all* soldiers and the goodness and villainy *everywhere*. This they experienced as a manifestation of their inherent human and female nature, not as dogma imposed on them by Soviet politics. This fact suggests a reconsideration of the degree to which Soviet ideology affected human behavior.

For some time, historians have been acknowledging the positive force of personal narratives and a cultural or social history of the Russian past. Research has shown that official discourse interacts with popular discourse, that language and other cultural forms acquire meaning in relationship with

the realities of material life. In an introductory essay on one such methodology, critical cultural theory, Mark Steinberg reviews three articles calling
into question the historical assumption of the power of official authority in
late Imperial Russia or early Soviet Russia.[1] Steinberg identifies three major
characteristics of the methodology: 1) "a new appreciation of the telling
power of small stories and of particular voices, of the revealing significance
of the seemingly marginal"; 2) "the influence that language, images, sym-
bols, myths, ethics, and other structures of signification and of subjective
value have had in shaping people's perceptions and actions"; and 3) "the
critical questioning of texts to reveal silences, multiple and conflicting meanings, paradox, ambivalence, and ambiguity."[2] Although Steinberg based his
analysis on a review of late nineteenth-century and early twentieth-century
Russian/Soviet history, these personal narratives of the Siege of Leningrad
provide further encouragement for the historian to consider what Steinberg
terms "small stories."[3] Inclusion of a broader scope of narratives implies a
critical questioning by narratives of the "other" (Steinberg's second point)
—as well as a demand for similar questioning on the part of the reader
(Steinberg's third characteristic). Women who authored the texts published
in our collection represent these other, formerly marginalized, observers of
history. Through their diaries, reminiscences, and imagined narratives, they
discern and challenge the language, myths, and ethics of Soviet society. The
very variety of perceptions in these texts allows for revealing comparisons of
conflicting meanings and opposing attitudes (the Party line of Kropacheva
versus the dissonant and iconoclastic understandings of Ol'ga Freidenberg
or Liubov' Shaporina). The now standard linguistic and literary methods of
investigating the relationship of text (in its broadest understanding) and
context can be used equally effectively to discern the influences on historical events. A variety of personal perceptions can be projected on the background known as the "History of the Siege of Leningrad." An aggregate
picture provides greater perspective, and, as in the apocalyptic vision that
Ostroumova-Lebedeva describes in her diary, a multidimensional panorama
of the Siege prevails over a "two-dimensional" (spatio-temporal) design.

Foreword

1. David M. Glantz, *The Siege of Leningrad, 1941–1944: 900 Days of Terror* (Osceola, Wisconsin: MBI Publishing Co., 2001), 180. For Soviet military losses on different fronts during the war, see G. F. Krivosheev, *Grif sekretnosti sniat: poteri vooruzhennykh sil SSSR v voenakh, boevykh deistviiakh i voennykh konfliktakh* (Moscow: Voennoe izdatel'stvo, 1993), 128–393.

2. G. L. Sobolev, "Blokada Leningrada v svete perestroiki istoricheskoi nauki (Ob osveshchenii nekotorykh voprosov istorii blokady Leningrada v knigakh D.V. Pavlova)," in *Voprosy istorii i istoriografii Velikoi Otechestvennoi voiny*, ed. A. P. Kriukovskikh et al. (Leningrad: Izdatel'stvo Leningradskogo Universiteta, 1989), 74–75.

3. An early precursor of the liberalizing effect that *glasnost'* would have on the Soviet historical profession during the Gorbachev years was the publication of a large group of memoir accounts, edited by Ales Adamovich and Daniil Granin under the title *Blokadnaia kniga* (Moscow: Izdatel'stvo Sovetskii pisatel', 1982). This book was translated into English as *A Book of the Blockade* (Moscow: Raduga Publishers, 1983). It dealt more frankly with many issues, including popular attitudes, but still encountered censorship problems. *Blokadnaia kniga* has been republished in many revised editions.

4. Nikita A. Lomagin has recently compiled two document collections: *Mezhdunarodnoe polozhenie glazami Leningradtsev, 1941–1945* (St. Petersburg: Evropeiskii dom, 1996); and *V tiskakh goloda: Blokada Leningrada v dokumentakh germanskikh spetssluzhb i NKVD* (St. Petersburg: Evropeiskii dom, 2000). Andrei R. Dzeniskevich has assembled the most comprehensive set of documents on the siege, *Leningrad v osade: Sbornik dokumentov o geroicheskoi oborone Leningrada v gody Velikoi Otechestvennoi voiny, 1941–1944* (St. Petersburg: Liki Rossii, 1995). Lomagin, together with V. M. Koval'chuk and V. A. Shishkin, edited a collection of essays on

the siege, *Leningradskaia èpopeia: Organizatsiia oborony i naselenie goroda* (St. Petersburg: Izdatel'stvo KN, 1995).

5. A. R. Dzeniskevich, *Voennaia piatiletka rabochikh Leningrada, 1941–1945* (Leningrad: Lenizdat, 1972), 102

6. See Richard Bidlack, "Workers at War: Factory Workers and Labor Policy in the Siege of Leningrad," in *The Carl Beck Papers in Russian and East European Studies* (Pittsburgh: University of Pittsburgh Center for Russian and East European Studies, 1991), 3–6.

7. A. P. Kriukovskikh et al., *V gody surovykh ispytanii: Leningradskaia partiinaia organizatsiia v Velikoi Otechestvennoi voine* (Leningrad: Lenizdat, 1985), 90.

8. Ibid., 89–90; and M. M. Kozlov, ed., *Velikaia Otechestvennaia voina, 1941–1945: Èntsiklopediia* (Moscow: Sovetskaia Èntsiklopediia, 1985), 401.

9. A. V. Karasev, *Leningradtsy v gody blokady, 1941–1943* (Moscow: Nauka, 1959), 92, 94.

10. Dzeniskevich, *Leningrad v osade*, 442.

11. Finland did take one city east of Lake Ladoga, Petrozavodsk, that had not been part of Finland before 1939. The Finnish government, which depended heavily on Germany for food, supplies, and munitions, subsequently turned down repeated requests to dismantle its part of the blockade and sign a separate peace with the USSR.

12. About 30,000 defense-plant workers, 13,000 wounded soldiers, and 7,000 very ill civilians were evacuated by air from Leningrad during October 10–25, 1941. This was the only time during the siege that Moscow sent a large air fleet to Leningrad. Food was brought into Leningrad on the thirty planes that were part of this operation. I. V. Kovalev, *Transport v Velikoi Otechestvennoi voine: 1941–1945* (Moscow: Nauka, 1981), 227.

13. For more information on this subject, see Richard Bidlack, "Survival Strategies in Leningrad," in *The People's War: Responses to World War II in the Soviet Union*, ed. Robert W. Thurston and Bernd Bonwetsch (Urbana and Chicago: University of Illinois Press, 2000), 84–107. The quotation from Adamovich and Granin is the title of chapter eleven of their book, *Blokadnaia kniga*.

14. These examples are from pp. 12–14, 19 of the L. S. Rubanov file, general manuscript collection, Bakhmeteff Archive, Columbia University.

15. Bidlack, "Survival Strategies in Leningrad," 95–96.

16. Ibid., 94.

17. Several groups successfully petitioned for worker status for rationing purposes. For example, doctoral candidates were considered workers from 9 February 1942. *Sbornik ukazov, postanovlenii, reshenii, rasporiazhenii i prikazov voennogo vremeni, 1941–1942* (Leningrad: Lenizdat, 1942), 202.

18. Bidlack, "Survival Strategies in Leningrad," 91–92.

19. Vladimir Putin, *First Person: An Astonishingly Frank Self-Portrait by Russia's President Vladimir Putin with Nataliya Gevorkyan, Natalya Timakova, and Andrei Kolesnikov* (New York: Public Affairs, 2000), 5–9.

20. Lomagin, *V tiskakh goloda*, 236; Bidlack, "Survival Strategies in Leningrad," 98–99.

21. Recent works that rely on party and NKVD assessments of popular mood include: N. A. Lomagin, "Nastroeniia zashchitnikov i naseleniia Leningrada v period oborony goroda, 1941–1942," in Koval'chuk and Shishkin, eds., *Leningradskaia èpopeia;* and Richard Bidlack, "The Political Mood in Leningrad during the First Year of the Soviet-German War," *The Russian Review*, 59 (January 2000): 96–113. Chapter 6 of Dzeniskevich's *Leningrad v osade* (463–86) includes ten documents on popular mood.

22. There were about 200,000 Jews in Leningrad, approximately 6 percent of the city's population, on the eve of the German invasion. The city's population comprised almost as many Jews as all other ethnic minorities combined. Jews were well represented in several professions, including law, medicine, teaching, journalism, and retail trade. See M. Beizer, "The Jewish Minority in Leningrad, 1917–1939," paper presented to the BASEES conference, Cambridge, England, March 1995, 8, 10; as in Sarah Davies, *Popular Opinion in Stalin's Russia* (Cambridge: Cambridge University Press, 1997), 83–85. The Soviet wartime press largely ignored German anti-Semitism and atrocities committed against Jews. On 26 July 1941, however, *Leningradskaia pravda* reported on Poland's ghettos and murders of Jews. Aileen G. Rambow, "The Siege of Leningrad: Wartime Literature and Ideological Change," in *The People's War: Responses to World War II in the Soviet Union*, ed. Robert W. Thurston and Bernd Bonwetsch (Urbana and Chicago: University of Illinois Press, 2000), 166.

23. Bidlack, "The Political Mood in Leningrad," 101–03.

24. Ibid., 105–06.

25. This fact was noted by Lomagin at a panel on the Siege of Leningrad during the 1997 annual convention of the American Association for the Advancement of Slavic Studies held in Seattle.

26. Bidlack, "Survival Strategies in Leningrad," 102.

27. Recent works on wartime food supply and popular culture highlight the rise in spontaneous initiative and freedom. See William Moskoff, *The Bread of Affliction: The Food Supply in the USSR during World War II* (Cambridge: Cambridge University Press, 1990); and Richard Stites, ed., *Culture and Entertainment in Wartime Russia* (Bloomington and Indianapolis: Indiana University Press, 1995).

28. M. V. Shkarovskii, "V ogne voiny: Russkaia pravoslavnaia tserkov' v 1941–1945 gg." in *Russkoe proshloe*, 5 (1994): 259–77; Shkarovskii, "Religioznaia zhizn' Leningrada v gody voiny," in Koval'chuk and Shishkin, eds., *Leningradskaia*

èpopeia, 260–93; Nathaniel Davis, *A Long Walk to Church: A Contemporary History of Russian Orthodoxy* (Boulder: Westview Press, 1995), 17.

29. Stites, *Culture and Entertainment in Wartime Russia*, 69–70; Harrison Salisbury, *The 900 Days: The Siege of Leningrad* (New York: Harper & Row, 1969), 284, 496.

30. Dzeniskevich, *Leningrad v osade*, 442, 461.

31. V. M. Koval'chuk, ed., *Ocherki istorii Leningrada*, vol. 5 (Leningrad: Nauka, 1967), 298–99; and N. N. Amosov, "Rabochie Leningrada v gody Velikoi Otechestvennoi voiny," unpublished candidate dissertation, (Leningrad, 1968), 118.

32. *Leningradskaia pravda*, June 3 and July 18, 1942; and Koval'chuk, *Ocherki istorii Leningrada*, 291.

33. Dzeniskevich, *Voennaia piatiletka*, 101–02.

34. I. C. B. Dear, *The Oxford Companion to World War II* (Oxford and New York: Oxford University Press, 1995), 686; V. M. Koval'chuk, *Doroga pobedy osazhdennogo Leningrada* (Leningrad: Nauka, 1984), 178; Iu. S. Tokarev et al., eds., *Deviat'sot geroicheskikh dnei* (Moscow: Nauka, 1967), 215–16; V. G. Zakharov et al., *Ocherki istorii Leningradskoi organizatsii KPSS, 1918–1945* (Leningrad: Lenizdat, 1980), 415–17; A. V. Burov, *Blokada den' za dnem* (Leningrad: Lenizdat, 1979), 310.

35. Amosov, "Rabochie Leningrada," 232, 246; Kriukovskikh et al., *V gody surovykh ispytanii*, 273–74; N. A. Manakov, "Èkonomika Leningrada v gody blokady," *Voprosy istorii*, no. 5 (1967): 29.

36. Karasev, *Leningradtsy v gody blokady*, 296–97. More than 11,000 shells were fired at the city that month.

37. Manakov, "Èkonomika Leningrada," 29.

38. Karasev, *Leningradtsy v gody blokady*, 304, 309.

39. According to the Soviet testimony at Nuremberg, 632,253 Leningrad civilians died of hunger, and another 16,747 were killed by bombs and artillery shells, for a total of exactly 649,000. Deaths in Pushkin and Peterhof, both of which Germany occupied, raised the totals to 641,803 starvation deaths and 671,635 deaths from all war causes. Salisbury, *The 900 Days*, 514.

40. Dmitri Volkogonov, *Stalin: Triumph and Tragedy*, ed. and trans. Harold Shukman (New York: Grove Weidenfeld, 1991), 510, 519–23

Preface

1. On the creation of the album, see N. Sinitsyn, *Graviury Ostroumovoi-Lebedevoi* (Leningrad: Iskusstvo, 1964), 122–34. An introduction to its use as propaganda is given in *Zhenshchiny goroda Lenina: Rasskazy i ocherki o zhenshchinakh v dni blokady* (Leningrad, 1944).

2. *Avtobiograficheskie zapiski*, vol. 1 (Leningrad: LOSKh, 1935), vol. 2 (Leningrad-Moscow: Iskusstvo, 1945); vol. 3 (Moscow: AKhSSSR, 1951).

3. The disparities range from the absurd censoring of the word "paradise" (*rai*), used metaphorically by Ostroumova-Lebedeva in her diaries, to the unexplained interpolation of passages in *Avtobiografisheskie zapiski* that are unaccounted for in the diaries.

4. Vera Inber, *Pochti tri goda: Leningradskii dnevnik* (Moscow: Sovetskii pisatel', 1946).

5. Vera Inber, *Almost Three Years* (London: Hutchinson, 1971), 31.

6. Ibid., 117.

7. Salisbury, *The 900 Days*. A translation has recently been published in Russia.

8. Leon Goure, *The Siege of Leningrad* (Stanford: Stanford University Press, 1962), 277, 282–83.

9. Salisbury's book had a tremendous impact on the writing of Siege history. The Soviet government feared its potential influence—during the more repressive years, Soviet citizens were arrested for possession of *samizdat* (underground-publishing) editions of *The 900 Days.*

10. *Blokadnaia kniga* (Sovetskii pisatel', 1982) was translated in 1983 as *A Book of the Blockade* (Moscow: Raduga). All page-number citations refer to the English translation.

11. Ol'ga N. Grechina was compelled to write her memoirs not only by the birth of her granddaughter. She writes with indignation about the lack of respect afforded survivors, now old women, who are asked not to take up places on public transportation during working hours or who are silenced when they attempt to speak of the blockade because, after all, "Everyone suffered during the War." "Spasaius' spasaia," *Neva* 1 (1994): 224.

12. Adamovich and Granin, *A Book of the Blockade*, 26.

13. Ibid., 82.

14. Ibid., 105.

15. Ibid., 106.

16. Ibid., 246.

17. The tenth edition of *Blokadnaia kniga* was published in 1994 by *Pechatnyi dvor*. It varies from the original by including more of the interlocutors' direct statements. However, these additions do not constitute a substantial reworking of the book. Daniil Granin has expressed his intention not to make significant changes in the future. His coauthor, Ales Adamovich, has since died, and the process of conducting interviews among Siege survivors was a harrowing experience (both authors became physically ill during the process), which Granin does not wish to repeat. When asked to elaborate on the authors' rationale for choosing among the many

interviews, Granin commented in general that apart from stylistic differences, they were both aware of what was publishable and what not. He cited their innate sense of respect for their interviewees as the motivation to exclude confessions of human sacrifice or cannibalism (interview with Daniil A. Granin, Komarovo, July 1995). In his most recent contribution to the history of the Siege (*Neva* 1 [1999]), Granin advocates caution, or as he terms it "*razumnyi pessimizm*," in the contemporary revision of historical accounts.

18. Elena Skriabina, *Gody skitanii: Iz dnevnika odnoi leningradki* (Paris: Piat' Kontinentov, 1975); Galina Vishnevskaia, *Galina* (San Diego: Harcourt Brace Jovanovich, 1984); Elena Kochina, *Blockade Diary* (Ann Arbor: Ardis, 1990).

19. Vishnevskaia, *Galina*, 28–29.

20. In A. V. Darinskii and V. I. Startsev, *Istoriia Sankt-Peterburga: XX Vek* (St. Petersburg: Glagol, 1997), for example, written and in use as a school textbook, a palpable tenor of resentment underlies the chapter on the history of the Siege.

21. Lidiia Ginzburg, *Chelovek za pis'mennom stolom* (Leningrad: Sovetskii pisatel', 1989), 517.

22. For a more detailed discussion of Ginzburg's memoirs and the writing of the history of the Siege, see Cynthia Simmons, "Lifting the Siege: Women's Voices on Leningrad 1941–1944," *Canadian Slavonic Papers* 1–2 (1998): 43–65.

23. I. M. Grevs, *Ocherki po istorii rimskogo zemlevladeniia* (SPb., 1899); N. P. Antsiferov, *Dusha Peterburga* (Petrograd, 1922); M. M. Bakhtin, *The Dialogic Imagination* (Austin: University of Texas Press, 1981); M. Bloch, *The Historian's Craft* (Manchester, 1954); Isaiah Berlin, *Russian Thinkers* (New York: Penguin, 1977); Nicola Chiaromonte, *The Paradox of History* (Philadelphia: University of Pennsylvania Press, 1985); Viktor Vinogradov, "O iazyke khudozhestvennoi prozy," in *Izbrannye trudy* (Moscow: Nauka, 1980).

24. The phrase "an infinitesimally small integral of history" originates in Lev Tolstoy's *War and Peace*. Significantly, Grevs, Antsiferov, Berlin, and Chiaromonte all studied Tolstoy's opus with considerable enthusiasm.

25. Chiaromonte, "Tolstoy and the Paradox of History," in *The Paradox of History*, 38. Through reference to Levi-Strauss, Chiaromonte provides his own interpretation of Tolstoy's philosophy of history in *War and Peace*. In the same essay (p. 18), he also refers to Isaiah Berlin's "The Hedgehog and the Fox" and highlights the passage in which Berlin demonstrates how Tolstoy, while debating with himself the grandiose aim "to write the genuine history of present-day Europe," ended up with a semifictional, semiconfessional "History of Yesterday."

26. In confronting the topic of fictionalization, we have eschewed the genres of poetry and drama, whose "doubly stylized" modes of thinking are of a different nature.

Introduction

1. Ol'ga Grechina, "Spasaius' spasaia," *Neva* 1 (1994): 237–38.

2. N. I. Baryshnikov et al., eds., *Leningrad v osade* (St. Petersburg: Liki Rossii, 1995), 298.

3. A. R. Dzeniskevich, *Voennaia piatiletka rabochikh Leningrada, 1941–1945* (Leningrad: Lenizdat, 1972), cited in Richard Bidlack, *Workers at War: Factory Workers and Labor Policy in the Siege of Leningrad,* in *The Carl Beck Papers in Russian and East European Studies* (Pittsburgh: University of Pittsburgh Center for Russian and East European Studies, 1991). A recent high school textbook cites an even higher percentage of women workers, although without reference to any data: "In the cold shops of factories, workers, 96 percent of whom were women, worked one of two twelve-hour shifts, manufactured mines, shells, and other armaments, repaired weapons, ordnance, and other military equipment" (*Istoriia Sankt-Peterburga: XX Vek* (St. Petersburg: Glagol, 1997): 137–38.

4. Here and elsewhere, citations from Homer's *The Iliad* are from the translation by Robert Fagles (New York: Viking, 1990).

5. We should always keep in mind that women also fought at the front, in the land and air forces. Although historians have recognized the unprecedented participation of Russian women in combat in World War II, their contribution has yet to be studied or appreciated adequately. This oversight has resulted in part from the official stance of the Soviet government, according to which any person who entered the armed services ceased to be man or woman and became simply "soldier." See, for example, John Erickson, "Soviet Women at War" in John Garrard, ed., *World War II and the Soviet People* (New York: St. Martin's Press, 1990), 50–77; and Svetlana Alexiyevich, *War's Unwomanly Face* (Moscow: Progress Publishers, 1988).

6. On the various ways in which women's more active participation in war affects them and notions of warfare alike, see Margaret Randolph Higonnet et al., *Behind the Lines: Gender and the Two World Wars* (New Haven: Yale University Press, 1987).

7. Harrison Salisbury, *The 900 Days: The Siege of Leningrad* (New York: DeCapo, 1985), 172.

8. Baryshnykov et al., *Leningrad v osade,* 44.

9. "Postanovlenie Voennogo Soveta Oborony Leningrada o formirovanii batal'onov Narodnogo Opolcheniia," in Baryshnykov et al., *Leningrad v osade,* 47.

10. Salisbury, *The 900 Days,* 329.

11. Richard Bidlack, "Rabochie leningradskikh zavodov v pervyi god voiny," *Leningradskaia èpopeia* (St. Petersburg: Izdatel'stvo KN), 172.

12. The German triad of *Kinder, Küche,* and *Kirche* is used in this study as now-common terms in feminist scholarship that denote women's traditionally pre-scribed domain. They are certainly not intended to invoke Nazi ideology. It is worth noting that both the Nazi and Soviet governments found it appropriate to co-opt this coinage of Bismarck's—his being likewise a patriarchal and autocratic regime.

13. Lidiia Ginzburg, *Chelovek za pis'mennym stolom* (Leningrad: Sovetskii pisatel', 1989), 575.

14. Freidenberg praises A. Ostroumova-Lebedeva as such a person. Ironically, Ostroumova-Lebedeva in her diary laments the cowardice of "the Jews" during the Siege, who, according to hearsay, conspired to evacuate only themselves and their own. On the valorous contributions of Jews to the war effort, see, for example *Kniga zhivykh* (Book of the living) (St. Petersburg: Akropol', 1995).

15. For a notable exception, see "Religioznaia zhizn' Leningrada v gody voiny," in *Leningradskaia èpopeia* (St. Petersburg: Izdatel'stvo KN, 1995), 260–93. The au-thor cites numerous archival documents. The only research article he refers to, "Dukhovnaia zhizn' Leningrada vo vremia blokady (1941–1944)," by S. Pavlov (1983), remains unpublished.

16. Ginzburg, *Chelovek za pis'mennym stolom,* 521.

17. The literal titles of Ginzburg's memoir of the Siege, "notes of a besieged *person,*" and of the entire corpus of her memoirs, "a *person* at the writing table" attest to her attempt to maintain a genderless rhetorical position in her observation of events. For instance, she does not distinguish between men and women in her in-dictment of the intelligentsia. Yet in her observations on her own physical changes, the body disappearing was a woman's body. For a further discussion of Ginzburg's generally gender-neutral stance, see Sarah Pratt, "Lidiia Ginzburg, A Russian De-mocrat at the Rendezvous," *Canadian-American Slavic Studies* 28 (1994): 183–203.

18. On the exploitation of representations of the body, especially in Fascist states, see Dorinda Outram, *The Body and the French Revolution: Sex, Class and Political Culture* (New Haven: Yale, 1989).

19. From the perspective of the West, Russian women form remarkably close relationships. Their interdependence during the Siege only strengthened the bonds of close friends. Certainly not all the *blokadnitsy* would have defined their loss of a youthful intimate relationship in heterosexual terms, nor would they have defined a life fulfilled as one that necessarily included children. However, our contributors wrote and spoke of a traditional woman's youth and future that was not to be.

20. Regenia Gagnier, *Subjectivities: A History of Self-Representation in Britain 1832–1920* (New York and Oxford: Oxford University Press, 1991), 39.

21. Barbara Heldt, *Terrible Perfection* (Bloomington: Indiana University Press, 1987), 68.

22. Beth Holmgren, *Women's Works in Stalin's Time* (Bloomington: Indiana University Press, 1993), 10.

23. Toby W. Clyman and Diana Greene, eds., *Women Writers in Russian Literature* (Westport, Conn.: Greenwood Press, 1994), 140.

24. Research in women's studies has documented the liberating effect on women of the chaos of war; particularly, with respect to the women's movement in the West, of World War I (cf. *Behind the Lines: Gender and the Two World Wars*). Russian women felt the repercussions of World War I as well. See, for example, the documents by Russian women in *Lines of Fire: Women Writers of World War I*, edited by Margaret R. Higonnet (New York: Plume, 1999).

Diaries and Letters

1. Veronique Garros, Natalia Korevskaya, and Thomas Lahusen, *Intimacy and Terror* (New York: The New Press, 1995), 333–81.

2. Ibid., 334. Palekh, a settlement in the Ivanovo region, is famous for its artisans community. Its most famous artist of the time, A. I. Zubkov, was arrested in 1938.

3. Ibid., 378.

4. Terrioki (now Zelenogorsk) is a resort area on the Finnish Bay that was annexed by the Soviet Union at the close of the Soviet-Finnish War. The German army occupied Terrioki on 31 August 1941. Kolpino is a railway station and Ivanovskoe is a harbor on the Izhora, a tributary of the Neva River, twenty-five kilometers from Leningrad.

5. M. M. Gipsi-Khipsei (d. 1942), actor with the Theater of the Young Spectator (*Teatr iunykh zritelei*).

6. Vladimir Stepanovich Cherniavskii, a musician with the Leningrad Philharmonic.

7. Elena Ivanovna Glen, an acquaintance of L. V. Shaporina.

8. Vasilii Yurevich Shaporin is an artist and the son of L. V. and Yu. A. Shaporin. On his strained relations with his mother, see Garros, Korevskaya, and Lahusen, *Intimacy and Terror*, pp. 334–40.

9. Gavriil Nikolaevich Popov (1904–1972) composed "Divertissement in Ten Miniatures" and an aria for cello and orchestra, "In memory of Aleksei Tolstoi," which were performed by the Leningrad Symphony Orchestra in May 1938 and March 1944.

10. Shaporina here cites the phrase Pushkin used in *Poltava* to symbolize the hardships that rendered Russia a more resilient nation: "No v iskushen'iakh dolgoi kary/Pereterpev sudeb udary/Okrepla Rus'. Tak tiazhkii mlat/Drobia steklo, kuet bulat" (Fortune's harsh blows and long denials/Steeled Rus. The heavy hammer

thus/Shapes iron while it shatters glass. Trans. by Walter Arndt). Furthermore, the archaic '*mlat*' varies only slightly from the modern Russian word for hammer, '*molot*', of the Soviet '*serp i molot*' (sickle and hammer).

11. Shaporina's choice of the term "Manducus," masticator, might imply both a metaphor and a pun, that is, Stalin *and* the corporeal manducation of the Siege.

12. Sergei Ėrnestovich Radlov (1892–1958) was the artistic director of the Youth Theater (Lensovet Theater) in Leningrad. Radlov staged Nikolai Ostrovskii's novel *How the Steel Was Tempered* in 1936.

13. For more on Shaporina's negative opinion of the writer Aleksei Nikolaevich Tolstoi (1882–1945), see Garros, Korevskaya, and Lahusen, *Intimacy and Terror*, 340, 360–69.

14. N. Sinitsyn, *Graviury Ostroumovoi-Lebedevoi* (Moscow: Iskusstvo, 1964), 124.

15. B. Suris, *Bol'she chem vospominan'ia: pis'ma leningradskikh khudozhnikov 1941-45* (St. Petersburg: Kul'tinformpress, 1993), 1: 43.

16. For the history of *The Scottish Album*, see Margaret Henderson, *Dear Allies: A Story of Women in Monklands and Besieged Leningrad* (Monklands District Libraries, 1988); and Vera Miliutina in this collection.

17. Suris, *Bol'she chem vospominan'ia*, 1: 46–47.

18. Soviet citizens were completely misinformed about the military actions in Egypt. In January 1941, Churchill wrote about "a serious menace of mines to the Suez Canal." From March to May 1941, the German Air Force, established in Syria, attacked the Suez Canal and made it difficult for Great Britain to hold Egypt. From June 1941 to June 1942, the crisis in Egypt grew steadily worse. See Winston Churchill, *The Second World War* (Cambridge: Houghton Mifflin, 1950), III: 5–7, 71; IV: 393.

19. Jacques Bossuet (1674–1704) referred to England as "*la perfide Angleterre*." By the time of the French revolution, the expression had become "*Albion perfide*." The Soviet coverage of events in the West minimized the significance of Britain's resistance to Germany between the fall of France and the summer of 1941, and exhibited no pro-British bias after the war began in the Soviet Union. See Alexander Werth, *Russia at War, 1941–1945* (New York: Dutton, 1964), 91–100.

20. On 10 May 1941, Rudolf Hess, member of the Secret Cabinet Council for Defense of the Reich and leader of the Nazi Party, landed alone by parachute in Scotland. His mission was to outline proposals for Anglo-German settlement. However Churchill "never attached any serious importance to this escapade," for he "knew it had no relation to the march of events" (*The Second World War*, III: 51, 49). The Soviet government was afraid that such a settlement would bring the war in Europe to an end and make it possible for Germany to concentrate all of its military forces on Russia. Soviet newspapers insisted that Hess should be treated not

as a prisoner of war, but as a war criminal. See, for example, a "violent editorial on Rudolf Hess," in *Pravda*, 15 October 1942, cited by Werth in *Russia at War*, 487.

21. Ostroumova-Lebedeva makes an inverted analogy and snide reference to the situation in tsarist Russia, where there had been a 5 percent quota for the admission of Jews into high schools, institutions of higher education, and the professions.

22. During World War II, no chemical (gas) weapons were used in combat.

23. Lilia (Elizaveta Petrovna Filonenko, 1880–1942) was Ostroumova-Lebedeva's younger sister.

24. Semen Semenovich Girgolav (1881–1957) was the assistant chief surgeon of the Red Army and a member of the Academy of Medical Sciences.

25. Aleksandra Nikandrovna Verkhovskaia was the sister of Yurii Nikandrovich Verkhovskii, a poet, translator, literary historian, and friend of Aleksandr Blok.

26. Cheremiss is the former name of the Mari. The Mari Autonomous Republic, with its capital, Ioshkar-Ola (until 1918, Tsarevokokshaisk), is located in the basin of the mid-Volga.

27. In his memoirs, Churchill described the situation from January to the end of February 1942 as very serious. He spoke of "the temporary disablement of our whole Eastern Fleet." See Churchill, *The Second World War*, IV: 113. He stressed the necessity to fight the enemy in the Atlantic, in Egypt, and in the Indian Ocean. He mentioned also "the bitter and confused fighting with the German fighters, in which we suffered more severe losses than the enemy with his superior numbers" (114–18).

28. This trip is described in *Avtobiograficheskie zapiski* (Moscow: Izobratel'-noe isskustvo, 1974), II: 465–80.

29. Anastasiia Iosifovna Yakubchik (1894–1973) was a professor of chemistry at Leningrad State University and a student of Sergei Vasil'evich Lebedev, Ostroumova-Lebedeva's husband.

30. Apparently these children are, in fact, cousins. It is not uncommon in the Russian tradition, however, for cousins to refer to each other as brothers and sisters.

31. The first wave of persecution of Soviet citizens of German ancestry began in Leningrad in 1928–1930. In the academic year 1929–1930, German classes were canceled at the time-honored Petersburg schools Peterschule and Annenschule. In 1930, Aleksandr Germanovich Vul'fius/Wulfius, the director of the German schools and a historian and instructor at Leningrad State University, was arrested and exiled to Siberia for three years. See *Bolschewistische Wissenschaft und Kulturpolitik*, ed. Bolko Freiherr von Richtofen (Königsberg, Berlin: Ost-Europa Verlag, 1942).

32. Vorkuta, a town in the northeastern part of the Komi Autonomous Soviet Socialist Republic, became one of the centers of the GULAG.

33. The Stray Dog, a restaurant in Petrograd (St. Petersburg), served, in the second decade of the twentieth century, as a meeting place for the artistic elite.

34. A. E. Obrant was the ballet master for the children's dance studio of the Palace of Pioneers. The costumes for his productions in 1943 were designed by Vera Miliutina, one of the contributors to this volume. Obrant also led the Leningrad Front-Line Ensemble (*Leningradskii Frontovoi Ansambl*).

35. Mikhail Aleksandrovich Glukh (1907–1973) was a composer whose works include the operetta "Oreshek" (1944). Nataliia Levi (Natal'ia Nikolaevna Smyslova, pseud., 1901–1972) was the composer of the children's opera "Karel'skaia skazka."

36. *Pulkovo Meridian* (1942–1946) is a narrative poem for which Vera Inber received a Stalin Prize.

37. The lifting of the Siege was announced on the radio 27 January 1944 at 7:59 P.M.

38. An old miller, the hero of Pushkin's narrative poem *Rusalka* (The Mermaid), goes mad from grief and shock and in his insanity imagines himself to be a crow.

39. Gabriela Komleva, "Khranitel'nitsa baletnykh tain" (The curator of ballet's mysteries), *Nevskoe vremia*, 19 January 1996.

40. The speaker of Russian who also knows French will recognize this phrase as a pun. The French word for cat, *chat*, pronounced *sha*, in Russian is an interjection demanding silence (the English "sh"). Eating cat meat was for some a clandestine activity.

41. Kostrovitskaia alludes to the fact that the drummer, who in a marching band serves also as the drum major (*udarnik*), could hardly serve in that capacity while sitting or lying on his cot.

42. The man was apparently heading for the Finland Station in the hope of getting out of Leningrad on Lake Ladoga, the "Road of Life."

43. Tager refused to use her influence (or supplies) to save the promising dancer Petia Kosar'kov, who, cut off from his family by the Siege, and sleeping in the halls of the ballet school, could not receive the supplemental nourishment that was necessary for a male adolescent to survive. This hideous exhibition drained his last reserve of energy. He took to bed and eventually died in a children's hospital.

44. Peter Kenez, *The Birth of the Propaganda State: Soviet Methods of Mass Mobilization, 1917–1929* (Cambridge: Cambridge University Press, 1985), 4.

45. C. Leonard Lundin, *Finland in the Second World War* (Bloomington: Indiana University Press, 1957), 150.

46. "Order #227 of the People's Commissar for Defense" (Stalin) was published 28 July 1942. Stalin demanded that the soldiers of the Red Army and the entire Soviet citizenry cease retreating and act decisively to stop the enemy. "Not one step back—this must now be our slogan" was printed at the time in the newspapers. On 29–31 July, the secretaries of the party organizations called meetings to discuss how Leningrad could be turned into a military stronghold.

47. Sevastopol' was surrendered on 4 July 1942.

48. Local partisans were given nicknames to hide their identity and, in case of arrest, to protect members of their families, who often lived in nearby villages.

49. During the war Aleksei Fedorvich Pakhomov (1900–1973) worked on two large series of posters: "Leningrad during the Blockade" (1942–1944) and "In Our City" (1944–1948). Pakhomov wrote to his colleague: "When (in 1941) publishing came to a halt, I went to draw in the morgue of the Erisman Hospital, I drew in the therapy department, at the Serafimov Cemetery, I sketched on the street, I froze, I starved, I went to the Little Neva for water, I acted and lived like all ordinary Leningraders. In March, I began to work on the series 'Leningrad during the Patriotic War.'" Suris, *Bol'she chem vospominan'ia*, 2: 231.

50. Vladimir Aleksandrovich Serov painted such canvases as "Lenin in Smolnyi" and "Capturing the Winter Palace by Storm." During the war he was the president of the Leningrad Chapter of Soviet Artists (LOSKh). He produced numerous political posters and paintings of the atrocities of the German occupation.

51. Georgii Semenovich Vereiskii (1886–1962), a painter and graphic artist, created the cycle of lithographs "The Red Air Force" (Krasnyi Voennyi Vozdushnyi Flot, 1932–1936). During the blockade, he painted on board the ships of the Baltic fleet. Vereiskii painted the portrait of Iosif Orbeli, the director of the Hermitage, when he himself was a patient at the temporary convalescent center set up at the Hermitage, where he was suffering from severe exhaustion. In the summer of 1942, Vereiskii was commissioned for a work in Moscow and thus was saved from death by starvation.

52. In 1901 the workers of the Bolshevik Factory (at that time the Obukhov Factory) took part in a strike, a clash with the police (the "Obukhov Defense"), and a struggle with the government. In the Soviet period, before and after World War II, the factory manufactured equipment for the oil industry and electric power plants; during the war it served the needs of the front.

53. Kropacheva fails to explain that parents and guardians gave up children in hope of finding a job. Thereby they would receive a worker's ration, and their children would receive more food in an orphanage than they would as dependents at home.

54. José Julian Marti (1853–1895) was a Cuban poet, political journalist, and famous patriot.

55. Evacuees were sometimes given chocolate instead of sugar for their food rations.

56. Doctors distinguished three stages of dystrophy due to starvation. The first stage is characterized by emaciation and a constant feeling of hunger, but is not accompanied by a disruption of the body's vital functions. Second-stage (*statsionarnyi*) dystrophy, which was treated, when possible, with supplemental nourishment in a

convalescent hospital, is recognized by a sudden drop in body weight, muscle weakness, the inability to work, and perhaps the loss of the feeling of hunger and the advent of psychological changes. In the third, critical, stage, striking metabolic changes occur. Food cannot be digested—a symptom of the general suppression of physical and psychological functions of the organism. The third stage results in death.

57. The system of supplemental nourishment was devised to correspond to the recognized stages of dystrophy. First-stage dystrophy was treated with supplemental nourishment made available in cafeterias. Second-stage dystrophy required supplemental nourishment in a convalescent hospital (*statsionar*), which, during the blockade, was difficult to provide.

58. *Khriapa* refers to the outer leaves of the cabbage soaked in water. It was used to make soup.

59. Volodia was Likacheva's husband.

60. Hydrochloric acid, a chemical component of gastric juices, was given to raise the acidity of gastric fluids.

61. Boris Pasternak, *The Correspondence of Boris Pasternak and Olga Freidenberg 1910–1954,* compiled and edited, with an introduction by Elliott Mossman, trans. Elliot Mossman and Margaret Wettlin (London: Harcourt Brace Jovanovich, 1982); originally published in Russian under the title *Boris Pasternak: Perepiska s Ol'goi Freidenberg* (New York: Harcourt Brace Jovanovich, 1981).

62. On 6 March 1943, "for outstanding service as leader of the Red Army," Stalin was awarded the title of "Marshal." This event was celebrated with a flood of festive ceremonies attended by the party leadership and writers from the front.

63. In his "My Tour of Duty in the Soviet Union," American Ambassador to the Soviet Union William H. Standley discusses at length "the apparent ingratitude of Soviet Government officials for the aid that the United States Government and the American people were extending to Russia to carry on their war against the Nazis." William H. Standley and Arthur Ageton, *Admiral Ambassador to Russia* (Chicago: Henry Regnery, 1955), 331.

64. The lines cited by Freidenberg originate not from "someone in America" who raised his voice in defense of the Soviet Union, but from V. Molotov's pronouncement, which he, as the Peoples' Commissar of Foreign Affairs, made to Standley on 10 March 1943. Ibid., 342–43. On 8 March 1943, the newspaper *Pravda* referred to Standley's complaint that Russia was getting American supplies in quantity, but was keeping the fact from the people and was leading them to believe that Russia was fighting unaided (ibid., 346–47). A few days later the Soviet "press published a very full account of a statement . . . showing just how much had been sent to the Soviet Union since the beginning of the war." Werth, *Russia at War,* 627–28.

65. In August 1942, a crisis arose in India. The British war cabinet endorsed the proposal of the Viceroy Council to arrest and intern Mahatma Gandhi, Jawaharlal Nehru, and other leaders of India's Congress Party whose activities "threatened to jeopardize the whole war effort of India in face of the Japanese invasion menace." In February 1943, Gandhi, who was being kept in detention in a palace at Poona, announced he would fast for three weeks. This act of protest drew worldwide support, and nearly all the Indian members of the Viceroy's Executive Council demanded Gandhi's release. By the end of the month Gandhi had abandoned his fast.

66. General Vladislav Sikorski (1887–1943) was the leader of the Polish émigré government in England. Freidenberg's chronology is slightly inaccurate. The Soviet government began direct negotiations with Prime Minister Sikorski not on 22 July, but on 30 July 1941. As a result of the negotiations, a Polish embassy was opened in Moscow, and a Polish Army was formed within the USSR (30,000 soldiers drawn from prisoners of war on Soviet territory). The meeting between Sikorski and Stalin occurred not in 1942, but on 3 December 1941. By negotiating with the Kremlin, Sikorski hoped to save the lives of 1.5 million Polish citizens who were interned in the USSR. Later on Freidenberg writes about the tragic fate of General Sikorski—about the fabrication in Moscow of false documents incriminating Sikorski in the aiding and abetting of fascism and of his death in an airplane disaster under suspicious circumstances.

67. The participants in the Polish uprising of 1863 (the Confederates) made a square-tapped cap the emblem of their Confederation.

68. In *The Hinge of Fate* (Boston: Houghton Mifflin, 1950), 757–60, Churchill discusses a breach that "occurred between the Soviet Government and the Polish Government in exile in London." Alexander Werth provides a thorough analysis of Stalin's "technique of building a new Poland" in *Russia at War*, 635–67.

69. On 16 February 1943, after heavy fighting, Soviet troops entered Khar'kov. However, on March 15, the Germans forced the Soviet Army to abandon the city. This recapture of Khar'kov (which the Germans held until September 1944) was the Nazis' "revenge for Stalingrad."

70. Nina Deikina, a young nurse, lived in the same apartment building as the Freidenbergs. She offered them her generous help during the harsh years of starvation; in return, Olga Mikhailovna helped Nina, a poorly educated orphan, with the high school program and prepared her for the university entrance exams.

71. Petr Sergeevich Popkov (1903–1950) was, from 1939 and during the war, chairman of the Executive Committee of the Leningrad City Soviet. In March 1946, he was appointed first secretary of the Leningrad District and Town Committees. He was arrested in 1949 in connection with the "Leningrad Affair" and died in prison. *Leningradskoe delo* (Leningrad: Lenizdat, 1990), 317–21. Freidenberg

was quite critical of this Party functionary and called Popkov a governor out of Shchedrin with the character of Gogol's Manilov (that is, a petty bureaucrat who simultaneously harbored idyllic illusions).

72. Vasilii Spiridonovich Spiridonov (1878–1952), textual critic and bibliographer, lived in the same apartment building as Ol'ga Freidenberg. From 1943, he chaired the Department of Russian Literature at the Herzen Institute.

73. TsGIAL (Central Government Historical Archives of Leningrad) was located in the building of the former Senate, on the Embankment of the Red Navy (formerly, and again now, the English Embankment).

74. In the Soviet Union, all archives belonged to the People's Commissariat of Internal Affairs (NKVD).

75. The secretary of the group Tsvibak was the cousin of the historian I. M. Tsvibak, supporter of the so-called "Marxist theory of historical progress." In 1931 he was one of those who denounced the "sabotage by Tarle and Platonov on the political front." *Problemy marksizma* (Problems of Marxism) (1931), 3: 66–126. In 1937 he was himself repressed and died in prison.

76. Vera Arkad'evna Michurina-Samoilova was an actress at the Pushkin Drama Theater, an Honored Artist of the USSR, and the author of *Shest'desiat let v iskusstve* (Leningrad, 1946). She dedicated the last three chapters of her memoir to the Siege. Due to illness Michurina-Samoilova could not be evacuated. She lived during the blockade with the actress S. I. Muromtseva in an "improvised dormitory" in the building of the Pushkin Theater. A long-time actress of the theater, V. P. Streshneva, lived there as well. See Ostroumova-Lebedeva's diary in this collection.

77. Mariia Kapitonovna Petrova (1874–1948) was a physiologist and the student and common-law wife of Ivan Petrovich Pavlov. During the Siege she studied the problem of "absolute starvation" on dogs in the laboratory.

78. See Mariia Kropacheva's "The Way We Worked" in this volume.

79. Mariia Veniaminovna Yudina (1899–1970) was an outstanding pianist, religious activist, and political nonconformist. In February 1943, she was sent with a group of Moscow musicians to give concerts in Leningrad. There, on the request of Boris Pasternak, she sought out Ol'ga Freidenberg and her mother. Yudina came a second time to Leningrad on 26 June 1943 and stayed until the middle of October. In her memoir "Nemnogo o liudiakh Leningrada" (A few words about the people of Leningrad), Yudina relays a vivid impression of Freidenberg. See *Stati'i vospominaniia materialy* (Moscow: Sovetskii kompozitor, 1978), 220.

80. Elena Lifshits was a high-school friend of Ol'ga Freidenberg.

81. This is a quote from Chekhov's story (and later play) "Kalkhas" (1886), which itself refers to Jean Offenbach's operetta *La Belle Hélene*. Calchas is the celebrated seer who accompanied the Greeks in their expedition against Troy and foretold its outcome.

82. Sof'ia Petrovna Preobrazhenskaia was a mezzo-soprano with the Kirov Theater. Her patriotic repertoire included the roles of Marfa in Mussorgsky's *Khovanshchina* and Joan of Arc in Tchaikovsky's *Orleanskaia Deva* (The Maid of Orleans).

Memoirs and Oral Histories

1. *Vera Miliutina i o nei* (Moscow: Prometei, 1991).

2. Ibid., 8.

3. Tamara Talbot-Rice, "From Russia with Thanks: 'The Album' by Vera Miliutina," *The Week-End Scotsman*, 14 February 1970; Kira Ingal, "The Story of Two Albums," *Soviet Woman*, 3 (1972): 9.

4. Beginning in 1917, the Leningrad City Council and the headquarters of the Communist Party were located in Smolnyi Institute.

5. For more information on the compiling of the greetings, the choice of Burns's poetry, and other work on the book, see Margaret Henderson, *Dear Allies: The Story of Women in Monklands and Besieged Leningrad* (published by Monklands District Libraries, 1988).

6. A. F. Volkova was the editor of the anthology *Zhenshchiny goroda Lenina: Rasskazy i ocherki o zhenshchinakh Leningrada v dni blokady* (Women of the City of Lenin: Stories and Sketches about Leningrad Women during the Siege) (Leningrad, 1944). It included "Zarubezhnye sestry—s nami" (Our Foreign Sisters Are with Us) and excerpts from letters sent from Scotland to besieged Leningrad. Of the authors included in our anthology, two were contributors to Volkova's book: M. V. Kropacheva, "Umelye ruki, zheleznoe uporstvo" ("Adroit Hands and an Iron Will," about women Stakhanovites and heroines of labor), and L. Frankfurt, "Na bibliotechnoi vakhte" ("The Librarians Keep Watch"), on the functioning of the reading rooms of the library during the worst winter of the Siege, with letters from library patrons addressed to the staff.

7. A slightly different account of these events is given in Henderson, *Dear Allies,* 33–40.

8. Tamara Talbot-Rice is one of the leading experts on the history of the Russian arts.

9. The USSR–Great Britain Society eventually brought Miliutina together with one of the initiators of *The Scottish Album*. On 29 July 1971, at an exhibit of the album at the Museum of the History of Leningrad, an emotional meeting took place between Miliutina and Agnes Maxwell (Miss Plant had by that time died).

10. Valentina N. Gorokhova, "The Eve of War and ÈG [evacuation hospital] 1012," 64.

11. Ibid., 37.

12. Ibid., 39.

13. Ibid., 44.

14. A political instructor held a Party administrative position and was appointed by local Party committees to Soviet institutions.

15. The Luga line, a system of fortifications, ran along the shores of the Luga River. It was constructed hastily (12–23 July 1941). The town of Luga was captured by the Germans on 24 August.

16. Increased rations for the military.

17. In addition to the regular stores, there were special "commercial stores" (*kommercheskie magaziny*) in Leningrad that sold a broader assortment of groceries for higher prices. On 1 July the commercial stores announced rigid ration limits for most of the food products: butter—no more than one hundred grams per person; meat products—no more than five hundred grams; candies or sugar—five hundred grams. O. Freidenberg, *The Race of Life*, VII: 12.

18. Grigorii Aleksandrovich Gukovskii (1902–1950), historian of Russian literature of the eighteenth and nineteenth centuries, and professor of Russian Literature at Leningrad State University, was arrested during the anticosmopolitan campaign and died in prison. His two major monographs on Pushkin and Gogol were published posthumously after his rehabilitation.

19. Vladislav Iosifovich Ravdonikas was an archeological historian and a specialist on the Neolithic Age.

20. Aware of military censorship, Yura conveys to his mother that he will be either killed (transferred to *Narkomzem*) or severely wounded (placed with *Narkomzdrav*).

21. "Takimi my schastlivymi byvali,/takoi svobodoi burnoiu dyshali,/chto vnuki pozavidovali b nam." From the poem "February Diary" (January-February 1942), in Ol'ga Berggol'ts, *Poems, Prose* (Moscow, 1961), 318.

22. A. A. Andreev, according to Harrison Salisbury, was one of the senior members of the Politburo "long since forgotten, but in those days often spoken of as a possible successor to Stalin." *The 900 Days: The Siege of Leningrad* (New York: DeCapo, 1985), 141.

23. Leningrad University was evacuated to Saratov by three trains 26 February–3 March 1942. Classes were resumed there on 1 April 1942. In the overpopulated city of Saratov, the living conditions were very harsh—people from Leningrad were short of clothing, food, and living space (O. Freidenberg, IX: 48). In June 1943, there were several air raids on the city. Alexander Werth, *Russia at War* (New York: Dutton, 1964), 675.

24. Yurii Mikhailovich Lotman (1922–1993), the founder of the Tartu School of Semiotics, whose interests ranged from philosophical analyses of medieval Russian texts to literary criticism of modern works, was a fellow student at the university. Lotman was serving in the Red Army when the war started. He managed

to survive, ending up in Berlin. Grechina was completing her reminiscences for a collection of memoirs dedicated to Lotman.

25. Vladimir Yakovlevich Propp (1895–1970) was a specialist in folklore and the author of *Morphology of the Folktale* (1928) and *The Historical Roots of the Wondertale* (*Istoricheskie korni volshebnoi skazki*, 1946). Both studies were severely criticized during the infamous anticosmopolitan campaign.

26. Pavel Naumovich Berkov (1896–1969) was a specialist in eighteenth-century Russian literature, a professor at Leningrad State University, and a corresponding member of the Academy of Sciences.

27. Ol'ga Borisovna Vrasskaia (1905–1991) was a medievalist and student of Ivan Mikhailovich Grevs and Nikolai Pavlovich Antsiferov, historians of urban culture. She published "Arkhivnye materialy I. M. Grevsa i M. P. Antsiferov po izucheniiu goroda," *Arkeograficheskii ezhegodnik za 1933 god* (Moscow, 1982). Tat'iana Nikolaevna Kopreeva (1917–1988) was a specialist on the history of bookmaking and a bibliographer. Liudmila Alekseevna Mandrykina (1906–1989) was an archivist and researched the Decembrist movement. On the evacuation of the library collections and the preservation of materials during the blockade, see the report by L. Frankfurt in this collection.

28. Tat'iana Solomonova Grigor'iants (1917–1996) was a research assistant for the library's main catalogue and was an author of the index *Periodicheskaia pechat' v Rossii v 1917 g.* (Leningrad, 1987).

29. Elizaveta Petrovna Fedoseeva (1920–1989) was an archivist and author of *Nikol'skii Aleksandr Sergeevich: Katalog chertizhei i arkitekturnykh rabot* (Leningrad, 1980). Valerii Nikolaevich Sazhin (b. 1945) is a literary scholar and research assistant in the Manuscript Department of the Russian National Library, and the editor of the journal *Russian Studies* (St. Petersburg).

30. A. N. Tsamutali contributed an overview of the work of high-school teachers and university professors during the Siege, "Kul'turnaia i nauchnaia zhizn' v Leningrade," to the anniversary collection *Leningradskaia èpopeia* (St. Petersburg: Izdatel'stvo KN, 1995), 132–51.

31. *Zhenshchiny goroda Lenina* (Leningrad: Lenizdat, 1963), 262–71.

32. On this period, see, for example, C. V. James, *Soviet Socialist Realism: Origins and Theory* (New York: St. Martin's Press, 1973); Regine Robin, *Socialist Realism: An Impossible Aesthetics* (Stanford: Stanford University Press, 1992); *Peterburgskii zhurnal*, 12 (1993): 9–66, 183–202.

33. Here and elsewhere in the interview, Petrova refers to her cousin as her sister—a practice not uncommon in Russia.

34. Rozhdestveno was the Nabokov estate.

35. The Radio Committee as a military target is discussed in L. Magrachev, *Reportazh iz blokady* (Leningrad, 1989).

36. On V. A. Khodorenko, see ibid., 66–76. N. A. Khodza was the author of stories dealing with the lives of adolescents during the Great Patriotic War. In 1965, he published *Ispytanie*.

37. The idea for the organization of a theater at the House of Radio came from the editor of the literary department, Yakov Babushkin, and the first play to be produced was K. Simonov's *Russkie liudi* (The Russian People). I. Gorin, V. Yarmagaev, and Nina Cherniavskaia were actors and readers of Leningrad Radio. For more on their literary broadcasts and performances of the radio theater, see M. G. Petrova, "V dome radio" in *Zhenshchiny goroda Lenina* (Leningrad: Lenizdat, 1963), 269–72.

38. Lev Abramovich Kassil' (1905–1970), writer, whose children's books depict the October Revolution through the eyes of a middle-class child of the intelligentsia. Gaidar (pseudonym of Arkadii Petrovich Golikov, 1904–1941) was a journalist and writer of children's books, many of which became Soviet classics (*School, Timur and His Team*).

39. L. Magrachev points out (see *Reportazh iz blokady*, 78–85) that at the end of December 1941, a colleague from the Russian Service of the BBC spent some time in the "Latest News" department of Leningrad Radio. Magrachev's memoirs reflect the distrust and dislike that at that time characterized Soviet sentiments toward the Allies. In June 1943 a correspondent from United Press, Henry Shapiro, came to Leningrad, and in September of that year, the English journalist Alexander Werth (who had been born in St. Petersburg and who had left Petrograd in 1918). See Alexander Werth, *Leningrad* (London, 1944), and *Russia at War* (New York: Dutton, 1964), 297–359.

40. Mikhail Aleksandrovich Dudin (b. 1916)—author of the collections of patriotic poems *Fliaga* (The Flask), *Voennaia Neva* (The Neva at War, 1943), *Doroga Gvardii* (The Guard's Road, 1944). Aleksandr Germanovich Rozen (b. 1910) made the heroic defense of Leningrad the main theme of his documentary works: "Zimniaia povest'" (A Winter Tale, 1942); "Polk prodolzhaet put'" (The Regiment Continues on Its Way, 1947). Liudmila Mikhailovna Popova (1898–1972) in 1942 volunteered for the front; in her poems "Schast'e letat'" (The Joy of Flight, 1941) and "Kryl'ia zhizni" (The Wings of Life, 1941), she describes the military victories of the Soviet Air Force and hails the heroism of the Soviet female pilots Osipenko and Baidukova.

41. Georgii Panteleimonovich Makogonenko (b. 1912) worked at the Radio Committee from February 1941 for the literature and drama department. In collaboration with O'lga Berggol'ts he wrote the play *Oni zhili v Leningrade* (They Lived in Leningrad, 1944). In 1944 he began postgraduate study and became a professor and then the chairman of the Department of Russian Literature at Leningrad State University. Izrail' Moiseevich Metter—a writer of children's books and a playwright. With L. Levin he wrote several plays dedicated to soldiers and victims of

World War II; among these, *Nash korrespondent* (Our Correspondent, 1942) and *Severnoe siianie* (Northern Lights, 1943).

42. The day described is 18 January 1943, when the blockade was broken. *Volki i ovtsy* (1879) is a play by A. N. Ostrovksii.

43. Viktor Andronikovich Manuilov was a specialist on Mikhail Yu. Lermontov, a professor at the Herzen Institute and, later, at Leningrad University.

44. At the Herzen Pedagogical Institute, classes resumed for the academic year 1943–1944; Leningrad University returned from evacuation in Saratov toward the beginning of the academic year 1944–1945.

45. For a more recent and detailed account of religious life in Leningrad during the war, see M. V. Shkarovskii, "Religioznaia zhizn' Leningrada v gody voiny," in *Leningradskaia èpopeia* (St. Petersburg: Izdatelstvo KN), 260–90.

46. These badges looked like large buttons, contained phosphate, and therefore glowed in the dark.

47. These scraps served as makeweights to ensure that each person got the exact weight of bread being rationed.

48. "The International," the hymn of the worldwide proletarian movement, was also, until 1944, the national anthem of the Soviet Union.

49. Lidiia Alekseevna Charskaia (pseud. of Churilova, 1875–1937) was a popular writer of children's stories describing the lives of privileged girls in boarding schools.

50. Bystrov, Butusov, and Dement'ev were all stars before the war of the soccer teams Central House of the Red Army, Zenith, and Dynamo.

51. See note 15.

52. For three days during the fourth week of January 1942, no bread was delivered to the bakeries in Leningrad.

53. Here Bushueva's memory must have failed her. By early March the ration for the "dependent" category had been raised to three hundred grams of bread.

54. On 4 March 1942 the Party Town Council (*gorkom*) addressed the question of extracting peat. On 24 March, 1,500 women were mobilized to work in the peat bogs.

55. "*Topliak*" is derived from the verb "to sink" (*topit'*). It refers to pieces of wood so saturated with water that they lose buoyancy.

56. On 7 February 1943 the first train with provisions, from Cheliabinsk in the Urals, arrived at the Finland Station.

57. When liberated from the Germans, Shlissel'burg was renamed Peter's Fortress (*Petrokrepost'*).

58. In his memoirs, "How We Stayed Alive" ("Kak my ostalis' zhivy," *Neva* 1 [1991]: 18), Dmitrii S. Likhachev writes that the icy road across Lake Ladoga "they called the road of death (and not at all the road of life, as it has been white-washed subsequently by our writers)."

59. The Palace of Pioneers, located in the former Anichkov Palace on the Fontanka, is now called the Children's Palace for the Arts (*Dvorets tvorchestva iunykh*).

60. Buried in Piskarevskoe Cemetery are approximately 470,000 defenders of Leningrad, both civilians and soldiers of the Red Army.

61. The Rossi Pavilion was built in 1817–1818 as part of the architectural ensemble of Aleksandrinskii Theater Square, now Ostrovskii Square.

62. The Catherine Garden, a square with a statue of Catherine the Great, is located on Ostrovskii Square, between Nevskii Avenue and the Pushkin Drama Theater (before the Revolution the Imperial Aleksandrinskii Theater). Saraeva-Bondar' is somewhat mistaken in her recollection. It is not the Catherine Garden that is enclosed by a railing, but the Garden of Relaxation, located between Ostrovskii Square and the Fontanka embankment. Located within the Garden are the Rossi Pavilion and the Palace of Pioneers.

63. The air-raid shelter of the Pushkin Theater was used as a dormitory for artists whose apartments had been destroyed by bombs and fires.

64. "Russian Warriors" (*drevnerusskie vitiazi*) refers to a bas-relief at the entrance to the Rossi Pavilion.

65. School #218 was located in the building of the old Petersburg German school Peterschule.

66. Since 1802, the Petersburg Philharmonic Society had been located in the house of Vasilii Vasil'evich Èngel'gardt (1785–1837). The building, constructed in 1759–1761 by Rastrelli, was destroyed during World War II as a result of a direct hit and was reconstructed after the war. Building No. 18 on Nevskii Avenue housed the famous candy store of Wolf and Berange, where Pushkin met with his seconds on the day of the duel that led to his death (27 January 1837).

67. Throughout the Siege, the daily newspaper *Leningrad Truth* was published every day but one. On 25 January 1942, the Volodarskii printing plant lost electricity, and the printer's ink froze in the presses.

68. Matus is mistaken. It was the first concert of the Symphony Orchestra that took place on 5 April; rehearsals had begun in March. Èliasberg was the lead conductor of the Leningrad Radio Orchestra. See Salisbury, *The 900 Days*, 8, 512; Boris Schwarz, *Music and Musical Life in Soviet Russia 1917–1970* (New York: Norton, 1972), 177; Yurii Alianskii, *Teatr v kvadrate obstrela* (Leningrad: Iskusstvo, 1985), 45–61.

69. Vladimir Ivanovich Kastorskii (1870–1948) was a bass who performed roles in operas by Mussorgsky and Glinka (*Ivan Susanin*).

70. On Shostakovich's talk on Leningrad Radio 1 September 1941 and the performances of the Seventh Symphony in Leningrad, Moscow, other cities in the Soviet Union, the United States, and England, see Salisbury, *The 900 Days*, 283, and Schwarz, *Music and Musical Life in Soviet Russia*, 177–80, 190–93.

71. In conversation with Solomon Volkov, Shostakovich said: "It saddens me that people don't always understand what it's all about, yet everything is clear in the music. Akhmatova wrote her *Requiem* and the Seventh and the Eighth Symphonies are my requiem." *Testimony: The Memoirs of Dmitry Shostakovich as Related to and Edited by Solomon Volkov* (New York: Harper and Row, 1979), 136.

72. The guard's crew was the prerevolutionary name for a group of ships. The crew included naval officers, mechanical engineers, and a military orchestra.

73. Leonid Aleksandrovich Govorov (1897–1955) was a Marshal of the Soviet Union. In 1941–1942, he commanded military forces in Leningrad. In 1943 he became commander of the Leningrad Front.

74. The hotel and restaurant Astoria is located on St. Isaac's Square. During the war it served as a convalescent hospital for artists weakened by starvation.

75. Vsevolozhskaia is a resort town forty kilometers from Leningrad.

76. As the ration-card system was introduced in Leningrad on 18 July 1941 and Leningrad was cut off on 8 September, the events described by Matus took place primarily in August 1941.

77. Rzhevka is a railway station and suburb of Leningrad/St. Petersburg on the bank of the river Bol'shaia Okhta.

78. The rank of military commissar was abolished on 9 October 1942.

79. It was not uncommon for urban schools, orphanages, and hospitals to keep their own gardens and orchards.

80. Quotations are taken from Frankfurt's personal file and the transcripts of her interrogations at the Leningrad branch of the People's Commissariat of Internal Affairs (NKVD), which her daughters Èsfir' Genina and Tat'iana Zhidkova were kind enough to provide us.

81. Nikolai Osipovich Lerner (born 1877, Odessa—died 1934, Leningrad) was a bibliophile and the author of *Trudy i dni Pushkina*, *Proza Pushkina*, and *Pushkinskie ètiudy*.

82. The Larionov brothers were historians of the Russian Navy, including the Battle of Tsushima. The battle, which took place in May 1905 near the island of Tsushima in the Korean Strait, ended with the defeat of the Russian Navy.

83. *Russkoe bogatstvo*, a journal of literature and culture, was published in St. Petersburg from 1876 to 1917.

84. "Bat" (*letuchaia mysh'*) was the name given to a portable kerosene lamp with a glass shade.

85. Bogdan Khmel'nitskii was a Ukranian hetman and leader of the anti-Polish uprising of 1648–1654.

86. Aleksandr Alekseevich Brusilov (1853–1926) commanded the southwestern front during World War I. In 1916 his troops broke through the Austro-German lines.

87. Voltaire was elected an honorary member of the Russian Academy of Sci-

ences. After his death, his library (6,902 books and 20 volumes of manuscripts) was obtained by Catherine II, transported to St. Petersburg, and in the nineteenth century was given to the Imperial Public Library.

88. I. A. Bychkov was a collector and publisher of manuscript materials on the history of medicine in the era of Peter I.

89. *Leningradskoe delo* (Leningrad: Institut Istorii Partii, 1990). This work is the (authoritative) source for information on the Leningrad Affair given below.

90. Ibid., 7.

91. Ibid., 352–63.

92. The first Museum of the Defense of Leningrad was located along Market Street and Salt Lane (*Solianyi pereulok*) between Tchaikovsky and Pestel' Streets, in an area of warehouses known as Salt Town. Salt and wine were warehoused here from the date of its construction in 1782 until the mid-nineteenth century (and the abolition of the salt monopoly). The buildings of Salt Town were subsequently used for various exhibitions.

93. In 1953–1954 the archives of the Museum of the History of Leningrad "were enriched by the collections of the former Museum of the Defense of Leningrad, which reflected the life of the city during the Great Patriotic War." L. S. Shaumian, ed., *Leningrad: Èntsiklopedicheskii spravochnik*, (Leningrad: Bol'shaia Sovetskaia Èntsiklopediia, 1957), 615.

94. In February 1945, in two night-time air-raid attacks on Dresden, 135,000 people perished. In his memoirs, Churchill expressed no regret in this regard.

95. The chronological framework of the museum is thus determined by the advent of Hitler and the death of Stalin. However, the museum's exposition includes no documentary materials that make reference to these events.

96. The Eliseev store is located on Nevskii Avenue. Tram service began on Nevskii Avenue in 1907 and continued until 1947.

97. Tania Savicheva was evacuated in the spring of 1942 and died in the summer of 1943, in Orphanage No. 48 in the village of Shakhty (Gor'kii region). See Salisbury, *The 900 Days*, 484–85.

Documentary Prose

1. Tamara Staleva, *Vechnye deti blokady: Dokumental'nye ocherki* (Moscow, 1995), 99.

2. The institute was located in the famous building with the "tower," where, in the beginning of the twentieth century, Symbolist poets and artists met in the studio of Viacheslav Ivanov.

3. Staleva, *Vechnye deti blokady,* 108–09.

4. On Hitler's prescripts to have Leningrad surrounded and to starve to death

the city's population of three million, see Aileen Rambow, *Überleben mit Worten: Literatur und Ideologie während der Blokade von Leningrad 1941–1944* (Berlin: Arno Spitz, 1995), 32–35.

5. *Olifa* is a paint that contains oil as a dissolvent. It was consumed as food during the Siege.

6. Razumovskaia describes the wedding as "*gor'ko.*" This word literally means "bitter," and it is shouted to the bride and groom during the wedding party, in response to which they must kiss and "make it sweet."

7. The author has not accurately recalled the circumstances and data with regard to the "Regulation." It was accepted on 10 September and the following day announced on radio and published in the newspapers. The following norms represented a second reduction: Blue-collar workers and technicians—500 grams; white-collar workers—300 grams; dependents—250 grams; children—200. See the Table of Rations in the front of this volume.

8. Lev Nikolaevich Oborin (1907–1974), winner of the First International Chopin Competition in Warsaw, was a Moscow pianist and professor at the Moscow Conservatory.

9. The father plays and sings to his daughter the famous song by Ludwig von Beethoven *Der Murmeltier*, set to the words of the poem "The Marmot," by Johann Wolfgang von Goethe.

10. Ernst Thälmann (1866–1944) was one of the leaders of the Third International and President of the Central Committee of the Communist Party of Germany. He was killed in a concentration camp (Buchenwald).

11. Ernst Busch (1900–1980) was a German singer, member of the Socialist Party of Germany, and one of the performers of the ensemble and theater of Helene Weigel and Bertolt Brecht. He toured the Soviet Union in 1936. In 1937–1939 he achieved renown in Spain, performing songs of the Civil War. Reference is made here to his famous songs "Wir sind die Moorsoldaten" and "Arise, The Party Is in Danger." From 1940 to 1945, he was a prisoner in Auschwitz.

12. The lyrical song "*Sinii platochek,*" music by Peterburgskii and lyrics by Ya. Galitskii (pseud. Yakov Markovich Gol'denberg), was written before the war and enjoyed great popularity, especially as sung by Klavdiia Ivanovna Shul'zhenko. Early in the war, the song appeared in a number of popular variants. Shul'zhenko herself began to add a patriotic ending, "*Strochit pulemetchik za belye nochi, za sinii platochek, milyi zhelannyi, rodnoi.*" ("The machine gunner fires away, for white nights, for the blue scarf, dear beloved, [our] own.") In the cities and at the front, a folk song arose that was sung to the melody of "*Sinii platochek.*" It is this song that Varia recalls.

13. "*Dvadtsat' vtorogo iiunia rovno v chetyre chasa Kiev bombili, nam ob'iavili, chto nachalasia voina.*"

237

14. Uncle Nartik had been sent to a labor camp, a victim of the Stalinist "Terror."

15. Vvedenskaia Street, in the Petrograd district, was named for Vvedenskaia Church. In 1953, it was renamed Oleg Koshevoi St. in honor of a hero of World War II. The copper-founding factory Krasnyi Vyborzhets located on this street was the reason for its suffering especially frequent bombardments.

16. Irena Dubitskaia includes a similar incident in her novel. See the excerpt from *Cold Sun.*

Conclusion

1. Mark D. Steinberg, "Stories and Voices: History and Theory," *The Russian Review*, 55 (July 1996): 347–54. Steinberg discusses articles by James von Geldern, Diane P. Koenker, and Michael Gorham, which follow his introductory essay.

2. Ibid., 348–49, 351.

3. It is striking that the literary scholar and researcher of the Russian National Library, Natal'ia Rogova, used exactly this term to describe the role of these women Siege survivors in preserving memory.

239